The Writer's Studio

Level A

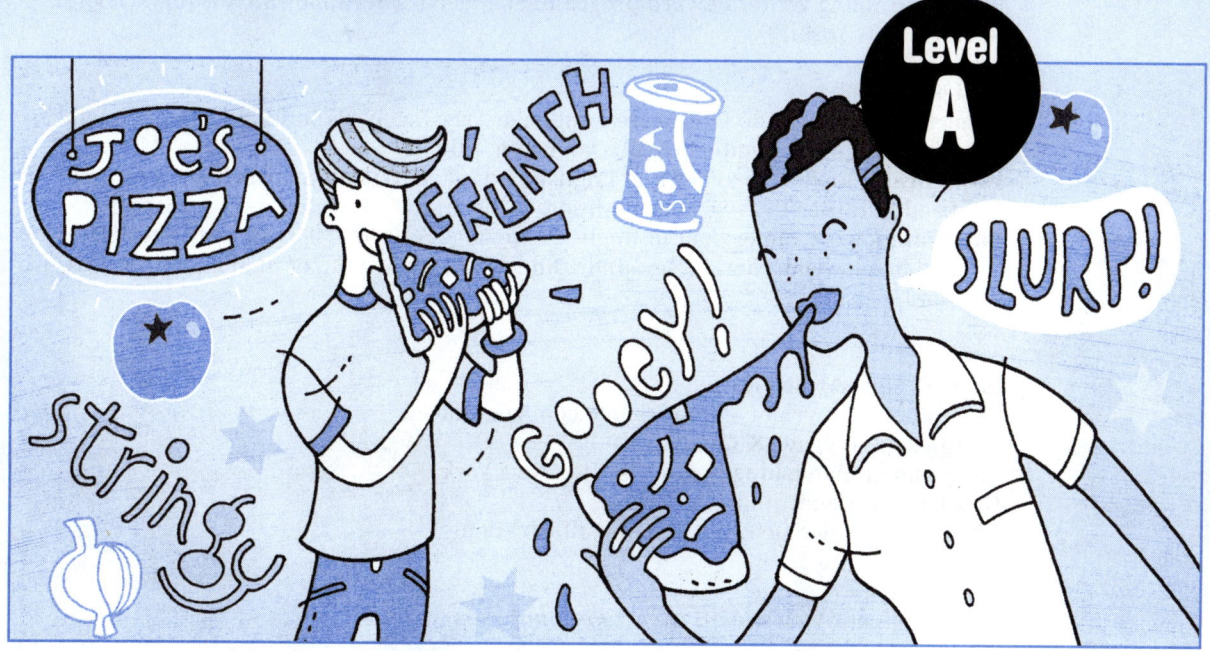

Lesli J. Favor, Ph.D.

AMSCO

Amsco School Publications, Inc.
315 Hudson Street
New York, N.Y. 10013

About the Author
Lesli J. Favor holds a Ph.D. in English from the University of North Texas. After graduating, she was assistant professor of English at Sul Ross State University Rio Grande College, in southwest Texas. She left that position to write full-time. She has written twelve English/language arts books and co-authored three more, all for Amsco School Publications. In addition, she has written twelve nonfiction books for middle school and high school readers. She lives near Seattle with her husband, young son, two dogs, and horse.

Consultant: Cathleen Greenwood
Cathleen Greenwood is an award-winning teacher, writer, and veteran presenter at national and local conferences on teaching and writing. She has written two books for teachers and has co-authored a book for young adults on writing. In addition, she has published poems, short stories, and essays in magazines and journals. She is a consultant for the National Council of Teachers of English (NCTE) and a judge for the NCTE Promising Young Writers award program. She teaches at Rippowam Cisqua School in Bedford, New York.

Reviewers:
Robert Gath, 8th-Grade Literature/Language Arts Teacher and English Department Head, Simmons Middle School, Oak Lawn, Illinois
Ivana Orloff, English Teacher and English Language Arts Standards Review Course Lead, Whittier High School, Whittier, California
Gary Pankiewicz, Supervisor of English Language Arts (6–12), District of South Orange and Maplewood, New Jersey, and adjunct writing instructor at Montclair State University

Cover Design: Armen Koyoyian
Cover Photo: Copyright © iStockphoto.com/zentilia
Text Design: Delgado & Company
Composition: Publishing Synthesis, Ltd., New York
Graphic Art: Hadel Studio
Illustrations: Clive Goodyer (Beehive Illustration)

Please visit our Web site at: *www.amscopub.com*

When ordering this book, please specify:
either **R 173 P** *or* THE WRITER'S STUDIO, LEVEL A.

ISBN: 978-1-56765-202-4 / *NYC Item: 56765-202-3*

Copyright © 2011 by Amsco School Publications, Inc.

No part of this book may be reproduced in any form without written permission from the publisher.

Printed in the United States of America

1 2 3 4 5 6 7 8 9 10   16 15 14 13 12 11

Contents

Welcome to *The Writer's Studio*   ix

Unit 1   Descriptive Writing   1

Get to Know the Genre: Descriptive Writing   1

Chapter 1: Describe a Person   5
Six Traits of Describing a Person   5
Your Turn to Write: Describe a Person   7
Prewrite 7   Draft 9   Revise 11
Edit 14   Publish 15

Chapter 2: Describe a Place   19
Six Traits of Describing a Place   19
Your Turn to Write: Describe a Place   21
Prewrite 22   Draft 24   Revise 25
Edit 30   Publish 30

Chapter 3: Describe a Scientific Subject   33
Six Traits of Describing a Scientific Subject   33
Your Turn to Write: Describe a Scientific Subject   35
Prewrite 35   Draft 37   Revise 38
Edit 42   Publish 42

Chapter 4: Test Writing: The Descriptive Essay   45
Six Traits of a Descriptive Test Essay   45
Preparing to Write Your Test Essay   46
Write a Descriptive Test Essay   54

Descriptive Writing Wrap-Up   55
Unit 1 Reflections   60

Unit 2 Expository Writing	61
Get to Know the Genre: Expository Writing	61

Chapter 5: Write a How-To Article — 67
Six Traits of a How-To Article — 67
Your Turn to Write: Compose a How-to Article — 69
Prewrite 69   Draft 71   Revise 73
Edit 77   Publish 77

Chapter 6: Write an Explanatory Essay — 81
Six Traits of an Explanatory Essay — 81
Your Turn to Write: Compose an Explanatory Essay — 83
Prewrite 83   Draft 85   Revise 87
Edit 89   Publish 89

Chapter 7: Write a Comparison-Contrast Essay — 93
Six Traits of a Comparison-Contrast Essay — 93
Your Turn to Write: Compose a Comparison-Contrast Essay — 95
Prewrite 95   Draft 98   Revise 99
Edit 104   Publish 105

Chapter 8: Test Writing: The Expository Essay — 109
Six Traits of an Expository Test Essay — 109
Preparing to Write Your Test Essay — 110
Write an Expository Test Essay — 119

Expository Writing Wrap-Up	120
Unit 2 Reflections	124

iv • The Writer's Studio   Level A

Unit 3 Persuasive Writing   125

Get to Know the Genre: Persuasive Writing   125

Chapter 9: Write an Editorial   131
Six Traits of an Editorial   131
Your Turn to Write: Compose an Editorial   133
Prewrite *133*   Draft *136*   Revise *138*
Edit *142*   Publish *142*

Chapter 10: Write a Persuasive Essay   145
Six Traits of a Persuasive Essay   145
Your Turn to Write: Compose a Persuasive Essay   147
Prewrite *147*   Draft *151*   Revise *153*
Edit *156*   Publish *156*

Chapter 11: Write a Review   159
Six Traits of a Review   159
Your Turn to Write: Compose a Review   161
Prewrite *161*   Draft *165*   Revise *165*
Edit *168*   Publish *169*

Chapter 12: Test Writing: The Persuasive Essay   173
Six Traits of a Persuasive Test Essay   173
Preparing to Write Your Test Essay   174
Write a Persuasive Test Essay   183

Persuasive Writing Wrap-Up   185
Unit 3 Reflections   189

Contents • v

Unit 4 Literary Writing — 191

Get to Know the Genre: Literary Writing — 191

Chapter 13: Write a Personal Narrative — 195
Six Traits of a Personal Narrative — 195
Your Turn to Write: Compose a Personal Narrative — 197
Prewrite *197*   Draft *200*   Revise *204*
Edit *207*   Publish *208*

Chapter 14: Write a Story — 211
Six Traits of a Story — 211
Your Turn to Write: Compose a Story — 213
Prewrite *214*   Draft *217*   Revise *219*
Edit *222*   Publish *222*

Chapter 15: Write a Poem — 225
Six Traits of a Poem — 225
Your Turn to Write: Compose a Poem — 227
Prewrite *227*   Draft *230*   Revise *231*
Edit *234*   Publish *236*

Chapter 16: Test Writing: The Narrative — 239
Six Traits of a Narrative Test Essay — 239
Preparing to Write Your Test Essay — 240
Write a Narrative Test Essay — 248

Literary Writing Wrap-Up — 249
Unit 4 Reflections — 253

Unit 5 Response to Literature	**255**

Get to Know the Genre: Response to Literature … 255

Chapter 17: Respond to a Narrative … 259
Six Traits of a Response to a Narrative … 259
Your Turn to Write: Respond to a Narrative … 261
Prewrite *262*   Draft *264*   Revise *266*
Edit *268*   Publish *271*

Chapter 18: Respond to a Poem … 273
Six Traits of a Response to a Poem … 273
Your Turn to Write: Respond to a Poem … 275
Prewrite *276*   Draft *277*   Revise *278*
Edit *282*   Publish *282*

Chapter 19: Respond to a Document-Based Question … 285
Six Traits of a Response to a DBQ … 286
Your Turn to Write: Respond to a DBQ … 288
Prewrite *291*   Draft *294*   Revise *296*
Edit *298*   Publish *298*

Chapter 20: Test Writing: The Critical-Lens Essay … 299
Six Traits of a Critical-Lens Essay … 299
Preparing to Write Your Test Essay … 300
Write a Critical-Lens Test Essay … 307

Response to Literature Wrap-Up … 308
Unit 5 Reflections … 311

Conventions Handbook … 313
Mini-Lessons Taught in This Book … 316
Acknowledgments … 317
Index … 319

Welcome to *The Writer's Studio*

A studio is a place where an artist develops a craft or skill. A photographer develops prints, a dancer practices a routine, a singer records an album, and a writer composes a story. Think of this book as *your* writing studio—a place where you will develop as a unique and skilled writer. As you work through this book, you'll learn about a variety of genres (kinds) of writing, examine model essays, and practice writing for a variety of audiences and purposes. You'll also learn how to add your own creativity and self-expression to your writing. Just like fingerprints, no two writers are alike. Your writing rings with your voice, your style, your experiences, and your perspective. The unique place you come from as a writer can help you succeed in this literary craft.

Take a moment to review where you stand as a writer. Complete the following activity. Your teacher may ask you to share your responses in a class discussion.

What Do You Think About Writing?

Read each of the following statements. Decide whether you strongly agree, strongly disagree, or stand somewhere in between. Then, draw an X to mark your position on the scale.

1. Strong writers are born that way.

   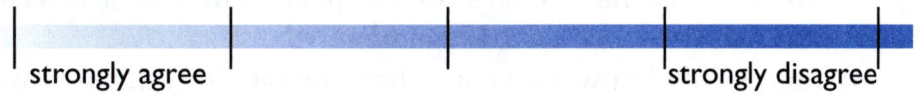

2. Writing is useful for school, but it's not very useful beyond that.

   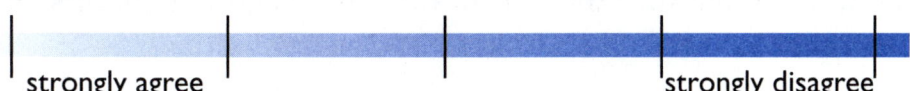

3. Strong writers usually get the words down right the first time, without needing to revise or get feedback.

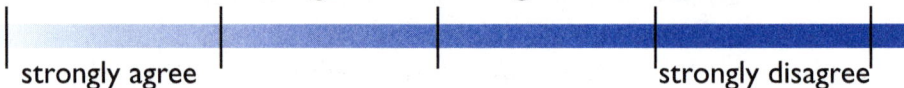

4. A writer should never write in the first person (use *I*).

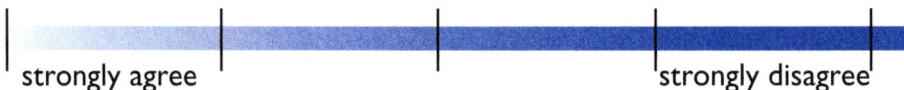

5. As long as your ideas are good, it doesn't matter if you use correct punctuation and grammar.

As you complete each unit in this book, take a moment to return to the questions above. Think about whether the placement of each X still represents your beliefs about writing. If necessary, move your X to a new position.

Your Writers' Network

The British poet John Donne wrote, "No man is an island, entire of itself; every man is a piece of the continent, a part of the main." Similarly, no writer is an island, working entirely alone. Each writer is a part of a larger group. For instance, writers in the workplace and professional writers turn to peers, editors, or a writers' group for feedback and encouragement.

Whom do you know who could become part of your own writers' network? In the box on the next page, write the names and contact information of at least three people who will form your network. Make sure that one of them is a classmate in this class.

> My Writers' Network
>
> *People to rely on for feedback and encouragement*

Why Study Writing?

The ability to write clearly and engagingly in a variety of genres is a sure sign of a solid education. It prepares you for success in school, in college, and beyond in careers and daily life. For this reason, students are asked to demonstrate their ability in various forms of writing. These forms, or genres, include descriptive, expository, persuasive, and literary writing as well as response to literature. Classroom tests, state tests, the SAT, and the ACT measure your ability to write clear, original, well-organized paragraphs and essays.

Teachers and other educators who evaluate your writing will check to see how well you use certain *traits of writing*. The following table explains six important traits.

Six Traits of Writing

Ideas	The writing is clear and focused. Each detail clearly relates to the topic.
Organization	Details are arranged in a logical manner, such as from least to most important or in chronological order.
Voice	The writer shines through as a real person behind the writing. The writing style fits with the purpose and audience of the piece.
Word Choice	Words are vivid and accurate, helping to draw in the reader while making ideas clear.
Sentence Fluency	A variety of sentence types and structures creates a pleasing rhythm to the writing.
Conventions	Capitalization, spelling, punctuation, and grammar are correct.

These six traits of writing form the backbone of the lessons in the books in this series.

About This Series

This is the first book of *The Writer's Studio*, a three-volume writing instruction series. In this book, *Level A*, you'll get instruction, review, and practice in five important genres of writing. In *Level B*, you'll sharpen your writing skills and increase your knowledge of the traits of writing. In *Level C*, you'll continue to build your abilities of writing in different genres while learning more sophisticated writing skills and techniques. All three levels contain detailed sections on test writing to help you prepare for writing in different genres on school, state, and national tests.

What's Inside This Book

The Writer's Studio, Level A contains a variety of lessons, features, and activities.

Unit Opener: This section introduces you to a particular genre of writing. You'll learn why the genre is important, and you'll read an example of this genre.

> **Six Traits of Writing:** For each unit, the table of writing traits is tailored to explain a specific genre of writing.
>
> **Real-World Examples:** These are short models of writing taken from books and Web sites. They show how writers use a particular genre outside the classroom.
>
> **Learning Tips:** These are suggestions for linking your classroom study to your life outside of school.
>
> **Rubrics:** Each chapter includes a 4-point rubric, or scoring guideline, tailored for a specific genre of writing.
>
> **Models:** In each chapter, one model of writing helps to teach the traits of writing. A second model provides an opportunity for you to use the rubric to evaluate the strength of the writing.
>
> **Writer's Toolkit** and **Tips:** Strategies and tips for the stages of the writing process.
>
> **Checklists:** Revising and editing checklists in of each chapter help you improve your writing.
>
> **Mini-Lessons:** These lessons target some of the trouble spots that face writers. Topics range from grammar to sentence structure to thesis statements.
>
> **Test Writing:** These chapters prepare you for writing tasks on school tests, on state tests, and on national tests.

Unit Wrap-Up: In this section you will summarize and reflect on what you have learned.

> **You Be the Judge:** You will evaluate an essay that was written by a real student.

Ideas for Writing: This is a bank of additional writing prompts from which you or your teacher can choose. One choice asks you to Write Across the Curriculum, using information from a subject such as social studies or science.

Reflections: In a graphic organizer, you will organize your thoughts, accomplishments, and goals regarding a genre of writing.

Conventions Handbook: Rules and definitions of key terms in the areas of sentences, the eight parts of speech, how words work in sentences, and punctuation.

This book is a valuable resource that will help you become a stronger writer in many different genres and writing situations. Complete the series, and you'll see big improvements in your ability to write clearly, powerfully, and engagingly.

Good luck!
Lesli J. Favor, Ph.D., *Author*

Unit 1

Descriptive Writing

The Unit at a Glance
Get to Know the Genre   1
Ch. 1 Describe a Person   5
Ch. 2 Describe a Place   19
Ch. 3 Describe a Scientific Subject   33
Ch. 4 Test Writing: The Descriptive Essay   45
Descriptive Writing Wrap-Up   55

Get to Know the Genre: Descriptive Writing

Think about a time when you saw a great movie, and you told a friend all about it. Or imagine a time when you saw the perfect haircut, ate a mouth-watering dessert, or held a squirming puppy, and you eagerly told a friend. Chances are, you described these things by telling how they looked, sounded, felt, smelled, or tasted. You were using descriptive details to bring something to life for your audience—in this case, your friend. In the same way, you can bring people, places, things, and experiences to life in descriptive writing. **Descriptive writing** tells about a person, place, thing, or experience in a way that helps readers connect to the subject as though they were right there. **Sensory details**—those that appeal to sight, hearing, taste, touch, and smell—help to do this.

Unit 1

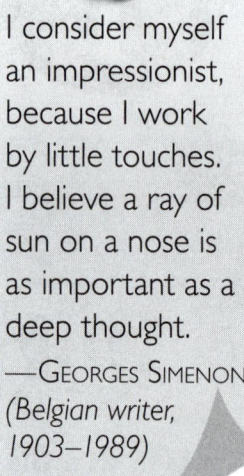

I consider myself an impressionist, because I work by little touches. I believe a ray of sun on a nose is as important as a deep thought.
—GEORGES SIMENON
(Belgian writer, 1903–1989)

Give It a Try: Explore Sensory Details

On separate paper, complete each of the following sentences.

1. I'll always remember the smell of…
2. I couldn't believe my eyes when I saw…
3. The worst taste in the world is…
4. I was surprised the first time I touched…
5. The first thing I usually hear in the morning is…

On page xii, you read about six traits of good writing. Now look at the following table. It shows how these traits link to descriptive writing.

Six Traits of Descriptive Writing

Ideas	The topic is narrowed to a specific person, place, thing, or experience. Each detail clearly relates to the topic.
Organization	Details are arranged with care, such as from least to most important or in time order.
Voice	The writer shines through as a real person behind the writing. The writing style fits with the purpose and audience of the description.
Word Choice	Nouns, adjectives, adverbs, and verbs are specific and lively. Sensory details bring life to sights, sounds, textures, smells, and/or tastes.
Sentence Fluency	A variety of sentence types and structures creates a pleasing rhythm to the writing.
Conventions	Capitalization, spelling, and punctuation are correct.

2 • The Writer's Studio   Level A

Real-World Example

You've reviewed the traits of good descriptive writing. Now read this descriptive paragraph from the novel *Everything on a Waffle* by Polly Horvath. In this paragraph the narrator, Primrose, describes her uncle, Jack. Primrose recently moved in with Uncle Jack when her parents were lost at sea.

Ideas: one clear subject of the description

Sentence fluency: This complex sentence has one main clause and two dependent clauses.

Word choices: delightful adjectives

Conventions: Commas separate items in the series.

Voice: The voice is that of Primrose. She shines through here in her opinion of Uncle Jack.

Word choices: details about smells

Organization: chronological (time) order

Word choices: not just "cookies," but "lemon cookies"

Conventions: Proper nouns are capitalized.

Word choices: lively verb and adverb

> Just then Uncle Jack pulled up. He got out of his car with his big, bouncing, catlike step that I found so reassuring, especially when I was cowering between the front door and my guidance counselor, unable to say thank you, now go away. He was dressed in a suit, starched shirt, and tie. I could smell him from the top of the steps. He wore a lot of aftershave when he worked and used a lot of breath freshener. It didn't make him smell good exactly, more as if he was trying hard. He bounded up to us and when Miss Honeycut, who was taking in the crisp shirt and suit in an approving way, handed him the plate of lemon cookies, he gave her a huge smile that was wall-to-wall teeth from beneath his blond mustache. The smile was both a warm and gracious welcome and a polite dismissal. Miss Honeycut launched into her tea at Buckingham Palace anecdote and the grin never left Uncle Jack's face for one moment. When she finished there was silence for thirty seconds or so, then Miss Honeycut snapped it off crisply by saying through her teeth, "I hope that everything is running smoothly since the adjustment."

Give It a Try: Examine the Real-World Example

Can you find additional examples of the six traits of good writing in the model paragraph above? On separate paper, list two traits of good writing. For each one, quote or describe an example from the model.

Unit 1

Get Ready to Write

Now that you've explored the qualities of descriptive writing, you're ready to create some descriptions of your own. In the chapters that follow, you'll write about a person you know, a place you go for fun, science in your world, and an ideal escape. You'll use the stages of the writing process—prewriting, drafting, revising, editing, and publishing—and you'll be presented with models and mini-lessons along the way.

As you work through these chapters, you can enrich your understanding by trying the suggestions below. These tips will help you connect what you're learning in this unit to your own life and the world around you.

LEARNING TIPS

- Watch for descriptive writing in the reading you do for school. Think about how descriptive writing helps you understand ideas in math, science, and social studies.

- Watch for descriptive writing in magazines, in stories, in e-mails, and on menus. Think about the purpose of these descriptions. How does the writer seem to want the reader to respond?

- Listen for descriptive writing in television commercials and radio advertisements. Pay attention to what kinds of experiences the descriptive writing creates for you.

- Practice writing—and speaking—descriptively. Write e-mails and make phone calls simply to describe something to someone. Use description in your writing for other classes.

4 • The Writer's Studio   Level A

Chapter 1

Describe a Person

As you've learned, you can use your powers of description to bring things alive for readers. By using fresh word choices and sensory details, you can create lifelike images of people and other subjects.

You describe people all the time. Think of a time when you described your favorite actor to a friend. Or think of your best friend and how you described him or her to a parent. Perhaps a striking person caught your eye in a shopping mall. You grabbed your cell, called a friend, and said, "I have to tell you about this person I just saw!"

In this chapter, you will build on your natural skills of describing people. You will continue to use the Six Traits of Descriptive Writing that you studied on page 2. Here are the traits again. This time they are linked to the subject of this chapter: describing a person.

Six Traits of Describing a Person

Ideas	The topic is narrowed to a specific person. Each detail clearly relates to this person.
Organization	Details are arranged logically, such as from most to least important, in spatial order, or in time order.
Voice	The writer shines through as a real person behind the writing. The writing style fits with the purpose and audience of the description.
Word Choice	Nouns, adjectives, adverbs, and verbs are specific and lively. Sensory details are present.
Sentence Fluency	A variety of sentence types and structures creates a pleasing rhythm to the writing.
Conventions	Capitalization, spelling, and punctuation are correct.

Ch. 1 Describe a Person

In the following model paragraph, the writer describes his next-door neighbor.

> I met Carly last summer when her megaphone voice woke me up one morning. "Who left their bike in my new driveway?" she was yelling. She had just moved in next door. Her hair is carrot red and long. I yanked on it one time, and it felt thick and coarse, like my dog's long hair. Her eyes are denim blue and tilt up at the corners. On her nose she's got reddish brown freckles, and her smile shows a gap between two front teeth. She usually wears a shirt with a waffle-weave, which is a square bumpy pattern. Her short fingernails are always dirty, and this is proof of how much fun she has. Her feet, stuck into red high-top sneakers, are always in motion. She taps her toes, jiggles one foot, dances a jig, or breaks out in a run. As she races past, she trails the scent of bubble gum.

Give It a Try: Examine the Model Paragraph

Answer the following questions about six traits in the model paragraph above. Write your answers on separate paper.

1. **Ideas.** Whom is this paragraph about?
2. **Organization.** In general, how did the writer organize details (for example, order of importance or top of the person to bottom of the person). How can you tell?
3. **Voice and word choice.** List three words or phrases that catch your attention and make you have a sense of the real person who is writing this paragraph.
4. **Sentence fluency.** Copy the sentence that begins, "Her short fingernails . . . " Then circle the connecting word in this compound sentence.
5. **Conventions.** Why does the writer use quotation marks in the paragraph?

Describe a Person Ch. 1

Your Turn to Write: Describe a Person

Now you'll write your own descriptive paragraph about someone you know. Read the assignment carefully and follow the strategies and instructions for each stage of the writing process.

Assignment

You and a study partner have agreed to meet after school tomorrow. After you make the arrangements, another person asks if he or she can join in. Since you will be late to the meet time, you need to write an e-mail to your study partner. The purpose of the e-mail is to describe the additional person so that your study partner can recognize the person when he or she shows up. Write one paragraph of 100 to 150 words in which you describe the person who will join your study session. Be sure to use sensory details to bring this person alive.

Prewrite

Analyze the Prompt. What does this assignment require you to do? Reread the assignment above to find answers to the following questions. Write your answers on separate paper.

1. What is the purpose of this paragraph?
2. Who is the audience for this paragraph?
3. How long does the paragraph need to be?

Choose a Topic. Choose a person to describe. Follow the instructions below and write your answers on separate paper.

1. List three people whom you could describe in your paragraph. After each name, tell why you might write about that person.

Unit 1 • Descriptive Writing • **7**

Ch. 1 Describe a Person

2. Answer the following questions by writing names from your list in step 1. You can list more than one name in each answer.
   a. Who has hair or a clothing style that stands out?
   b. Who has an interesting voice or accent?
   c. Who has a special way of standing or walking?
   d. Who makes you think of a certain scent, such as cologne, shampoo, or mints?
   e. Who makes you think of a certain texture, such as rough denim or fuzzy sweaters?
3. Based on the ideas in steps 1 and 2, which person would make the best subject for your descriptive paragraph?

Gather Ideas and Details. Create a table like the one below to jot down sensory details about the person you chose to write about. Some details have been filled in as examples.

Sensory Details About _____ (the name of your person)

sight	sound	touch	smell
caramel-colored hair	husky voice	denim jacket	scent of breath mints

Organize Ideas and Details. Decide how you will arrange ideas and details in your description. Remember that the purpose of the description is to describe a person so that someone else can recognize him or her. The next page explains three methods of organization that work well in descriptions of people. Read about each method; later, you'll be asked to try one of them.

8 • The Writer's Studio   Level A

- **Order of importance.** Include details from most to least important. Start with the most noticeable detail about this person. Move on to the detail that your friend will probably notice next, and so on, in order to build a complete picture.

- **Time order.** Provide a context for your description, such as having the subject move from a doorway to a study table. Include details in the order in which your friend would notice them as the subject moves across this space.

- **Spatial order.** Describe your subject from top to bottom. Begin with the bright red hair, for example, and conclude with the squeaky shoes.

Organize Your Description. Follow the steps to organize your own description.

1. Review the details that you recorded in the Sensory Details table on page 8.
2. Circle two or three of the strongest details in each column of the table.
3. Choose one of the organization methods described above. Write the name of the method.
4. On your paper, list details in the order in which you will present them, based on your answer in step 3.

Draft

Now it's time to get your ideas on paper in a paragraph format. Three ingredients of a strong descriptive paragraph are a topic sentence, the body, and the closing sentence.

The **topic sentence** should introduce the subject of your description in a way that hooks the reader's interest. For example, you can include a sensory detail that helps the reader immediately form a mental image of the person being described. Here are two examples.

> The first thing you'll notice about Travis is that he will be carrying drumsticks. (visual detail)

Ch. 1 Describe a Person

> You'll probably hear Travis tapping his drumsticks together before you even see him. (sound detail)

Each of these examples introduces Travis with a different key detail. However, both examples show that Travis is a drummer. Additional descriptive details should support this image of Travis as a drummer.

Write Your Topic Sentence. On separate paper, write a topic sentence for your paragraph.

What do you think of your first effort? Want to try a different way of opening the paragraph? Write another topic sentence, and this time use a different attention-getting detail.

The **body sentences** of your paragraph build on the image that the topic sentence introduced. This part of the paragraph brings your subject to life. In the body sentences below, notice how the writer uses sensory details and vivid words to build her mental portrait of Travis. Since this is a rough draft, you'll notice rough spots in the writing.

Word choice: sight detail

Word choice: touch detail

Word choice: vivid adjective

Voice: personal detail that lets the writer's voice shine through

Word choice: smell detail; the noun *whiff* is vivid

Travis's caramel-colored hair is straight and silky. It's cut long and shaggy around the ears. He smiles a lot, and you'll see that his teeth are straight and sparkly. They remind me of a row of square breath mints. Speaking of mints, he always has a box of mints in his pocket. Up close, you may catch a faint whiff of the scent. Up close he is shorter than he seems from a distance. Maybe because he is thin with the posture of a dancer. But he doesn't dress like a dancer; he wears jeans and T-shirts.

Voice: personal opinion helps the writer's voice to shine

10 • The Writer's Studio   Level A

Describe a Person Ch. 1

Write the Paragraph's Body Sentences. Look back at Organize Your Description on page 9. There, you listed details of your description in a logical order. Use this list to write the body of your paragraph on a separate sheet of paper.

The paragraph's **closing sentence** brings the description to an end. A strong closing sentence makes your mental portrait stay in the reader's mind.

In a rough draft, the closing sentence may start out as two or three related sentences. Later, you can combine the related sentences into one strong sentence. In the example below, the writer uses three sentences to write her closing thought.

> He'll probably slide into a chair at your study table. He'll line his drumsticks up straight on the table. He'll say, "Hey," in his husky voice.

Write Your Closing Sentence. On separate paper, write the idea that will bring your description to an end. Then write a clean copy of your entire paragraph, including the topic sentence, body sentences, and closing sentence.

Revise

When you wrote the rough draft of your paragraph, you focused on getting your ideas down on paper. Now you will revise your paragraph to make it stronger. One way of making your paragraph stronger is to revise it for sentence fluency.

Mini-Lesson: Sentence Fluency

Sentence fluency is the rhythm and flow of the sentences in a paragraph. A well-written paragraph has a pleasing rhythm when you read it aloud or silently. The writer has used a mix of short and long sentences and a variety of sentence types.

Unit 1 • Descriptive Writing • **11**

Ch. 1 **Describe a Person**

The first draft of a paragraph often contains lots of short sentences. As a result, the rhythm is choppy or awkward. You can revise a paragraph that has too many short, choppy sentences. One way is to combine two *simple sentences* into one *compound sentence*.

➡ A **simple sentence** has one subject and one verb. It is a main (independent) clause.

I met Selena at the bus stop.

She smiled at me in a friendly way.

➡ A **compound sentence** is a combination of two or more simple sentences.

<u>I met Selena at the bus stop</u>, and <u>she smiled at me in a friendly way</u>.

As in the example above, you can join simple sentences using *coordinating conjunctions*.

➡ A **coordinating conjunction** is a word that is used to join two main clauses. Coordinating conjunctions include the words *for*, *and*, *nor*, *but*, *or*, and *yet*.

In the example above, the coordinating conjunction *and* joins two simple sentences to form one compound sentence. Notice that a comma is placed before the conjunction.

Give It a Try: Combine Simple Sentences to Form Compound Sentences

In each item that follows, combine the short, choppy sentences to form one compound sentence. To join the sentences, use a comma and a coordinating conjunction from this list:

    for   and   nor   but   or   yet

Write your new sentences on separate paper.

1. Her complexion is smooth and dark. Her eyelashes are long and curly.

Describe a Person Ch. 1

2. Selena's smile is shy. It lights up her face.
3. She has a chipped tooth. It just makes her more interesting.
4. She laughs a lot. She has a great sense of humor.
5. She usually wears faded jeans. She might dress up in a bright floral skirt.

Give It a Try: Revise Your Paragraph for Sentence Fluency

Revise your descriptive paragraph by looking for short, choppy sentences to combine. Use coordinating conjunctions and commas to create more pleasing compound sentences.

Revise Your Paragraph. Revise your rough draft, this time looking at more than sentence fluency. Here is a checklist that will help you decide what to change, remove, or leave in place. Also use the rubric on page 16 to guide your revisions.

Ideas
- ❏ Reread your topic sentence. Does it introduce the person in a way that gets your reader's attention? If so, place a check mark next to it. If not, revise it to make it more interesting.
- ❏ Place a check mark next to each main detail in your description. If a detail does not describe the person, cross it out.

Organization
- ❏ What is your paragraph's method of organization? Underline words in your paragraph that show your organizational method.

Voice
- ❏ Find two words or phrases that show how your writing style fits with your audience (a classmate). Write *voice* above each one. Then find two words or phrases that show your attitude or opinion about the person. Write *voice* above each one.

Ch. 1 — Describe a Person

Word choice
- ☐ Circle three specific and expressive words you used to describe the person.
- ☐ Underline three different kinds of sensory details you included.

Sentence fluency
- ☐ Make sure you have a variety of long and short sentences. If necessary, combine short, choppy sentences into longer, smoother sentences.

Edit

To edit your writing means to find and correct mistakes in capitalization, spelling, and punctuation. Here are three ways to find and correct mistakes in your writing:

Use reference tools. If you are unsure of a word's spelling, use a dictionary. If you are unsure of capitalization or punctuation rules, use a conventions handbook like the one on page 313 of this book.

Get feedback. Ask a classmate, family member, or tutor to circle mistakes in your writing. Then use reference tools to figure out how to correct the mistakes.

Learn from your work. As you correct mistakes, make sure you understand *why* something was a mistake. By learning the rules of conventions, you will begin to find and correct mistakes more quickly and easily.

> **T!p** Do not rely solely on Spell Check. It can be useful for catching mistakes, but it can also introduce new errors into your essay by substituting the wrong word if it thinks you mean something else. Check your essay yourself in addition to using Spell Check and look up words you're not sure about in an online dictionary like Merriam-Webster (www.m-w.com).

14 • The Writer's Studio   Level A

Edit Your Paragraph for Conventions. Edit your revised draft, using the checklist below.

Capitalization
- ❏ Did you capitalize proper nouns, such as the subject's name?
- ❏ Did you begin each sentence with a capital letter?

Punctuation
- ❏ Did you use a comma when you joined sentences with a co-ordinating conjunction?
- ❏ Did you use a comma when you began a sentence with a subordinate clause?

Spelling
- ❏ Did you correct spelling mistakes, either with a friend's help or by using a dictionary? Did you make sure that Spell Check used the right words?

PUBLISH

Presentation. Prepare your descriptive paragraph for publication by writing or typing the final, edited copy.

Publish Your Paragraph. Here are a few ideas for publishing your descriptive paragraph.
- ❏ Give a copy to the person whom you described in the paragraph.
- ❏ In a small group, read the paragraph aloud but leave out the name of the person being described (for example, *Travis* in the model paragraph). Find out if anyone can guess whom the paragraph describes.
- ❏ Add a copy to your writer's portfolio.
- ❏ Paste a copy in your scrapbook (along with copies of any paragraphs that were written about you).

Ch. 1 • Describe a Person

Descriptive Paragraph Rubric

	4 **Strong**	**3** **Effective**	**2** **Developing**	**1** **Beginning**
Ideas	One subject is described. Each detail clearly relates.	The subject is clear, but some details do not relate.	The writer is beginning to make the subject clear.	The subject is not clear. Most details do not relate.
Organization	Sensory details are arranged logically.	Most details are arranged logically.	Organization of details is awkward.	Details are in random order.
Voice	The writing style is distinctive and helps the reader connect to the description.	The writing style draws the reader into the description but doesn't have a personal flair.	The writing style of one or two sentences, but not all, draws in the reader.	Writing is mechanical, making it hard for readers to connect to the description.
Word Choice	Specific and lively words are used. Sensory details are used with skill.	Many words are specific and lively. Many sensory details are included.	Words are simple but mostly correct. A few sensory details are used.	Vocabulary is limited. Sensory details are not present or not clear.
Sentence Fluency	A variety of sentence types are used in a pleasing rhythm.	A variety of sentence types are used, but some may be awkward.	Sentences are complete but are mostly short and simple.	Sentences are mostly of one type or are incomplete.
Conventions	Capitalization, spelling, punctuation, and grammar are correct.	There are few errors in capitalization, spelling, punctuation, and grammar.	There are many errors in capitalization, spelling, punctuation, and grammar.	Errors in conventions make it hard to understand the writing.

Describe a Person   Ch. 1

Evaluate Your Paragraph

Your teacher will either assess your paragraph, ask you to self-assess your paragraph, or ask you to switch with a partner and assess each other's work.

Evaluate the Model Paragraph

Work with a partner to evaluate the completed model descriptive paragraph below. Use the rubric from page 16 and write your score here: _____. In a class discussion, explain the score that you gave.

> The first thing you'll notice about Travis is that he will be carrying drumsticks. He may be tapping them lightly together, sounding out a rhythm. His caramel-colored hair is silky straight, and it is cut long and shaggy around the ears. When he smiles, you'll see that his teeth are as straight and sparkly as a row of square breath mints. Speaking of mints, he always has a square, green metal box of mints in his pocket. Up close, you may catch a faint whiff of wintergreen on his breath. Also, up close he is shorter than he seems from a distance. Maybe this trick of the eye is because he is thin and has the posture of a dancer. Anyway, he'll probably slide into a chair at your study table, line his drumsticks up straight on the table, and say, "Hey," in his husky voice.

Describe a Place

If you search your memory, chances are you'll find lots of favorite places. Favorite places can be small, like "your" chair at the dinner table, and they can be large, like the Grand Canyon. They can be personal, like your room, and they can be public, like a school auditorium. All these places together make up a life—your life. What do they say about you?

In this chapter, you'll write about a place where you like to go to have fun. You'll continue to use your skills of description. Whereas in Chapter 1 you focused on writing a single paragraph, in this chapter you'll write an essay. Perhaps you'll enjoy your writing almost as much as you enjoy your favorite place.

Some information in the following table will be familiar to you from Chapter 1. Some new details have been added to link to this chapter's topic—describing a place—and the essay format.

Six Traits of Describing a Place

Ideas	The topic is narrowed to a specific place. Each detail clearly relates to this place.
Organization	The essay includes a catchy introduction, body paragraphs that describe the place, and a satisfying conclusion. Ideas and details throughout the essay are arranged logically.
Voice	The writer shines through as a real person behind the writing. The writing style fits with the purpose and audience of the description.
Word Choice	Nouns, adjectives, adverbs, and verbs are specific and lively. Sensory details are present.
Sentence Fluency	A variety of sentence types and structures creates a pleasing rhythm to the writing.
Conventions	Capitalization, spelling, and punctuation are correct.

Unit 1 • Descriptive Writing • 19

Ch. 2 **Describe a Place**

In the following model paragraph, the writer describes a favorite place for having fun.

> A day at Splash World is a refreshing way to cool off and have fun with friends. As I enter the park, my nose detects the scents of water, sunscreen, and food all luring me into enjoyment. My first stop is always Water Town, where there are twenty different water rides. I slide, ride, wade, and spin my way to coolness. When I'm tired, I relax by the pool in Swim Town, shaded by blue and green umbrellas. Then I step over to Food Town and order favorites like crispy chicken fingers or minivegetables with ranch dressing. Finally, I walk through Shop Town. I pose with friends for goofy pictures, record a song at the mini-recording studio, and buy an inexpensive souvenir for my little sister. A day at Splash World always adds fun to *my* world!

Give It a Try: Examine the Model Paragraph

Answer the following questions about six traits in the model paragraph above. Write your answers on separate paper.

1. **Ideas.** What place does the writer describe?
2. **Organization.** What method does the writer use to organize details (such as most to least important, spatial order, time order)? How can you tell?
3. **Voice.** Which point of view does the writer mainly use? Choose one of the following:
   - first-person point of view, which uses first-person pronouns such as *I*, *me*, and *my*
   - second-person point of view, which uses second-person pronouns such as *you* and *your*

20 • The Writer's Studio   Level A

- third-person point of view, which uses third-person pronouns such as *he*, *she*, and *their*

4. **Word choice.** Copy each verb in the paragraph. (Your teacher may ask you to work with a partner to do this.) Then, on your paper, list five verbs that, in your opinion, really make the paragraph sparkle.

5. **Sentence fluency and conventions.** Write one example of a sentence from the paragraph that begins with an introductory element and a comma.

Your Turn to Write: Describe a Place

Now you'll write your own descriptive essay about a special place. Read the assignment carefully and follow the strategies and instructions for each stage of the writing process.

Assignment

Each state in our nation has a tourism office whose job is to attract visitors to the state. Your state tourism office has invited students to send in descriptions of their favorite place in the state. Winning entries will be used on a brochure for students and teachers to encourage class trips to these locations. Here are the writing guidelines:

> Across our state, people gather for fun in special places. These places include fairgrounds, shopping malls, summer camps, lakes, zoos, and more. Where is your favorite place to gather for fun? Write an essay of 400 words in which you describe your favorite place in the state. Write your description so that young readers will feel as if they are there with you in this place.

Ch. 2 **Describe a Place**

Prewrite

Analyze the Prompt. The following questions will help you identify important details in the writing assignment. Write your answers on separate paper.

1. What is the purpose of this essay?
2. Who is the audience for this essay?
3. How long does the essay need to be?

Choose a Topic. Complete the following steps to select a topic for your essay.

1. Choose *two* different fun places where you have been. Then choose one of the people on your Writers' Network from page xi. E-mail or talk to that person and tell him or her briefly about each place. Ask a few questions such as, "Which place sounds more fun?" or "Which place would you rather read about?"
2. Review the e-mails or conversations from step 1. Then choose one of the places to be the subject of your essay.

Gather Ideas and Details. The following strategies will help you gather ideas and details to use in your description of a fun gathering place. Try one or more of these strategies.

- **Freewriting.** Write the name of your place at the top of a sheet of paper. For five minutes, write about your topic without stopping. Let one idea lead to the next, and don't worry about spelling, grammar, or organization. In your mind, notice sights and other sensory details. Let them all flow out onto the paper. After five minutes, stop writing and read your freewriting. Circle ideas and details that you could use in your essay.

- **Blind writing.** This is a variation on freewriting. On a computer, open a word-processing program so that you can type in your ideas. Then, either close your eyes or turn off the monitor so that you are "blind." Write for five minutes without stopping.

22 • The Writer's Studio   Level A

Describe a Place Ch. 2

Record sensory details, images in your memory, and so on. After five minutes, stop and read what you have written. Underline ideas and details that you could use in your essay.

- **Listing.** Write the name of your place at the top of a sheet of paper. Make several columns on your paper, such as *activities*, *animals*, *foods*, *nature*, *sounds* or other useful categories. Then list as many details in each column as you can. Finally, review your lists and circle details that you could use in your essay.

Organize Ideas and Details. Now it is time to plan the arrangement of ideas and details in your descriptive essay. The following model shows part of an informal outline for a descriptive essay. The writer uses the organizational method of time order. First, he introduces Marymoor Park; then he describes parts of the park in the order that a visitor would see them during a visit.

1. Marymoor Park
   --time of year: autumn
   --first impression of park when I arrive
2. Entering the park
   --5 mph speed limit
   --dirt bicycle path
   --sound details: *whoosh* of bikes and *ding* of bells
   --my bicycle
3. Kids in park
   --guy my age with ice cream
   --playground with kids on swings
   --skateboard course

Which method of organization would work best for your essay—time order, order of importance, or spatial arrangement? Choose one of these methods.

Organize Your Description. At the top of a sheet of paper, write the name of your place and the method of organization that you chose. Then use a numbered list or outline format to plan the structure of your essay.

Ch. 2 **Describe a Place**

 **Draft**

Now it's time to write the first draft. As you know, your essay needs an introduction, a body, and a conclusion.

Introduction. A strong essay begins with an introduction that catches the reader's interest. In your descriptive essay, the introductory paragraph should introduce your place by name, tell what kind of place it is, and give readers an idea, image, or detail that will make them want to know more.

Here are a few strategies for catching your reader's interest.

- Give interesting facts or figures.
  More than three million people visit Marymoor Park each year.
- Include one or more sensory details that will spark your reader's imagination.
  As you enter the park, you'll hear cheers from the ballpark, laughter from the playground, and the ding! ding! of bicycle bells on the bike path.
- Give an overview of the most interesting features of this place.
  Marymoor Park is like a miniworld, complete with food, playgrounds, sports fields, a dog park, picnic areas, and more.

Write Your Introduction. On a clean sheet of paper, write an introductory paragraph for your essay. Be sure to
  ❏ introduce your place by name
  ❏ tell what kind of place it is
  ❏ include an idea, image, or detail that will make your readers want to know more about this place

Body paragraphs. The body of a descriptive essay is the middle part, the part that comes after the introduction and before the conclusion. In this part, describe your place in a way that makes readers feel as though they are right there. Use sensory details and follow a clear method of organization.

Write Your Body Paragraphs. Write the paragraphs that form the body of your descriptive essay. As you write, be sure to
- review the ideas and details you gathered during prewriting
- follow the outline you wrote
- use a consistent point of view

Conclusion. Your essay's conclusion brings your description of the place to an end. A strong conclusion adds something new to the image of the place while giving the sense that the description is now complete. Here is the conclusion to the essay about Marymoor Park.

> The highlight of the day will be at dusk, when a movie will be shown on the giant outdoor screen at the far end of the grassy field. People will gather to sit on blankets and lawn chairs. We'll eat kettle corn, sip lemonade, murmur quietly to one another, and watch the family-friendly movie with lazy interest. I might even fall asleep before the movie is over, just like at home. The perfect place.

Write Your Conclusion. Now write a paragraph that will bring your essay to a satisfying close.

Revise

Why revise an essay if you got all your ideas written down in the rough draft? This is like asking why you should practice batting *again* when you hit two home runs in last week's game. The reason is that, by going over your work again, you can add that spark that makes your audience sit up and pay attention. Your work gets stronger with each careful pass.

One way to make your writing stronger is to add sentence variety. Sentence variety refers to a mix of sentence types, sentence lengths, and sentence beginnings. The mini-lesson on the next page explains how to vary the beginnings of your sentences.

Ch. 2   **Describe a Place**

Mini-Lesson: Using Introductory Elements

One of the traits of good writing is sentence fluency. Sentences flow fluidly, or pleasingly, for the reader when there is variety in sentence structure. When most sentences have the same structure, the rhythm is predictable and even boring.

You can examine the structure of sentences in a paragraph by writing the sentences in a list format, like this:

> Our car slows to obey the 5-mile-per-hour speed limit.
>
> A row of bicyclists zips along up ahead on a dirt path.
>
> They flick the little bells on their bikes.
>
> They pass my car window with a whoosh.
>
> I reach down to check for my bike helmet in the bag at my feet.
>
> My bike is stowed on a rack on the top of the car.

Next, study the placement of subjects and verbs. Underline each subject once and each verb twice, as shown above. Notice that all the examples above begin with a subject and verb. This pattern is used over and over, creating a dull, repetitive pattern.

To create sentence variety, some of the sentences need to have different types of beginnings, such as introductory words, phrases, or clauses. The introductory elements may be formed of words from another part of the sentence or with new words.

> Our car slows to obey the 5-mile-per-hour speed limit.
>
> **Up ahead,** a row of bicyclists zips along on a dirt path.
>
> **As they come near our car,** they flick the little bells on their bikes.
>
> **With a whoosh,** they pass my car window.
>
> **Automatically,** I reach down to check for my bike helmet in the bag at my feet.
>
> My bike is stowed on a rack on the top of the car.

Describe a Place Ch. 2

Give It a Try: Revise Sentences to Add Variety in Structure

On separate paper, rewrite each sentence by adding a word, phrase, or clause to the beginning. You can move words from another part of the sentence, or you can add your own words.

1. Dog owners pile out of their cars near the dog park.
2. A youth softball league whoops and shouts in the ball fields.
3. Bats ring against neon-yellow softballs.
4. Canadian geese honk and fly in long V formations.
5. They land with a whisper of webbed feet.

Give It a Try: Revise a Paragraph with a Partner

With your teacher's permission, get together with a partner. Together, revise a paragraph in your essay for sentence variety. Follow these steps:

1. Write the sentences from the paragraph in a list format.
2. With your partner, underline each noun once and each verb twice.
3. If several sentences begin in the same way, choose some to revise.
4. Revise sentences by adding an introductory word, phrase, or clause.
5. Be sure to insert a comma after the introductory element.

Revise Your Descriptive Essay. You have already made some revisions to the rough draft of your essay. Now, review the following checklist and make additional revisions to your work. The Descriptive Essay Rubric that follows the checklist will help you determine how strong your essay is and where to make your revisions.

Unit 1 • Descriptive Writing • 27

Ch. 2 Describe a Place

Ideas
- ❏ Find the sentence where you introduce the place. Place a check mark next to the sentence if it introduces the place in a way that catches your reader's attention. If not, revise it.
- ❏ Underline three details and ideas that help to describe the place. Cross out any details that are off topic.

Organization
- ❏ Are the descriptive details arranged in a logical order? Rearrange any details that are out of order.

Voice
- ❏ Find words or phrases that show your attitude or opinion about the place. Write *voice* above them. Then find words or phrases that show you're aware of your audience (young people who are looking for a fun gathering place). Write *voice* above them.
- ❏ Check that you have used a consistent point of view (first, second, or third person).

Word choice
- ❏ Circle two specific and expressive words you used to describe this place.
- ❏ Circle two sensory details you used.

Sentence fluency
- ❏ Have you used a variety of sentence structures? Revise sentences if necessary.

Describe a Place — Ch. 2

Descriptive Essay Rubric

	4 Strong	**3 Effective**	**2 Developing**	**1 Beginning**
Ideas	One place is described. Each detail clearly relates.	The subject is clear, but some details do not relate.	The writer is beginning to make the subject clear.	The subject is not clear. Most details do not relate.
Organization	Descriptive details are arranged logically.	Most details are arranged logically.	Organization of details is awkward.	Details are in random order.
Voice	The writing style is distinctive and helps the reader connect to the description.	The writing style draws the reader in to the description but doesn't have a personal flair.	The writing style of one or two sentences, but not all, draws in the reader.	Writing is mechanical, making it hard for readers to connect to the description.
Word Choice	Specific and lively words are used. Sensory details are used with skill.	Many words are specific and lively. Many sensory details are included.	Words are simple but mostly correct. A few sensory details are used.	Vocabulary is limited. Sensory details are not present or not clear.
Sentence Fluency	Sentence variety creates a pleasing rhythm	Sentences are varied in structure, but some are awkward.	Sentences are complete but are mostly short and simple.	Sentences are mostly of one type or are incomplete.
Conventions	Capitalization, spelling, punctuation, and grammar are correct.	There are few errors in capitalization, spelling, punctuation, and grammar.	There are many errors in capitalization, spelling, punctuation, and grammar.	Errors in conventions make it hard to understand the writing.

Unit 1 • Descriptive Writing

Ch. 2 **Describe a Place**

 ## Edit

How is editing your writing different from revising it?

When you revise your essay, you make changes to strengthen ideas, organization, word choice, sentences, and voice. The changes at this stage can be large or small. You move around sentences and paragraphs, for example, or add and delete details.

After revising comes the editing stage. Now you look for mistakes in spelling, punctuation, capitalization, and grammar, and you fix them. These edits are usually small. You add a comma, for instance, instead of four supporting details. Even though edits are small changes, they are absolutely necessary. Doing a good job at the editing stage is like cleaning a spotty window that is interfering with a majestic view.

Edit Your Descriptive Essay. Edit the revised copy of your descriptive essay. The following questions will help you decide what to change, remove, or leave in place.

Conventions
❑ Did you capitalize proper nouns, such as the place's name?
❑ Did you use a comma after each introductory word, phrase, or clause?
❑ Did you use a comma when you joined sentences with a coordinating conjunction?
❑ Did you correct spelling mistakes, either with a friend's help or by using a dictionary?

PUBLISH

Presentation. Prepare your descriptive essay for publication by writing or typing the final, edited copy.

Publish Your Descriptive Essay. Here are a few ideas for publishing your work.
❑ With classmates, create a Web site where you can publish descriptions of fun gathering places.

30 • The Writer's Studio   Level A

Describe a Place — Ch. 2

- Visit your place with a camera and capture images that illustrate your written description. Use the photos and written description to create a travel brochure. Friends and family will enjoy reading the brochure, and it makes a great keepsake to remind you of a fun trip.
- Read your descriptive essay aloud to the class. Then ask for a show of hands to find out who would like to visit the place you described.

Evaluate Your Essay

Your teacher will either assess your essay, ask you to self-assess your essay, or ask you to switch with a partner and assess each other's work.

Evaluate the Model Essay

Work with a partner to evaluate the following descriptive essay. Use the rubric on page 29 and write your score here: _____. In a class discussion, explain the score that you gave.

Fun at Marymoor

It is late August in Marymoor Park, a place where residents of the East Side gather for year-round fun. It is a miniworld, complete with food, playgrounds, sports fields, a dog park, hiking, biking, outdoor entertainment, picnic areas, clean restrooms, and room to spread out and enjoy yourself. When we get to the park's entrance, I roll down the car window. Immediately, sounds fill my ears, smells tickle my nostrils, and sights delight my eyes.

Our car slows to obey the 5 mile-per-hour speed limit. Up ahead, a row of bicyclists zips along on a dirt path. They pass my car window. *Whoosh!* They flick the little bells on their bikes. *Ding! Ding!* Automatically, I reach down to

Ch. 2 Describe a Place

check for my bike helmet in the bag at my feet. My bike is stowed on a rack on the top of the car.

Now I see a boy who is around my age. A sweet, sticky trail of melted ice cream drips down his wrist. He jogs toward the playground where kids shout, "Watch me!" as they pump their legs hard to rise high in the swings. Older kids gather on a skateboard course that runs along two sides of the playground area. I can hear the rattle of boards as they land after jumps.

Around a curve in the road, dog owners pile out of their cars. Their furry friends bounce like happy rabbits into the grassy fields of the off-leash dog park. Across the parking lot, in the ball fields, a youth softball league whoops and shouts. The *thwack* of an aluminum bat against a neon-yellow softball splits the crisp autumn air. Overhead, Canadian geese honk as they fly in long V formations. They land with a whisper of webbed feet on the pond.

Here, near the water, my family spreads out a red-checked blanket and settles in for another unforgettable day at Marymoor. Lana opens a basket of food while Will dumps charcoal in the grill. Soon, the mouthwatering smell of grilled hot dogs floats in the air.

The highlight of the day will be at dusk, when a movie will be shown on the giant outdoor screen at the far end of the grassy field. People will gather to sit on blankets and lawn chairs. We'll eat kettle corn, sip lemonade, murmur quietly to one another, and watch the family-friendly movie with lazy interest. I might even fall asleep before the move is over, just like at home. The perfect place.

Chapter 3

Describe a Scientific Subject

Scientific writing helps readers understand the world they live in. For instance, think of questions you had about the world when you were younger. *Why is it dark at night? Why can birds fly and I can't? Why does rain fall down and not up?* As you learned more about science, you learned answers to some of these questions. You began to apply your new knowledge to the world around you. In this chapter you will use your knowledge of gravity and your powers of observation to write a scientific description.

Six Traits of Describing a Scientific Subject

Ideas	The purpose of the description is clear. Each idea and detail helps to accomplish this purpose.
Organization	The article contains a beginning, a middle, and an end. The ideas and details are arranged logically.
Voice	The writer uses an objective, fact-focused tone. The writer shines through as a trustworthy source of the information.
Word Choice	Scientific words and terms make the description precise.
Sentence Fluency	The writer uses a variety of sentence types and structures. Transition words and phrases link ideas clearly.
Conventions	Capitalization, spelling, punctuation, and grammar are correct.

Unit 1 • Descriptive Writing • 33

Ch. 3 **Describe a Scientific Subject**

In the following description of a fountain, the writer uses scientific words and terms to help make the subject clear.

> The fountain in front of City Hall shoots water fifteen feet into the air. The sight is like poetry in motion. The water goes only so high before it begins to fall. Gravity pulls the water back to Earth with force. As a result, it crashes through the water that is moving upward. Falling water hits the concrete and splatters, causing drops to bounce back into the air. However, it goes only a little way before gravity stops its upward motion. A metal grate at the fountain's base allows the water to flow down into the fountain's mechanism. From there, the cycle begins again.

Give It a Try: Examine the Model Paragraph

With your teacher's permission, work with a partner to answer the following questions about six traits in the model paragraph above. Write your answers on separate paper.

1. **Ideas and organization.** What is the writer's purpose in writing this paragraph?
2. **Word choice.** List two words that you think are examples of scientific vocabulary.
3. **Voice.** Which sentence expresses an opinion instead of a factual observation? Write the sentence.
4. **Sentence fluency.** List two transition words or phrases from the paragraph.
5. **Conventions.** Which word from the paragraph is a possessive noun?

Describe a Scientific Subject Ch. 3

Your Turn to Write: Describe a Scientific Subject

Now you'll write your own article about a scientific subject. Read the assignment carefully and follow the strategies and instructions for each stage of the writing process.

Assignment

You and Your World, a science magazine, is publishing a special issue on gravity. Writers are invited to submit an article for the issue. Writers must choose one of the following topics:
- Gravity and different kinds of ramps in the community
- Gravity and water in town or in nature
- Gravity and playground equipment

The article must describe the effects of gravity in the situation selected above. Articles are to be 350 words, written for students in grades 6–12.

Choose one of the topics listed above, and write a descriptive article for *You and Your World*.

Prewrite

Analyze the Prompt. Use the assignment above to answer the following questions. Write your answers on separate paper.

1. What is the purpose of this article?
2. Who is the audience for this article?
3. How long does the article need to be?

Explore Your Options and Choose a Topic. Take five minutes to explore the choices of writing topics. For each question that follows, spend a full minute thinking about and writing an answer. Use separate paper.

Unit 1 • Descriptive Writing • 35

Ch. 3 **Describe a Scientific Subject**

1. What do you know about gravity?
2. What do you know about ramps (what they're used for, etc.)?
3. What kinds of ramps, if any, have you used?
4. What kinds of playground equipment do you know about?
5. When you form a mental picture of moving water in nature, what do you see?

Now that you've looked at your choices, you can select a topic for your scientific description. On your paper, write your topic. Then write a sentence explaining why you chose that topic.

Gather Ideas and Details. When it comes to gravity and the specific topic you chose, what do you know already? What do you need to find out through observation? On a blank sheet of paper, create a 3Ws table like the one that follows. Use it to organize your knowledge, questions, and findings.

My writing topic: _____

What I Know	What I Need to Find Out Through	What I Found Out
your details here	your details here	your details here

Organize Ideas and Details. Follow these steps to organize the information in your descriptive article.

1. **Plan it.** Use an outline or list format to plan the organization of your article.
2. **Review it.** Meet with a writing partner to review your outline. Ask your partner the following questions.

36 • The Writer's Studio   Level A

Describe a Scientific Subject Ch. 3

❑ Do I clearly introduce the subject of my description?
❑ Does the topic of each paragraph relate to the subject of the article?
❑ Do I have a working idea for my conclusion? (You can always revise it later.)

3. **Revise it.** Make changes to strengthen your outline. Add, remove, and move ideas and details.

 **Draft**

> **Tip**
>
> As you outline your article, you may notice that you need additional supporting details. Create another 3W's table like the one on page 36. Then go back and observe your subject and collect the additional details you need.

One of the traits of good scientific writing is the correct use of scientific language. **Scientific language** is the special vocabulary used to express science-related facts and ideas. For instance, *glucose* is a scientific term for *sugar*, and *calorie* is a scientific term for *energy*. Compare the following definitions.

> **calorie** The amount of energy needed to raise the temperature of 1 gram of water by 1 degree Celsius. Chemical energy in foods is expressed in calories.

> **energy** The ability of a physical system to perform work.

In a general conversation, using the word *energy* is good enough. But if you are writing a scientific article to teach about calories, then scientific language allows you to be as accurate as possible.

Use Scientific Language. Write the first draft of your article about gravity. As you write, use scientific language to express ideas as accurately as possible. The following word bank contains some scientific words and terms that you might use, depending on your topic. As you write, add words to the box.

Unit 1 • Descriptive Writing • **37**

Ch. 3 **Describe a Scientific Subject**

Scientific Language Word Bank			
gravity	gravitational pull	mass	force
attraction	acceleration	deceleration	incline

Additional Science Vocabulary:

 Revise

No matter how good your ideas are, readers can misunderstand them if they have to guess how the ideas connect. Using transition words and phrases can help readers see exactly how one idea relates to another.

Mini-Lesson: Using Transition Words and Phrases

You can strengthen your descriptive article by clarifying how ideas connect. Words and phrases called *transitions* can help you do this.

Transitions are words or phrases that connect one idea to another, one sentence to another, or one paragraph to another.

38 • The Writer's Studio   Level A

Transition Words and Phrases

To Show Location

above	beneath	in front of	on top of
ahead	between	inside	outside
behind	beyond	near	throughout
below	in back of	next to	under

To Show Time

after	finally	later	until
at last	first, second, etc.	meanwhile	soon
before	in the past	next	then
during	last	now	following

To Add

also	as well	finally	furthermore
and	besides	for example	in addition
another	besides that	for instance	moreover

To Show Importance or Order of Importance

even greater	first, second, etc.	most significantly
finally	most important	next

To Show Comparison or Contrast

although	however	likewise	otherwise
but	in contrast	nevertheless	similarly
even though	like	on the other hand	yet

To Show Cause or Effect

as a result	consequently	since	therefore
because	for this reason	so	

Ch. 3 · **Describe a Scientific Subject**

In the following paragraph from an article on ramps and gravity, the writer has added transitions to show important connections between ideas.

Wheelchair ramps help people move from a low point to a higher point and back again safely and easily. These ramps are designed with gravity in mind. They allow the person in the wheelchair to conquer gravity bit by bit. *For this reason,* The ramp's incline must not be too steep. The steeper the incline, the stronger the force of gravity. *In contrast,* The gentler the incline, the easier it is to resist gravity in order to move upward.

Give It a Try: Use Transitions in Your Writing

Check your descriptive article for places where ideas, sentences, or paragraphs connect. Revise the draft by adding transitions to clarify these connections.

Revise Your Scientific Description. Use the following checklist to revise the rough draft of your descriptive article. The Descriptive Article Rubric that follows the checklist will help you determine how strong your article is and where to make revisions.

Ideas
- ❏ In the introduction, underline the sentence that makes clear the purpose of your article.
- ❏ Cross out any details and ideas that do not help to accomplish the purpose of your article.

Organization
- ❏ Move any details that are not arranged in a logical order.
- ❏ Circle your concluding sentence(s). If your article does not have a conclusion, add one.

Describe a Scientific Subject   Ch. 3

Voice
- ❑ Find two objective (nonemotional) words that show you're an authority on the topic. Write *voice* above each one.

Word choice
- ❑ Circle two scientific terms you used.

Sentence fluency
- ❑ Circle two transitions you used to link ideas.

Descriptive Article Rubric

	4 Strong	3 Effective	2 Developing	1 Beginning
Ideas	The writer describes the effects of gravity in a specific situation.	The writer describes a few effects of gravity in a situation.	The writer describes an effect of gravity in a situation.	The writer does not describe effects of gravity.
Organization	The article has a beginning, a middle, and an end.	The article has a beginning and middle, but the end is weak.	The article does not have a beginning or an end.	The article includes descriptions in random order.
Voice	The writer uses an objective tone.	The writer uses an objective tone in some paragraphs.	The writer uses an objective tone in some sentences.	The writer's tone is not objective.
Word Choice	The writer uses scientific language.	The writer uses some scientific language.	The writer uses a scientific word or term.	The writer does not use scientific language.
Sentence Fluency	Transitions connect ideas, sentences, and paragraphs.	Transitions connect some ideas and sentences.	One or two transitions are used.	Transitions are absent.
Conventions	Capitalization, spelling, punctuation, and grammar are correct.	There are few errors in capitalization, spelling, punctuation, and grammar.	There are many errors in capitalization, spelling, punctuation, and grammar.	Errors in conventions make it hard to understand the writing.

Unit 1 • Descriptive Writing • 41

Ch. 3 **Describe a Scientific Subject**

 ## Edit

As you know, editing your article means finding and correcting errors in capitalization, spelling, punctuation, and grammar. As you grow as a writer, you will develop your own system for identifying and fixing these kinds of errors. What system do you currently use? How could you make your system even more effective?

Share and Edit. In a class discussion, share your personal tips and techniques for identifying and correcting errors in one or more of these categories:

Conventions
- Capitalization
- Spelling
- Punctuation
- Grammar

Then use ideas from the class discussion to edit your descriptive article.

Presentation. Prepare your descriptive article for publication by writing or typing the final, edited copy.

PUBLISH

Publish Your Descriptive Article. Here are ideas for publishing your work.
- ❑ Share your article with a younger student who is learning about gravity.
- ❑ Work with classmates to create your own issue of *You and Your World* magazine. Create a magazine cover, a table of contents, and diagrams to go along with your articles. Make copies for each person who is published in the magazine—and make extra copies to pass out to friends.

Describe a Scientific Subject — Ch. 3

Evaluate Your Article

Your teacher will either assess your article, ask you to self-assess your article, or ask you to switch with a partner and assess each other's work.

Evaluate the Model Article

Here is the writer's final copy of the article on ramps. Use the rubric on page 41 and write your score here: _____. In a class discussion, explain the score you gave.

Ramps and Gravity

There is a saying that what goes up must come down. Gravity is the force that makes objects on Earth pull down toward Earth's center. Gravity keeps us all firmly on planet Earth instead of floating off into the atmosphere. The more mass an object has, the stronger the gravitational force. This means that heavy things are hard to lift. This is where ramps come in. Ramps such as wheelchair ramps, loading ramps, and skateboard ramps help us conquer gravity.

Wheelchair ramps help people move from a low point to a higher point and back again safely and easily. These ramps are designed with gravity in mind. They allow the person in the wheelchair to conquer gravity bit by bit. For this reason, the ramp's incline must not be too steep. The steeper the incline, the stronger the force of gravity. In contrast, the gentler the incline, the easier it is to resist gravity in order to move upward.

A second type of ramp is a loading ramp. I observed a loading ramp on the moving truck that my dad owns. Workers must load heavy items such as furniture and boxes of books into the trailer. Since the floor of the trailer is 48 inches above the ground, loading heavy items is a challenge. As with a wheelchair ramp, a loading ramp allows gravity to be conquered bit by bit until the things are lifted as high as they need to be.

Ch. 3 **Describe a Scientific Subject**

    A third type of ramp is a skateboard ramp. This kind of ramp uses the force of gravity for the purpose of sport and fun. Skateboarders must work up enough speed to roll up a ramp against the pull of gravity. Then, when they are skating down the ramp, they must control their speed and balance. If they don't, gravity will cause a huge wipeout. Skateboard ramps are designed with many different heights. The steeper the incline, the greater the challenge to the skateboarder.

    Wheelchair ramps, loading ramps, and skateboard ramps are just a few of the many types of ramps in a community. Ramps help people conquer gravity in order to live their daily lives, to work, and to have fun.

Chapter 4
Test Writing: The Descriptive Essay

A guitar recital, a basketball game, and the opening night of a play—what do all of these have in common? The people involved are demonstrating to an audience what they have worked hard to learn.

Similarly, as a student, you are sometimes asked to demonstrate your knowledge and skills by writing a test essay. A test essay is much like other types of essays you write, but with one key difference. On a test, you have a limited amount of time in which to plan and write your essay. This chapter will help you strengthen your skill at writing a descriptive test essay.

Six Traits of a Descriptive Test Essay

Ideas	The writer has written about the topic stated in the writing prompt. Each detail clearly relates to this topic.
Organization	The essay has a beginning, a middle, and an end. Ideas and details are arranged logically.
Voice	The writing style fits with the purpose and audience of the description.
Word Choice	The writer uses specific and lively words and sensory details.
Sentence Fluency	The writer uses a variety of sentence types and structures.
Conventions	Capitalization, spelling, punctuation, and grammar are correct.

Unit 1 • Descriptive Writing • 45

Ch. 4 **Test Writing: The Descriptive Essay**

Preparing to Write Your Test Essay

During your time in school, you will see essay prompts that are written and arranged in different ways. A prompt may be short and to the point, or it may include a list of tips or reminders. The prompt may be set in a box or set simply at the top of a page. Here is an example of a prompt for a descriptive composition.

Instructions

You have 25 minutes to complete the written composition. Read the prompt below. Then use separate paper to plan and draft your composition. Only your draft will be scored.

Writing Prompt

We all like to be treated special on our birthdays. If you could have an extraspecial meal on your birthday, what would it be? What would you have for dessert? How would the food and beverages look, taste, feel, and smell? Write an essay in which you describe your idea of the perfect birthday meal.

---

1. Study the Prompt

Before you begin to write your essay, take a few moments to study the prompt. Answer these important questions:

What is the purpose of the essay? Scan the prompt for key words that tell you what kind of essay to write.

> **Words That Signal a Descriptive Essay**
> describe
> description
> mental picture

Test Writing: The Descriptive Essay Ch. 4

What should you write about? Study the prompt to determine exactly what you must write. Look for an *imperative sentence*: a sentence that gives a command or makes a request. In the prompt above, the imperative sentence is this one:

Write an essay in which you describe your idea of the perfect birthday meal.

This sentence is your assignment in a nutshell. The other sentences in the paragraph give you ideas and inspiration, but this sentence tells you exactly what to write about.

How much time do you have to write? The sample prompt on page 46 states clearly that the student has 25 minutes in which to complete the assignment. If a prompt does not state a time limit, this information may be printed in another page in the test booklet, or your teacher may post the information in your classroom.

What other instructions are stated? Check the prompt for additional instructions. For example, the sample prompt gives directions about where to plan the essay and where to write the essay:

Then use separate paper to plan and draft your composition. Only your draft will be scored.

When responding to this prompt, a student who spends the whole time prewriting and doesn't move on to drafting will not get any credit for this essay.

2. Plan Your Time

After studying the prompt, make a quick plan for how to use your time. If you have 25 minutes in which to write the test, you could use your time as follows:

5–7 minutes:	Study the prompt and do your prewriting.
13–15 minutes:	Write the essay.
5 minutes:	Revise and edit the essay.

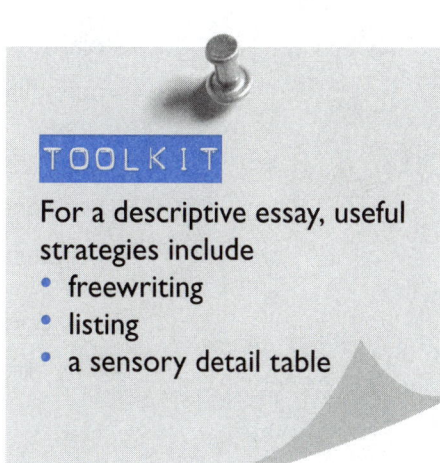

TOOLKIT

For a descriptive essay, useful strategies include
- freewriting
- listing
- a sensory detail table

Unit 1 • Descriptive Writing • 47

Ch. 4 **Test Writing: The Descriptive Essay**

3. Prewrite

During the time set aside for prewriting, you should gather ideas and details for your topic and organize the information.

Gather ideas and details. Use a few of your prewriting minutes to gather ideas and details. Choose one method and make it work for you.

Here is an example of organizing ideas in a list.

> **T!p**
> Since your prewriting will not be evaluated, use your own abbreviations and shorthand to save time.

desserts	drinks	main dishes	extras
choc. cake	grp. soda	cheeseburgers-- thick, juicy	ketchup
vanilla frosting	milk shakes-- choc. and vanilla	fries--crispy, salty	pickles
candles			mayonnaise
vanilla ice crm.			mustard

Organize the information. Use your remaining prewriting time to plan the arrangement of information in your essay. During a 25-minute testing period, it is reasonable to plan for a 3–5 paragraph essay. Don't try to create a formal or complicated outline. Instead, jot down key points to include in the introduction, body, and conclusion.

<u>beginning</u>
--birthday meal tradition in family
--quick list of food

<u>middle</u>
--paragraph 1: burgers and fries, sensory details
--paragraph 2: cake and candles, sensory details

<u>end</u>
--why this meal would make me feel special: grilling w/ Dad

Test Writing: The Descriptive Essay Ch. 4

Writing Your Test Essay

Now that you have studied the prompt and planned the essay's content, you can begin writing. To help yourself write quickly and purposefully, stick to the plan you made during prewriting. Refer to it between paragraphs to keep yourself on track.

The model essay below follows the outline you just read in the prewriting section. It contains some errors in capitalization, spelling, punctuation, and grammar. At this point, however, the writer is mainly concerned with getting the ideas down on paper.

An Unforgettable Meal

In my family, the birthday person gets to request a favorite meal for the big day. This year, I know exactly what I will ask for: hamburgers on the grill, along with french fries, all the extras, and chocolate cake with ice cream for dessert.

One of the best experiences of this birthday meal will be the sent of burgers grilling over charcoal. The smell will float across the backyard and into the house. Mom is making the fries. She has a secret coating that she puts on fresh-sliced potatoes, it has salt, garlic, pepper, and a little flour in it. She shakes the fries in a bag with the mixture until they are coated. She bakes the fries to a crisp. I like the edges dark brown and crunchy. The meal will not be complete without mayonnaise and mustard for the burgers ketchup for the fries and pickles on the side.

After that comes the birthday dessert--cake of course! My favorite is chocolate cake with vanilla frosting. My dream cake is so dark-chocolate that it is almost black. If you press your fork against crumbs on your plate they will cling together and give you one last bite. The vanilla frosting, which whipped cream in it, is the perfect topping to the rich cake. On top of this mouth-watering dessert would be colored candles. One for each year I been alive.

Unit 1 • Descriptive Writing • 49

Ch. 4 Test Writing: The Descriptive Essay

This meal of burgers, fries, and cake may seem average, it is special to me. This meal will be prepared by both my parents. It shows me that I am special to them. I get to help dad grill the burgers, and I get his undivided attention. This special meal on my birthday this year will be the first birthday meal that I share with my new family. My "mom" and "dad" are actually my foster parents, who have just adopted me. A birthday meal prepared by them is not just special, it is unforgettable.

Give your essay a title that will catch your reader's interest. Often, the best time to decide on a title is after you have written the essay. In the model, the writer uses a key word from the conclusion (*unforgettable*) to form the title.

Polishing Your Test Essay

Your reader will expect you to review your essay to correct errors in capitalization, spelling, punctuation, and grammar. Writing a test essay is different from preparing an essay outside of class. For a timed test, you don't have time to mark up a draft and then write a clean, revised copy. Instead, make your corrections directly on the copy to be scored. Using editing marks can help you revise and polish your essay as quickly as possible. Make all marks as neatly and cleanly as possible.

On the next page, you'll see how the writer of the model essay uses editing marks to add transitions and correct a capitalization error. The following table explains some commonly used editing marks.

Test Writing: The Descriptive Essay   Ch. 4

≡	Capitalize a letter.	i have a dog.
/	Change a capital letter to lowercase.	My D̸og is a beagle.
ℓ	Delete (remove).	My dogg is a beagle.
^	Insert here.	My dog ^Buster is a beagle.
⌄	Insert a comma here.	Buster is my best friend and I love him.
¶	Start a new paragraph.	A dog is a wonderful pet. ¶ Cats are good pets, too. I have a kitten named Roxy.

    This meal of burgers, fries, and cake may seem average, ~~it~~ but is special to me. ^For one thing, This meal will be prepared by both my parents. It shows me that I am special to them. ^For another thing, I get to help dad grill the burgers, and I get his undivided attention. ^Most of all, This special meal on my birthday this year will be the first birthday meal that I share with my new family. My "mom" and "dad" are actually my foster parents, who have just adopted me. A birthday meal prepared by them is not just special, it is unforgettable.

Evaluating a Descriptive Test Essay

Teachers understand that you have only a limited time to plan, write, and polish your test essay. They are not expecting this essay to be as polished as others you write for class. Despite the time limit, teachers do expect you to

- demonstrate your ability to write to the prompt
- include relevant details in an organized manner

Unit 1 • Descriptive Writing • 51

Ch. 4 Test Writing: The Descriptive Essay

- show your command of the conventions of capitalization, spelling, punctuation, and grammar

The rubric below shows guidelines for evaluating a descriptive test essay.

Descriptive Test Essay Rubric

	4 Strong	3 Effective	2 Developing	1 Beginning
Ideas	The writer wrote to the prompt. Each detail clearly relates.	The writer wrote to the prompt, but a few details do not relate.	The writer included some details relating to the prompt.	The writer did not write to the prompt.
Organization	Information is arranged logically.	Most information is arranged logically.	Organization of information is awkward.	Information is included in random order.
Voice	The writing style helps the reader connect to the description.	The writing style of some paragraphs draws the reader in.	The writing style of one or two sentences draws the reader in.	Writing is mechanical, making it hard for readers to connect.
Word Choice	Vivid words and sensory details are used.	A few vivid words and sensory details are used.	One or two vivid words or sensory details are used.	No vivid words or sensory details are used.
Sentence Fluency	A variety of sentence types are used in a pleasing rhythm.	A variety of sentence types are used, but some may be awkward.	Sentences are complete but are mostly short and simple.	Sentences are mostly of one type or are incomplete.
Conventions	Few errors in capitalization, spelling, punctuation, or grammar are present.	Several errors in capitalization, spelling, punctuation, or grammar are present.	Errors in capitalization, spelling, punctuation, and grammar do not prevent understanding.	Errors in capitalization, spelling, punctuation, and grammar prevent understanding.

52 • The Writer's Studio   Level A

Test Writing: The Descriptive Essay   Ch. 4

Evaluate a Model Test Essay

Work with a partner to evaluate the following model composition. Reread the prompt on page 46 and use the rubric on page 52. Write your score here: _____. In a class discussion, explain the score you gave.

An Unforgettable Meal

In my family, the birthday person gets to request a favorite meal for the big day. This year, I know exactly what I will ask for: hamburgers on the grill, along with french fries, all the extras, and chocolate cake with ice cream for dessert.

One of the best experiences of this birthday meal will be the sent [c] of burgers grilling over charcoal. The smell will float across the backyard and into the house, [where] Mom is making the fries. She has a secret coating that she puts on fresh-sliced potatoes, [and] it has salt, garlic, pepper, and a little flour in it. She shakes the fries in a bag with the mixture until they are coated. [Then] She bakes the fries to a crisp. I like the edges dark brown and crunchy. The meal will not be complete without mayonnaise and mustard for the burgers, ketchup for the fries, and pickles on the side.

After that comes the birthday dessert--cake, of course! My favorite is chocolate cake with vanilla frosting. My dream cake is so dark-chocolate that it is almost black. If you press your fork against crumbs on your plate they will cling together and give you one last bite. The vanilla frosting, which [has] whipped cream in it, is the perfect topping to the rich cake. On top of this mouth-watering dessert would be colored candles, One for each year I [have] been alive.

This meal of burgers, fries, and cake may seem average, [but] it is special to me. [For one thing,] This meal will be prepared by both my parents. It shows me that I am special to them. [For another thing,] I get to help dad grill the burgers, and I get his undivided attention. [Most of all,] This special meal on my birthday this year will be the first birthday meal that I share with my new family. My "mom" and "dad" are actually my foster parents, who have just adopted me. A birthday meal prepared by them is not just special, it is unforgettable.

Unit 1 • Descriptive Writing • 53

Ch. 4 **Test Writing: The Descriptive Essay**

Write a Descriptive Test Essay

Practice what you've learned by completing the following task.

Instructions

You have 25 minutes to complete the written composition. Read the prompt below. Then use separate paper to plan and draft your composition. Only your draft will be scored.

Writing Prompt

Many people have a special place where they go to daydream, to calm strong emotions, or to write in a journal. If you could design your own special place, what would it be like? Would it be indoors or outdoors? Would it smell of fresh air or scented candles? Would there be music, pets, or furniture? What items would be essential, such as a notebook and pen, snacks, or art supplies? Write an essay in which you describe your ideal place for being alone.

Descriptive Writing Wrap-Up

The activities and information in these pages will help you continue to strengthen your descriptive writing skills. In You Be the Judge, use the Descriptive Writing Rubric to evaluate a student's work. The Ideas for Writing are additional descriptive writing prompts you can use for practice. And finally, in the Unit 1 Reflections, you can list important ideas you have learned in this unit and set goals for future learning.

You Be the Judge

Use what you've learned about the traits of descriptive writing to evaluate a student essay. First, review the traits of descriptive writing on page 2, in the unit opener. Next, read the student essay printed below. Finally, in the rubric that follows the essay, assign the essay a score for each writing trait. In the space provided, explain each score that you assign.

Made in Thailand

by Daniel R., Albuquerque, NM

Every Sunday in Chiang Mai, Thailand, many shopkeepers travel on foot, by car, by auto-rickshaw, and by just about every other means imaginable to set up shop in and around the old city wall and moat.

Predominantly tourist-oriented, the market offers everything from bedspreads to pirated TV shows to offensive T-shirts. The stalls at the beginning of the market, outside the old wall, peddle different kinds of food--strawberry smoothies, dark coffee, guava, watermelon. Each type of merchandise or service can be found in several places throughout the bazaar.

Behind the blackened, battered brick wall, dozens of colorful umbrellas mark each stall lining the street. The sea of humans walking up and down the street stretches farther than the eye can see. Groups of camera-carrying Europeans cluster around people with overturned hats in front of them singing karaoke. A girl in vividly colored garments and jangling jewelry dances to traditional tunes blaring from a crackly amplifier.

Other common merchandise at the bazaar include knock-offs of expensive clothing and personal accessories, various Buddhas and idols, wooden figures and dishes, and long strings of Chinese-style paper lanterns that twinkle at night and swing in the breeze. In the underworld of the East, a place where Nike becomes Mike and Adidas lands another "d" to emerge as Addidas, crooks copy big-name Western brands and sell their own versions at a fraction of the price, sometimes alongside the genuine article. These cheap copycats can be found in street markets all over Asia, including those here in Chiang Mai.

The market's vendors import cashmere, known in Asia as pashmina, from India, and people of the Northern hill tribes maneuver their pickups and elephants loaded with hardwood into town. Exotic smells, foreign languages and a wide range of skin tones flood the senses from every direction.

In the daytime, the streets are choked with dust, the air is oppressive, and the sun is searing. Even as the sun sets and the lights of the many buildings, restaurants, shops, and street lamps blink on, the temperature still lingers in the 90s.

When the sky darkens, tuk-tuks (covered motorcycles with back seats) and song taus (red pick-up trucks with bench seats) whisk thirsty Aussies, Europeans, and assorted Westerners off to the bars and pubs.

Many tourists who vacation in sunny, tropical locales feel the need to wear flip-flops, straw hats and, well, little else; Chiang Mai's tourist population is no exception. Even at night, toasted tourists shine in all their sun-dried glory, sometimes appearing to be covered in melted glass. Still, getting one's hide tanned to such an extent must not feel as bad as it looks, because every season these rich foreigners return for more.

At the end of the day, although commonly flooded with visitors and sightseers from across the globe, Chiang Mai's market never fails to remind all they are still deep in the heart of Asia.

Unit 1

Descriptive Writing Rubric

	4 Strong	**3** Effective	**2** Developing	**1** Beginning
Ideas Score_____	*explanation:*			
organization Score_____	*explanation:*			
voice Score_____	*explanation:*			
word choice Score_____	*explanation:*			
sentence fluency Score_____	*explanation:*			
conventions Score_____	*explanation:*			

Ideas for Writing

The following assignments will give you additional practice with descriptive writing. Your teacher may choose one or let you pick one that's most interesting to you.

1. A television show about five teenage friends will be filming an episode in your city. The producers have invited young people in your city to describe their favorite hangout. From these descriptions, the producers will choose a hangout to use as a set in the episode. Here are the writing guidelines.

58 • The Writer's Studio   Level A

Where do you and your friends go to hang out? What do you do there? What do you eat and drink? What are the smells, sounds, and sights of this place? Write an essay of 350 words in which you describe your favorite hangout. Write your description so that the show's producers will feel as if they are there with you in this place.

2. Find a box to use as a time capsule and use it to collect written work and other items for one year. The first item for your time capsule will be a description of your ideal type of transportation. If you could own any mode of transportation, what would it be? Would you choose a dirt bike, a motorcycle, a horse, or a unicorn? Would you choose a jet plane or a rocket ship? Write a letter of about 300 words to yourself, describing your ideal mode of transportation. Use plenty of sensory details so that when you read the letter in the future, this image will come alive in your mind.

3. Art is all around us. Metal sculptures, bronze statues, paintings, fountains, murals, and even the design of a building are types of art. Your city's Committee for the Arts is preparing a full-color magazine with photographs and written descriptions of the city's art. The event coordinator has invited citizens to send in a written description of artworks that could be included in the magazine. Choose a piece of art in your community and write an essay of 300 words in which you describe it. Help your readers see, feel, smell, hear, and even taste what you do when you examine this artwork.

Unit 1 • Descriptive Writing • **59**

Unit 1 Reflections

How are you different as a writer now that you have completed this unit on descriptive writing? What new knowledge do you have? How is your writing stronger? What kinds of things could you work on to become even stronger as a descriptive writer? Use the following space to reflect on your work in this unit and to set goals for the future.

Focus on Me: My Achievements as a Descriptive Writer

What I've learned about descriptive writing in this unit:

Ways my descriptive writing is stronger now:

Things I can do to practice my descriptive writing skills:

60 • The Writer's Studio   Level A

Unit 2

Expository Writing

The Unit at a Glance
Get to Know the Genre 61
Ch. 5 Write a How-to Article 67
Ch. 6 Write an Explanatory Essay 81
Ch. 7 Write a Comparison-Contrast Essay 93
Ch. 8 Test Writing: The Expository Essay 109
Expository Writing Wrap-Up 120

Get to Know the Genre: Expository Writing

I see but one rule: to be clear. If I am not clear, all my world crumbles to nothing.

—STENDHAL
(FRENCH WRITER, 1783–1842)

Life is full of questions. *How do I hook this printer up to my computer? What makes someone a hero? How is softball different from baseball?* To find answers to life's questions, you can read (or write) expository writing.

Expository writing makes a subject clear for readers through the use of examples and evidence. A clear thesis statement, solid supporting ideas, and a strong conclusion help to form a successful expository essay.

Unit 2

Give It a Try: Explore the Genre

In the following table, spend five minutes listing questions that could be answered with different kinds of expository writing. A few questions are included to get you started.

Expository Category	My Questions
How-To (tells how to do, build, or accomplish something)	How do I create a Web page from scratch?
Explanatory (explains the reasons for an action or a viewpoint)	Why do I like science fiction stories?
Compare-Contrast (tells how two or more things are alike and different)	How am I alike yet different from my parent?

62 • The Writer's Studio   Level A

As with other forms of writing, a strong piece of expository writing includes specific traits. The following table explains traits of effective expository writing.

Six Traits of Expository Writing

Ideas	The topic is narrowed to a specific subject to be explained. Each detail clearly relates to the topic.
Organization	Details are arranged with care, such as in order of importance, from general to specific, or order of steps in a sequence.
Voice	The writing style fits with the purpose and audience of the explanation.
Word Choice	Specific nouns and verbs help the reader understand what the writer is explaining or how a process is completed.
Sentence Fluency	Declarative sentences are used to give information. A variety of sentence types and structures creates a pleasing rhythm to the writing.
Conventions	Capitalization, spelling, punctuation, and grammar are correct.

Real-World Example

As a student, you are probably familiar with encyclopedias. Encyclopedia articles, which explain topics, are a form of explanatory writing. The following article, taken from the online encyclopedia *Wikipedia*, explains what a blog is.

Unit 2

Blog
From *Wikipedia*, the free encyclopedia

Ideas: one clear topic

A blog (a contraction of the term "weblog") is a type of Web site, usually maintained by an individual with regular entries of commentary, descriptions of events, or other material such as graphics or video. Entries are commonly displayed in reverse-chronological order. "Blog" can also be used as a verb, meaning to maintain or add content to a blog. Many blogs provide commentary or news on a particular subject; others function as more personal online diaries. A typical blog combines text, images, and links to other blogs, Web pages, and other media related to its topic. The ability for readers to leave comments in an interactive format is an important part of many blogs.

Ideas: specific details

Word choice: specific nouns

Word choice: specific nouns

Voice: An objective voice fits with the purpose of giving a factual explanation.

Conventions: A semicolon joins two simple sentences, forming a compound sentence.

Organization: Ideas are arranged from general (the basic definition of *blog*) to specific (description of a typical blog).

Sentence fluency: Declarative sentences used throughout the explanation.

Give It a Try: Examine the Real-World Example

Can you find additional examples of the traits of good writing in the article above? On separate paper, list two traits of good writing. For each one, quote or describe an example from the article.

Get Ready to Write

Now that you've explored the qualities of expository writing, you're ready to create some expositions of your own. In the chapters that follow, you'll write a how-to article about a fun activity, an explanatory essay about friendship, a comparison-contrast essay about vacations, and an expository essay about communicating with friends. You'll use the stages of the writing process—prewriting, drafting, revising, editing, and publishing—and you'll be presented with models and mini-lessons along the way.

As you work through these chapters, you can enrich your understanding by trying the suggestions below. These tips will help you connect what you're learning in this unit to your own life and the world around you.

LEARNING TIPS

- Watch for expository writing in the reading that you do for school. Think about how expository writing helps you understand ideas in math, science, and social studies.

- Watch for expository writing in magazines, on Internet web pages, in e-mails, and in user's manuals. Think about the purpose of each type of expository writing that you find. Does it tell how to do something? Does it explain an idea or a viewpoint? Does it compare and contrast two things?

- Practice your skills of explaining ideas in everyday life. Write an e-mail to someone simply to explain an idea. In a conversation, explain to someone how to make something or perform a process. Use expository writing where it is appropriate in assignments for other classes.

- As you take part in sports or work on hobbies, think about how you could use expository writing to help someone else understand why you enjoy this sport or hobby.

Chapter 5

Write a How-To Article

Expository writing is, above all, *useful*. This type of writing teaches us about all kinds of topics, from bobsleds to brownies to birdhouses. With expository writing, we not only learn *about* things, but we also learn *how to do* things. We can learn how to steer a bobsled, how to bake brownies, and how to build a birdhouse. This category of expository writing—the how-to article—is one with which you're probably already familiar. Maybe you've searched the Internet for an article on how to fix a computer glitch, or maybe you read a magazine article on how to pull off a new fashion. How-to articles can be found online, in magazines, in textbooks, and in brochures. No matter where they appear, well-written how-to articles share the same traits.

Six Traits of a How-To Article

Ideas	The topic is narrowed to one specific goal to be accomplished. Each detail helps to explain a step in the process.
Organization	The article explains the steps in a process in the order in which they must be completed.
Voice	The writer uses a friendly, helpful tone.
Word Choice	Transition words make the order of steps clear. Specific nouns and verbs help the reader understand the process.
Sentence Fluency	Imperative sentences tell the reader what to do. Declarative sentences give information.
Conventions	Capitalization, spelling, punctuation, and grammar are correct. Contractions use apostrophes correctly.

Unit 2 • Expository Writing • 67

Ch. 5 Write a How-To Article

In the following how-to article, the author explains how to make a quesadilla in a toaster oven.

How to Make a Toaster-Oven Quesadilla

A *quesadilla* (kay-sah-DEE-ah) is like a cheese sandwich, except that it's made with tortillas instead of bread. Making a quesadilla is easy! Here's how.

Begin by laying one tortilla on a plate, and sprinkle shredded cheese on top. Next, lay another tortilla on top, like a sandwich. Then, carefully place the quesadilla on the rack in a toaster oven. Finally, toast the quesadilla for 2–3 minutes, until it turns golden brown and the cheese is melted. (If you don't have a toaster oven, heat your quesadilla on a cookie sheet in a regular oven at 400 degrees.)

Once the quesadilla is toasted, remove it carefully from the oven. Let it cool for a minute. Then slice it into wedge-shaped pieces. Enjoy your snack plain, or dip the wedges in guacamole, hot sauce, or sour cream.

Give It a Try: Examine the Model Article

Answer the following questions about six traits in the model article above. Write your answers on separate paper.

1. **Ideas.** What main goal does the article explain how to accomplish?
2. **Organization and word choice.** List three signal words that show the order of the steps in the process.
3. **Voice.** Does the writer mainly use the first-person point of view, the second-person point of view, or the third-person point of view? How do you know this?
4. **Sentence fluency.** Which type of sentence does the writer use most—declarative, imperative, or exclamatory?
5. **Conventions.** List three words from the article that use apostrophes. Why are apostrophes used for these words?

Write a How-To Article Ch. 5

Your Turn to Write: Compose a How-To Article

Now you'll write your own how-to piece. Read the assignment carefully and follow the strategies and instructions for each stage of the writing process.

Assignment

Splendid Adventures Summer Camp needs your help! The camp's staffers are collecting ideas for their daily How-To Adventure. Here is what they need from you:

> Help us by writing a how-to article! Each day, we will teach our campers how to do something new and fun. Write a 350- to 400-word article that tells us (the camp staff) how to do something fun. Categories include craft projects, cooking projects, life skills, and technology skills. We can't wait to read your how-to article!

Prewrite

Analyze the Prompt. Reread the assignment above and answer the following questions. Write your answers on separate paper.
1. What is the purpose of this article?
2. Who is the audience for this article?
3. How long does the article need to be?

Choose a Topic. With your teacher's permission, gather in a small group and follow these steps.
1. For five minutes, brainstorm for possible topics for a how-to article. Use a table like the one that follows to organize your ideas. A few ideas are included to get you started.

Unit 2 • Expository Writing • 69

Ch. 5 **Write a How-To Article**

2. After five minutes, stop brainstorming and review the table. Circle the idea you'd like to write about. Be sure to select a process that can be clearly explained in 350–400 words.

Craft Projects	Cooking Projects	Life Skills	Technology Skills
How To . . .			
tie-dye a T-shirt	make 7-layer dip	choose the right dog as your pet	use a digital camera

Gather Ideas and Details. Think through the process that you want to write about. If possible, complete the process yourself and take notes on what you do. On a blank sheet of paper, list each step, whether it is large or small.

Here is how one writer listed steps involved in making soap.

Steps in Making Surprise Soap

Get supplies: bars of soap, plastic surprises, paper cups, cooking oil, little boxes
Cut up the soap
Melt the soap in the microwave
Pour the soap into the cups and boxes
Put a surprise into each soap
Let it harden
Take the soap out of the molds

Write a How-To Article   Ch. 5

 After you gather ideas, think about the amount of material you have. Is there too little for your target word count? Just enough? Far too much? If necessary, choose a different process to explain.

Organize Ideas and Details. Organize the steps in your how-to article by making a sequence chain. A sequence chain lists each main step in the process, with substeps listed below the main steps.

Sequence Chain for Making Surprise Soap

1. Get supplies: bars of soap, plastic surprises, paper cups, cooking oil, little boxes
2. Prepare your molds.
   a. Set them out
   b. Oil them
   c. Set out the plastic surprises
3. Melt the soap
   a. Cut up the soap
   b. Put chunks in glass bowl
   c. Melt in microwave on high, 10 seconds
4. Make the soap bars
   a. Pour the melted soap into the molds
   b. Put a surprise into each soap
5. Wait
   a. Let the soap harden for 24 hours or more
   b. Take the soap out of the molds

While writing the sequence chain, you may realize that the previous list you made left out some steps. It's okay to add a main step or substeps now.

 ## Draft

When writing a how-to article, you want to use a friendly, helpful tone. A few strategies will help you create this tone.
- Use simple, everyday words instead of "big" words that may confuse your reader.

Unit 2 • Expository Writing • 71

Ch. 5 **Write a How-To Article**

- If you must use a specialized word or term, define it for your reader.
- Use some contractions, as you would when speaking to a friend.
- Use the second-person point of view to speak directly to your reader.

When using these strategies, it is important to use each one consistently. For instance, don't use simple words in one paragraph and then use difficult technical terms in the next paragraph.

Write Your How-To Article. Write your how-to article, using the sequence chain you created as your outline.

- Use a friendly, helpful tone throughout the article.
- Use transition words such as *first*, *next*, and *after that* to help your reader follow the sequence of steps. You can find a list of useful transition words in the table on page 39.

Here is a paragraph from the how-to article on making soap. Notice how the writer makes changes to create a friendly tone and to include transition words.

> Begin by getting
> ~~Get~~ several bars of transparent (see–through) glycerin soap. It's
> ~~It is~~ okay if the soap is tinted blue, green, or
> I like   Next,
> another color, but the colorless type ~~is~~ best. Look for little waterproof surprises to put in the soap. Plastic bugs, toy jewelry, coins, and even an old key will work. Choose a surprise that fits the person who will receive the gift. Choose some soap molds, such as paper cups or the little cardboard box that paper clips come in.
>   For instance, my brother loved the soap that had plastic eyeballs in it.
>   Finally,

72 • The Writer's Studio   Level A

Write a How-To Article   Ch. 5

Revise

You can strengthen your article by revising unnecessary shifts in point of view. The following mini-lesson explains this strategy.

Mini-Lesson: Using a Consistent Point of View

Point of view refers to the perspective from which you write. The following table explains the three points of view and why you might choose to use each one.

Point of View	Examples	Why Use It?
The **first-person** point of view uses mainly first-person pronouns such as *I, me, us,* and *we*.	*I built a birdhouse.* *We made quesadillas.*	Gives a personal tone to the writing. Useful when writing about personal impressions, feelings, and opinions.
The **second-person** point of view uses mainly second-person pronouns such as *you* and *your*. The writer speaks directly to the reader.	*First, you should find a clean white T-shirt. Crack the eggs into the mixing bowl.* (The subject, **you**, is implied.)	Helps to form a personal link between you (the writer) and the reader. Useful when writing how-to articles or chatty articles.
The **third-person** point of view uses mainly third-person pronouns such as *he, she,* and *they,* along with specific nouns.	**Students** *learn to use digital cameras, and* **they** *display their photographs in class.* *The* **chef** *spooned beans into the bowl, and then* **he** *added a layer of cheese.*	Creates a less personal, more objective tone. Useful for giving factual information and establishing a trustworthy tone.

Unit 2 • Expository Writing • 73

Ch. 5 **Write a How-To Article**

Whichever point of view you use in a piece of writing, make sure you use it consistently. For instance, in your how-to article, don't use the second-person point of view to explain some steps and then switch to the first-person point of view to explain other steps. In the model below, the writer has corrected an unnecessary shift in point of view.

> Next, cut the soap into one-half-inch chunks. If you don't normally handle knives, get help from someone who does. If ~~I am~~ *you are* using more than one color of soap, ~~I~~ keep the colors separate. Place soap chunks in a glass bowl and heat it in the microwave on high for 10 seconds. If the soap is not completely melted, heat it for 5 or 10 seconds more, but just until it is melted.

Give It a Try: Revise Your How-To Article for Consistent Point of View

Read your article, checking the point of view of each sentence. Underline each sentence that does not use the second-person point of view. Unless there is a specific reason to use first- or third-person point of view in that sentence, revise it to use the second-person point of view.

Revise Your How-To Article. Use the following checklist to revise the rough draft of your how-to article. The How-To Article Rubric that follows the checklist will help you determine how strong your article is and where to make revisions.

74 • The Writer's Studio   Level A

Write a How-To Article Ch. 5

Ideas
- ❑ Does your article explain how to accomplish *one specific goal*? If more than one goal is presented, or the goal is too general, revise your article to focus on one specific goal.
- ❑ Place a check mark next to each step that is clearly related to the process. If a step is unrelated, cross it out.

Organization
- ❑ Do you explain the steps in the order in which they should be completed? Revise any steps that are out of order.

Voice
- ❑ Do you use a friendly, helpful tone? Look for two words/ expressions that create your tone. Write *tone* above them.
- ❑ Do you use the second-person point of view consistently? Cross out any spots where you don't use the second-person point of view and revise them.

Word choice
- ❑ Underline three transition words you use to show sequence of steps.
- ❑ Circle three specific nouns and three specific verbs you use to make your ideas clear.

Sentence fluency
- ❑ Have you used imperative sentences to tell the reader what to do? Place a check mark next to each one.
- ❑ Have you used declarative sentences to give information? Place a check mark next to each one.

Ch. 5 Write a How-To Article

How-To Article Rubric

	4 Strong	3 Effective	2 Developing	1 Beginning
Ideas	One process is explained. Each step clearly relates.	One process is explained. Most steps clearly relate.	One process is explained, but many steps do not relate.	The process is not clear. Most steps do not relate.
organization	Each step in the process is explained in sequential order.	Most steps are explained in sequential order.	Steps in the process are explained, but many are out of order.	Few steps in the process are explained, and their order is random.
voice	The writer uses a friendly tone and consistent point of view.	The friendly tone and point of view are mostly consistent.	A few sentences use a friendly tone; point of view is inconsistent.	The tone is not friendly, and point of view is inconsistent.
word choice	Transition words and specific nouns and verbs are used skillfully.	Many transition words and specific nouns and verbs are used.	A few transition words or specific nouns and verbs are used.	Transition words and specific nouns and verbs are absent.
sentence fluency	A useful mix of imperative and declarative sentences is used.	Some imperative and declarative sentences are used.	A few imperative and declarative sentences are used.	More imperative sentences are needed.
conventions	Few errors in capitalization, spelling, punctuation, or grammar are present.	Several errors in capitalization, spelling, punctuation, or grammar are present.	Errors in capitalization, spelling, punctuation, and grammar do not prevent understanding.	Errors in capitalization, spelling, punctuation, and grammar prevent understanding.

Write a How-To Article Ch. 5

 **Edit**

Edit Your How-To Article. Edit the revised copy of your how-to article. The following questions will help you decide what to change, remove, or leave in place.

Conventions
❑ Did you use apostrophes correctly to form contractions?
❑ Did you use a comma when you joined sentences with a coordinating conjunction?
❑ Did you use a comma when you began a sentence with a subordinate clause?
❑ Did you correct spelling mistakes, either with a friend's help or by using a dictionary?

PUBLISH

Presentation. Prepare your article for publication by writing or typing the final, edited copy.

Publish Your Article. Here are ideas for publishing your work.
❑ Create a demonstration video based on your how-to article. Ask a friend to film you as you perform the process that your article explains. As you work, have another friend provide the voice-over by reading your how-to article aloud.
❑ Work with classmates to create a Babysitter's Survival Guide, a Summer Vacation Survival Guide, or another type of guide. Include a collection of how-to articles that babysitters, bored kids, or your target audience could use.
❑ Pass out copies of your how-to article to friends and then get together with them to have a how-to party. Bring the materials necessary to demonstrate your how-to article.

Unit 2 • **Expository Writing** • **77**

Ch. 5 **Write a How-To Article**

Evaluate Your Article

Your teacher will either assess your article, ask you to self-assess your article, or ask you to switch with a partner and assess each other's work.

Evaluate the Model Article

Here is the writer's published copy of "How to Make Surprise Soap." Using the rubric, decide what score you would give it. In a class discussion, explain your reasoning.

How to Make Surprise Soap

I love to give presents, and I like to make them myself. That way they are unique, reflect my personality, and—usually—are inexpensive. So far, the most popular gift I've created is Surprise Soap. This is a clear, glycerin soap with a plastic spider, flower, or toy in the center. The little surprises are recycled objects, of course. Here is how you can make your own Surprise Soap.

Begin by getting several bars of transparent (see-through) glycerin soap. It's okay if the soap is tinted blue, green, or another color, but I like the colorless type best. Next, collect little waterproof surprises to put in the soap. Plastic bugs, toy jewelry, coins, and even an old key will work. Choose a surprise that fits the person who will receive the gift. For instance, my brother loved the soap that had plastic eyeballs in it! Finally, choose some soap molds, such as paper cups or the little cardboard box that paper clips come in.

Start by setting out your soap molds. If you wish, spray the insides with oil to help the soap bars come out easily later on. Also, set out your supply of surprises.

Next, cut the soap into one-half-inch chunks. If you don't normally handle knives, get help from someone who does. If you are using more than one color of soap, keep the colors separate. Place soap chunks in a glass bowl and heat it in the microwave on high for 10 seconds. If the soap is not completely melted, heat it for 5 or 10 seconds more, but just until it is melted.

The Writer's Studio   Level A

Write a How-To Article Ch. 5

Carefully pour the melted soap into the molds to about 1/2" to 3/4" deep (enough to cover the surprise). Quickly set a surprise in the center of each soap. You might need to use a spoon to push the surprise beneath the surface of the soap.

    Now you simply wait. Set your filled molds in a dust-free spot indoors where they will not be disturbed. Check them after 24 hours. When they are hard, turn the molds upside down and tap the bottoms. The soap may slide right out. If it doesn't, tear off the paper cup or cardboard box. And there you have it! Your Surprise Soap is ready to wrap and give away!

Chapter 6
Write an Explanatory Essay

The purpose of explanatory writing is to explain something, such as an opinion, a perspective, or an experience, in order to inform the reader. Explanatory essays answer questions such as these:

How can people your age help to protect the environment?

What rules—fair and unfair—govern your life?

Are sports about winning or about having fun?

If you have ideas, opinions, and information about these questions, then you are already prepared to write an explanatory essay. In fact, you have probably already written many explanations in your life, both in and out of school. This chapter will help you strengthen your skills of explanatory writing.

Six Traits of an Explanatory Essay

Ideas	The topic is focused. Reasons and examples make the topic clear.
Organization	Reasons and examples are arranged logically, such as in order of importance.
Voice	The writer's voice shows confidence in the topic and an eagerness to help the reader understand.
Word Choice	Vivid, specific words make the writer's ideas memorable.
Sentence Fluency	A variety of sentence structures and lengths creates a pleasing rhythm to the writing.
Conventions	Capitalization, spelling, punctuation, and grammar are correct.

Unit 2 • Expository Writing • 81

Ch. 6 Write an Explanatory Essay

In the following model paragraph, the writer explains why she deserves respect.

> Even though I am "just" a teenager, I deserve respect at home, at school, and on the sports field. At home, I deserve respect from family members. They should knock on my door before entering, they should ask before borrowing my things, and they should take my opinions seriously. At school, I deserve respect from my friends. If someone has a problem with me, he or she should talk to me instead of spreading gossip. If I do my homework early, people should not ask to copy it. This is just using me. I also deserve respect on the sports field. During soccer games, I have been called names, bashed into, and ridiculed. Some of this disrespect came from players, and some came from parents in the stands. Disrespect in any area of my teenage life is not acceptable.

Give It a Try: Examine the Model Paragraph

With a partner, answer the following questions about six traits in the model paragraph above. Write your answers on separate paper.

1. **Ideas.** What main idea is the writer explaining?

2. **Organization.** What examples does the writer give to explain the main idea? Copy three sentences from the paragraph that express three main examples.

3. **Voice and word choice.** How would you describe the writer's voice in this paragraph? What words or expressions help you draw this conclusion?

4. **Sentence fluency.** Copy one sentence that begins with an introductory phrase or clause and circle this introductory element.

5. **Conventions.**
    a. Copy the sentence that begins, "They should knock . . ." Then circle the commas in this sentence.
    b. Do these commas link a series of phrases or clauses?

82 • The Writer's Studio   Level A

Write an Explanatory Essay Ch. 6

Your Turn to Write: Compose an Explanatory Essay

Now you'll write your own explanatory essay. Read the assignment carefully and follow the strategies and instructions for each stage of the writing process.

Assignment

Friendship is an important part of life. Who are your friends? How do they influence what you do, say, wear, eat, and laugh about? Most people have close friends; however, most people have different ideas about what makes a good friend. Write an essay explaining what, in your opinion, makes a good friend. Your essay should be suitable for presentation to your class, and it should be approximately 300 words long.

Prewrite

Analyze the Prompt. What does the prompt tell you about your goals for this assignment? Read the assignment closely to find answers to the following questions. Write your answers on separate paper.
1. What is the purpose of this essay?
2. Who is the audience for this essay?
3. How long does the essay need to be?

Gather Ideas and Details. Pair up with a partner to complete the following two steps.
1. **Say it out loud.** Take four or five minutes to tell your prewriting partner about some of your friends and what you like about them. The following sentence starters will help you get started.

Unit 2 • Expository Writing • 83

Ch. 6 Write an Explanatory Essay

- The first thing I look for in a friend is . . .
- Something I like about a friend of mine is . . .
- What I mean by that is . . .
- One thing I won't accept in a friend is . . .

After explaining your thoughts aloud, take a moment to jot down key qualities of friendship and reasons or examples that help make the qualities clear to your audience.

2. Get a response. Ask your partner, "What else do you want to know about my opinions about friendship?" Write down your partner's response. Now answer the question aloud. Add any useful ideas to your notes.

Organize Ideas and Details. Look over your prewriting, and circle the key qualities of a friend that you want to explain in your essay. Then number these ideas in order of priority, from least to most important. Think about the list you have formed.

- ❑ Do you have 3–4 solid qualities of friendship to explain in your essay?
- ❑ Do you have reasons or examples to support and explain each quality?
- ❑ Do you have too many qualities to explain in this essay? If so, which 3–4 qualities would your readers most want to learn about?
- ❑ If you don't have enough solid qualities listed, what can you add to your list?
- ❑ Do you need to change the order of importance of the qualities so that the strongest, most important quality is listed last?

In the following example, the writer has listed three important qualities of friendship and has added some supporting details.

> Qualities in a Good Friend
> 1. sense of humor
> --funny
> --doesn't take self too seriously
> --can laugh off your mistakes

> 2. common interests
> --seeing eye to eye when . . .
>   talking
>   supporting each other
>   playing
>   figuring out life
> 3. loyalty
> --friendships have high points, low points
> --loyalty makes or breaks a friendship

 **Draft**

An effective explanatory essay hinges on a strong thesis statement. The following mini-lesson will help you write a strong thesis statement for your essay on friendship.

Mini-Lesson: Writing a Thesis Statement

An essay's introductory paragraph does more than hook the reader's attention. It also tells the reader exactly what you intend to explain in the essay. This statement of your purpose for writing is your *thesis statement*.

A **thesis statement** declares exactly what the body of the essay will explain or prove.

Here is an example of a thesis statement:

Even though I am "just" a teenager, I deserve respect at home, at school, and on the sports field.

The essay that follows this thesis statement should explain the writer's ideas about respect at home, respect at school, and respect on the sports field.

Ch. 6 Write an Explanatory Essay

Here is another example of a thesis statement:

A good friend is someone who shares your sense of humor, shares your interests, and shares your loyalty to the friendship.

The essay that follows this thesis statement should explain the writer's ideas about a shared sense of humor, shared interests, and loyalty in friendship.

As you can see from these examples, a strong thesis statement is *focused*. The thesis statement makes a statement or claim that is narrow enough to be fully explained or proved in the essay.

Too broad: *Nobody gives teenagers the respect they deserve.* (The idea of *nobody* is too broad to prove in an essay. Likewise, the general category of *teenagers* is too broad to cover in an essay.)

Focused: *Even though I am "just" a teenager, I deserve respect at home, at school, and on the sports field.* (This thesis statement narrows the topic to one teenager and to three specific areas where she deserves respect.)

A strong thesis statement is also a complete sentence that does two things: It identifies a topic, and it states something specific about the topic.

Just a topic: *Friendship*

Just a topic: *This essay is about friendship.*

A thesis statement: *A good friend is someone who shares your sense of humor, shares your interests, and shares your loyalty to the friendship.* (This statement identifies the topic of friendship *and* states three points about it.)

Give It a Try: Write a Thesis Statement

Write your answer to each question on separate paper.
1. What is the topic of your explanatory essay?
2. What qualities or attitudes will you explain in the essay?
3. Using the information from your answers to questions 1 and 2, write a thesis statement for your explanatory essay.

Write an Explanatory Essay Ch. 6

Write Your Explanatory Essay. Now that you have gathered ideas and details, planned the organization of your essay, and written a thesis statement, you are ready to write your explanatory essay. Here are a few tips to keep in mind as you write:
- The first paragraph should include a thesis statement.
- Each body paragraph should explain one quality or attitude that makes a good friend. These paragraphs explain the qualities in order from least to most important.
- The concluding paragraph should offer a final thought about your opinion of what makes a good friend.

T!P

Don't forget to give your essay a title that gets your reader's attention and hints at your topic. An effective title may use a key word from the essay, ask a question that the essay answers, or use an interesting phrase to make the reader want to read more.

Revise

Revise Your Explanatory Essay. Use the following checklist to revise the rough draft of your explanatory essay. The Explanatory Essay Rubric that follows the checklist will help you determine how strong your essay is and where to make revisions.

Ideas
- ❑ Reread your thesis statement. Place one check mark next to it if it identifies a *focused* topic. Place another check mark next to your thesis if it says something *important* about your topic. If your thesis statement is missing one of these items, go back and revise it.
- ❑ Underline three reasons and three examples that support your main idea(s).

Organization
- ❑ Number each of your key points. Make sure they're in order from least to most important.

Voice
- ❑ Underline words and phrases that create your tone and show that you are confident and eager to explain your topic. Write *voice* above these words and phrases.

Word choice
- ❑ Circle at least three transition words you use to show order of importance.

Unit 2 • Expository Writing • **87**

Ch. 6 Write an Explanatory Essay

- ❑ Circle three specific, vivid words. Cross out and revise any plain or vague words.

Sentence fluency
- ❑ Check for a variety of sentence structures and sentence lengths.

Explanatory Essay Rubric

	4 Strong	3 Effective	2 Developing	1 Beginning
Ideas	One topic is explained using reasons or examples.	Most reasons and examples help to explain the topic.	Some reasons and examples help to explain the topic.	The topic and the reasons or examples are unclear.
Organization	Reasons and examples are arranged in order of importance.	One reason or example seems out of place.	Reasons and examples are in no particular order.	The order of reasons and examples is confusing.
Voice	The writer uses a confident tone, drawing the reader in.	Most paragraphs have a confident tone.	A mixture of confident and uncertain tones is used.	The writer's tone is uncertain and hesitant.
Word Choice	Vivid, specific words make the writer's ideas memorable.	Some vivid, specific words are used.	One or two vivid, specific words are used.	Key words are general, plain, or misused.
Sentence Fluency	A variety of sentence structures and lengths are used.	There is some variety in sentence structure and length.	A few sentences begin with an introductory element.	Sentence structure is repetitive and mechanical.
Conventions	Few errors in capitalization, spelling, punctuation, or grammar are present.	Several errors in capitalization, spelling, punctuation, or grammar are present.	Errors in capitalization, spelling, punctuation, and grammar do not prevent understanding.	Errors in capitalization, spelling, punctuation, and grammar prevent understanding.

Write an Explanatory Essay   Ch. 6

 **Edit**

Edit Your Explanatory Essay. Edit the revised copy of your explanatory essay. The following questions will help you decide what to change, remove, or leave in place.

Conventions
- ❏ Did you use commas to separate words, phrases, or clauses in a series?
- ❏ Did you use apostrophes correctly to form contractions?
- ❏ Did you use a comma when you joined sentences with a coordinating conjunction?
- ❏ Did you use a comma when you began a sentence with a subordinate clause?
- ❏ Did you correct spelling mistakes, either with a friend's help or by using a dictionary?

PUBLISH

Presentation. Prepare your essay for publication by writing or typing the final, edited copy.

Publish Your Explanatory Essay. Here are ideas for publishing your work.
- ❏ Give a copy to each of your friends who have some or all of the qualities in the essay.
- ❏ Use the essay as the first entry in a blog, either a real blog on the Internet or a hard copy that you share with friends.

Evaluate Your Essay

Your teacher will either assess your essay, ask you to self-assess your essay, or ask you to switch with a partner and assess each other's work.

Unit 2 • Expository Writing • **89**

Ch. 6 **Write an Explanatory Essay**

Evaluate the Model Essay

Here is the writer's published copy of the explanatory essay "What Makes a Good Friend?" What are the essay's strong points and weak points? Based on the rubric on page 88, how would you score this essay?

What Makes a Good Friend?

At home, work, school, and play we are around countless people. We bond with some of these people and become close friends. Sometimes, we dislike someone so strongly that we become enemies. How can we explain why some people become good friends and some people become enemies? It all boils down to what each person values in a friend. In my opinion, a good friend is someone who shares your sense of humor, shares your interests, and shares your loyalty to the friendship.

A sense of humor forms a good foundation for any friendship. For one thing, we all like to have fun with our friends. Someone who is funny, or who doesn't take himself or herself too seriously, is fun to be around. More important, someone with a good sense of humor is more likely to laugh off your mistakes rather than hold them against you.

A good sense of humor helps a friendship get off to a good start, but the two people also need to share interests. Friends spend a lot of time together talking, supporting one another, playing games or sports, and figuring out life. Unless the two people have lots in common, they won't see eye to eye. They'll lose interest in one another.

A friendship between people who have a sense of humor and share common interests can last only if both people are loyal to the friendship. This important quality--loyalty--can make or break a friendship. Any friendship naturally has high points and low points. Two people who are loyal enough to work on their problems and find solutions have a winning friendship.

In the search for friends, I try to keep in mind the fact that nobody is perfect. However, it is worthwhile to be a little demanding when it comes to choosing friends. Fun, interesting, loyal people make the best friends.

Chapter 7

Write a Comparison-Contrast Essay

Life is filled with decisions, big and small. Many decisions are life changing, while others simply determine what we'll eat for lunch. *Should the family rent an apartment or buy a house? Should I order fried chicken or grilled chicken? Should I be a math tutor after school or train for track season?*

Whenever we make decisions, form opinions, or select among choices, we make comparisons and contrasts. We review how the choices are alike and different, and we use this information to select one. We do this all the time in our minds and in our conversations. In this chapter, you'll practice making comparisons and contrasts in writing.

Six Traits of a Comparison-Contrast Essay

Ideas	The writer identifies specific topics to be compared and contrasted. Supporting details make the comparison and contrast clear.
Organization	The article includes a strong beginning, a middle that is organized point by point, and a strong conclusion.
Voice	The writing style fits with the purpose and audience of the description.
Word Choice	Transition words draw the reader's attention to comparisons and contrasts. Vivid words help to make key ideas memorable.
Sentence Fluency	A variety of sentence types and structures creates a pleasing rhythm to the writing.
Conventions	Proper nouns are capitalized. Spelling, punctuation, and grammar are correct.

Unit 2 • Expository Writing • 93

Ch. 7 Write a Comparison-Contrast Essay

In the paragraph below, the author explains how grilled chicken and fried chicken are alike and different.

> Most people have heard that it is healthier to eat grilled chicken than fried chicken. How different are these two options, really? Consider a 3-ounce chicken breast, boneless and skinless. Grilled with only herbs or spices, it has about 140 calories and 3 grams of fat. In contrast, this chicken fried in oil has about 160 calories and 4 grams of fat. This may not seem like a big difference, but consider this: The fried chicken in fast-food restaurants is usually fried with the skin on, coated in a secret-recipe batter. The same size piece of chicken, battered and fried with skin on, has a whopping 365 calories and 18 grams of fat. How different is a plain grilled chicken breast and a fried, battered chicken breast? You be the judge.

Give It a Try: Examine the Model Paragraph

Answer the following questions about six traits in the model paragraph you just read. Write your answers on separate paper.

1. **Ideas.** What two things does the writer compare and contrast?
2. **Organization and word choice.** How does the transition "In contrast" help to show the connection between ideas?
3. **Voice and word choice.** How does the word *whopping* show the writer's attitude about facts?
4. **Sentence fluency.** Why does the writer ask questions in this paragraph?
5. **Conventions.** Why does the writer use a colon in this paragraph?

Write a Comparison-Contrast Essay Ch. 7

Your Turn to Write: Compose a Comparison-Contrast Essay

Now you'll write your own comparison-contrast essay. Read the assignment carefully and follow the strategies and instructions for each stage of the writing process.

Assignment

Your family has decided to take a one-week vacation together this summer. In a family brainstorming session, the following types of vacation were suggested:

a beach
a state or national park
a city
a cruise ship

If money were not a problem, which two vacation types would be your top choices? Which *specific* beach, park, city, or cruise ship destination would you choose? Write a 350–400 word essay that compares and contrasts two specific vacation destinations. Your audience for this essay is your family.

Prewrite

Analyze the Prompt. What does the prompt tell you about your goals for this assignment? Read the assignment closely to find answers to the following questions. Write your answers on separate paper.

1. What is the purpose of this essay?
2. Who is the audience for this essay?
3. How long does the essay need to be?

Unit 2 • Expository Writing • **95**

Ch. 7 **Write a Comparison-Contrast Essay**

Choose a Topic. Create a T-chart by dividing a sheet of paper into two columns. Label each column with a vacation type (beach, state or national park, city, or cruise ship). Then list as many specific examples of each vacation type as you can think of. Finally, review your lists and choose one specific destination from each column to use in your essay. Here is an example of one writer's T-chart.

beach	state or national park
✗ any beach in Hawaii *(not specific)*	Yosemite National Park
Hollywood Beach in Florida *(circled)*	Yellowstone National Park
South Padre Island beach in Texas	Adirondack Park in New York
Florida Keys beach	**Rocky Mountain National Park** *(circled)*
Old Orchard Beach in Maine	Grand Canyon National Park

Gather Ideas and Details. Create another T-chart. This time, label each column with the name of a specific vacation destination. In each column, list fun things to do and useful facts about the vacation destination. On the next page is an example.

96 • The Writer's Studio   Level A

Write a Comparison-Contrast Essay Ch. 7

Hollywood Beach in Florida	Rocky Mountain National Park
located in southern Florida	located in Colorado, near Denver
temps around 80°	temps in 70s° day, 40° night
sun, sand, water	outdoor destination
shopping, dining, relaxing	mountains, valleys, forests
marine life	wildlife
outdoor destination	hiking, camping, relaxing
beautiful views to sketch/photograph	beautiful views to sketch/photograph

Organize Ideas and Details. You can use a Venn diagram to organize details about your two vacation destinations. In the following Venn diagram, the writer has listed similarities and differences between Hollywood Beach and Rocky Mountain National Park.

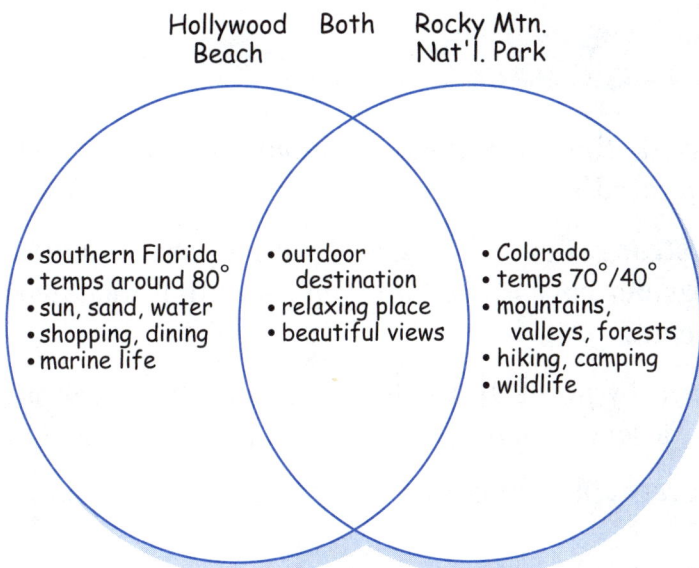

Unit 2 • Expository Writing • 97

Ch. 7 **Write a Comparison-Contrast Essay**

Use a Venn Diagram to Organize Ideas. Copy the following blank Venn diagram into your notebook and use it to organize your own details for your comparison-contrast essay.

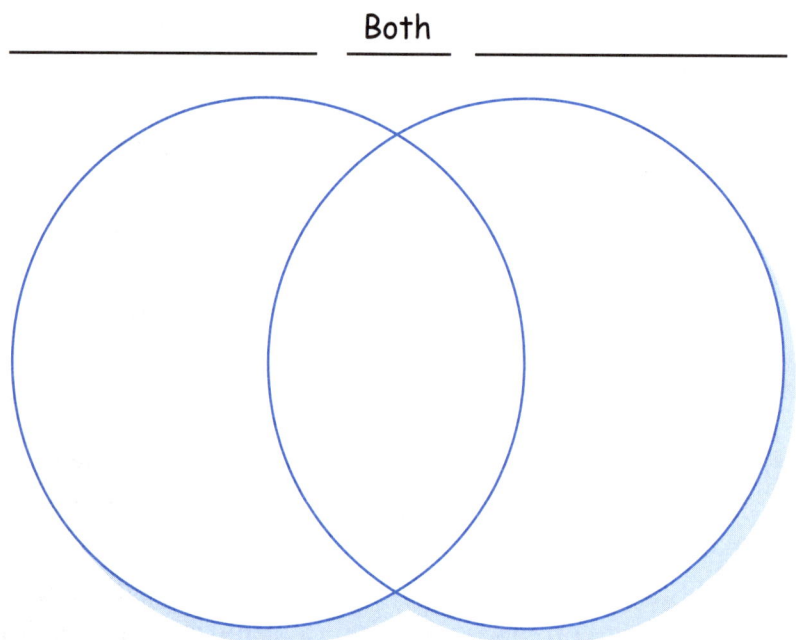

 Draft

When you write the draft of your comparison-contrast essay, keep these tips in mind.

- **Start strong.** Begin your essay with a paragraph that makes your reader care about your topic and that includes a thesis statement.

- **Go point by point.** In the body paragraphs, cover similarities and differences point by point. You could do this by writing
    - 1 paragraph that explains how the destinations are similar and
    - 1 paragraph that explains how they are different

98 • The Writer's Studio   Level A

Write a Comparison-Contrast Essay Ch. 7

OR
- 1 paragraph that explains how the destinations are similar,
- 1 paragraph on the unique qualities of the first place, and
- 1 paragraph on the unique qualities of the other place.

- **Finish strong.** Conclude your essay with a paragraph that sums up the choice your reader faces and offers guidance on making that choice.

Write Your Compare-Contrast Essay. Use the ideas and details that you gathered during prewriting to write a well-organized compare-contrast essay.

With the excitement and rush of getting your great ideas down on

Revise

paper, it's easy to make mistakes in sentence structure. A common error is the incomplete sentence. The following mini-lesson explains how you can identify and fix this type of error.

Mini-Lesson: Using Complete Sentences

Read the following sentences. Which ones are complete? Which are incomplete?

1. Colorado Springs, one of my favorite places.
2. Yosemite National Park is in east-central California.
3. Digging my toes in the hot, gritty sand.
4. The cruise to Alaska leaves from a port in Seattle.

If you said that sentences 1 and 3 are incomplete, then you have a good eye. You are probably familiar with the following definition of a complete sentence.

Unit 2 • Expository Writing • 99

Ch. 7 **Write a Comparison-Contrast Essay**

→A **complete sentence** contains a subject and a verb, and it expresses a complete thought.

→The **subject** is the word or words that perform the action of the verb or are talked about.

→The **verb** is the word or words that express the action or state of being of the subject.

Sentences 2 and 4 on the previous page are complete sentences. They each have a subject and a verb.

        subject   verb
Complete sentence: <u>Yosemite National Park</u> <u>is</u> in east-central California.
          subject verb
Complete sentence: The <u>cruise</u> to Alaska <u>leaves</u> from a port in Seattle.

The problem with sentence 1 is that it contains a subject but no verb.

         subject
Incomplete sentence: Colorado Springs, one of my favorite places.

To fix this error, the writer needs to say something about Colorado.

         subject verb
Complete sentence: <u>Colorado Springs</u> <u>is</u> one of my favorite places.
(The writer added a verb.)

        subject ← appositive
Complete sentence: <u>Colorado Springs,</u> (one of my favorite
     verb
places,) <u>offers</u> outdoor adventures.
(The writer used the phrase as an appositive and added a verb. Note the commas before and after the appositive.)

Write a Comparison-Contrast Essay Ch. 7

The problem with sentence 3 is that it contains a word group without a subject or a verb.

Incomplete sentence: Digging my toes in the hot sand.

To fix this error, the writer needs to add a subject and a verb.

Complete sentence: Digging my toes in the hot sand, I sighed happily.
(The writer added a subject and a verb.)

Complete sentence: I will be digging my toes in the hot sand.
(The writer added a subject and added helping verbs to create a verb phrase.)

Give It a Try: Revise Incomplete Sentences

On a separate sheet of paper, rewrite the following paragraph. Revise each incomplete sentence to form a complete sentence.

Even though these destinations seem very different, they offer the same types of activities. At either place, spending time outdoors in nature. Also being physically active. We could sit and read, and we could enjoy a fabulous view. Plenty of opportunities to sketch interesting outdoor subjects. Both vacations would be fun, and we would come home relaxed and filled with great memories.

Unit 2 • Expository Writing • **101**

Ch. 7 **Write a Comparison-Contrast Essay**

> **Give It a Try: Revise Incomplete Sentences in Your Own Essay**
>
> Work with a partner to identify incomplete sentences in your comparison-contrast essay. Discuss possible ways to make each sentence complete. Then revise each one to make it complete.

Revise Your Comparison-Contrast Essay. Use the following checklist to revise your rough draft. The Comparison-Contrast Essay Rubric that follows the checklist will help you determine how strong your article is and where to make revisions.

Ideas
- ❑ Does the essay compare and contrast two specific vacation destinations? Place a check mark next to your first mention of these destinations.
- ❑ Place a check mark above each detail that helps explain a point of similarity or a point of contrast.

Organization
- ❑ Do you explain the similarities and differences point by point? To be sure, write a *P* next to each point, and under each point, write *S* where you discuss similarities and *D* where you discuss differences.

Voice
- ❑ Do you use a tone suitable to an audience of my family? Underline three words or phrases that show tone and write *voice* above them.

Word choice
- ❑ Circle three transition words that show similarities and differences.
- ❑ Circle three vivid words that reveal your attitude about ideas or facts.

Sentence fluency
- ❑ Write *C* for complete above each complete sentence. If you have any incomplete sentences, revise them.
- ❑ Check for a variety of sentence types, sentence structures, and sentence lengths. Make revisions as necessary.

The Writer's Studio   Level A

Comparison-Contrast Essay Rubric

	4 Strong	3 Effective	2 Developing	1 Beginning
Ideas	The essay compares and contrasts specific subjects using relevant details.	The essay compares and contrasts specific subjects. Most details are relevant.	The subjects of comparison and contrast need to be more specific. Many details seem unrelated.	The subjects of comparison and contrast are general rather than specific. Details do not clearly relate.
Organization	Details of comparison and contrast are organized point by point.	A few details are out of place in the point-by-point arrangement.	A few details are arranged point by point.	Details are offered in no particular order.
Voice	The tone fits with the audience of family members.	In most paragraphs the tone fits with the audience.	A few sentences achieve a suitable tone.	The tone is stiff or otherwise does not fit with the audience.
Word Choice	Transitions and vivid words are used skillfully.	Some transitions and vivid words are present.	Two or three transitions or vivid words are present.	Transition words and specific nouns and verbs are absent.
Sentence Fluency	Sentences are complete. A variety of sentence types is used.	One or two sentences are incomplete. A variety of sentence types is used.	Many sentences are incomplete. There is some variety of sentence types.	Sentences are mostly of one type or are incomplete.
Conventions	Proper nouns are capitalized. Spelling, punctuation, or grammar are correct.	Several errors in capitalization, spelling, punctuation, or grammar are present.	Errors in capitalization, spelling, punctuation, and grammar do not prevent understanding.	Errors in capitalization, spelling, punctuation, and grammar prevent understanding.

Ch. 7 **Write a Comparison-Contrast Essay**

 **Edit**

To edit your writing means to find and correct mistakes in capitalization, spelling, and punctuation. Here are three strategies for identifying mistakes in your writing:

- **Use a checklist.** Use the checklists in the editing sections in this book. Use checklists that your teacher provides. Use checklists that you create based on your own particular needs.

- **Listen to your essay.** Make two copies of your essay and pair up with a partner. As your partner reads your essay aloud, follow along on your copy. Listen for incomplete sentences. Listen for times when your reader stumbles over a word that is spelled incorrectly or stumbles over a sentence that needs one or more commas. Circle each mistake so that you can go back later and fix it.

- **Highlight punctuation marks.** Highlight each mark of punctuation in your essay. Then consider each mark, one by one. Ask, "Did I use this mark correctly?" and "Is this the best mark to use here?" If you're not sure about the use of a mark, look it up in a handbook.

Edit Your Comparison-Contrast Essay. Edit the revised copy of your comparison-contrast essay. The following questions will help you decide what to change, remove, or leave in place.

Conventions
❏ Did you capitalize proper nouns?
❏ Did you find and correct punctuation errors, either with a friend's help or by using a handbook?
❏ Did you correct spelling mistakes, either with a friend's help or by using a dictionary?

Write a Comparison-Contrast Essay | Ch. 7

PUBLISH

Presentation. Prepare your essay for publication by writing or typing the final, edited copy.

Publish Your Comparison-Contrast Essay. Here are ideas for publishing your work.
- ❑ Read your essay to your family and take a vote: Which destination would your family most like to visit?
- ❑ Pass your essay around to friends and take a poll: Which destination would each friend prefer?
- ❑ Contact the visitor's center for each destination in your essay and request a tourist brochure. Most cities provide this information through their chamber of commerce. Most states provide tourist guides that include parks and beaches. Cities and states, as well as cruise lines, also offer information online. Use the photos in the brochures, along with your essay, to create a personal travel packet. Keep it for the day when you actually can go to one of these places.

Evaluate Your Essay

Your teacher will either assess your essay, ask you to self-assess your essay, or ask you to switch with a partner and assess each other's work.

Evaluate the Completed Model Essay

On the next page, you'll find the writer's published copy of the comparison-contrast essay "National Park or Beach?" What are the essay's strong points and weak points? Based on the rubric on page 103, how would you score this essay? Write your score here:_____

Unit 2 • Expository Writing • 105

Ch. 7 **Write a Comparison-Contrast Essay**

National Park or Beach?

A family vacation should be enjoyable to all family members. In our family, we like to be outdoors, and we like to be active. We enjoy nature, whether it is trees, animals, or water. We also like to have downtime when we can sit and read, take photographs, or sketch fabulous views. For these reasons, I suggest two possible vacation destinations: Rocky Mountain National Park and Hollywood Beach. This park and this beach are very different destinations, but each provides the opportunities that our family wants.

Rocky Mountain National Park has some exciting things that the beach does not. Located in Colorado near Denver, this park has forested mountains and valleys with stunning views. Elk, mule deer, moose, bighorn sheep, and black bears roam around, while coyotes and cougars slink through the trees. Eagles and hawks soar overhead. There are five drive-in campsites and 359 miles of hiking trails. In July and August, the daytime temperature is in the 70s, and it drops to the 40s at night. It has all the makings of a rugged wilderness adventure.

On the other hand, Hollywood Beach has all the makings of a sunny, sporty play place. Located in southern Florida, this beach is family-friendly, safe, and clean. The Hollywood Beach Boardwalk runs along a beach with sand that you'll want to sink your toes into. Shops and restaurants line the walk, ready to pamper you with gifts and fine food. To work up an appetite, you can bike, jog, or skate along the walk. At Hollywood North Beach Park, you can swim, sunbathe, fish, and play volleyball. In July and August, the temperature here is around 80 degrees.

Even though these destinations seem very different, they offer the same types of activities. At either place, we could spend time outdoors in nature,

Write a Comparison-Contrast Essay

we could be physically active, we could sit and read, and we could enjoy a fabulous view. There would be plenty of opportunities to sketch interesting outdoor subjects. Both vacations would be fun, and we would come home relaxed and filled with great memories.

The decision comes down to this: Do we want to be cool or hot during our outdoor adventures? Do we want to hike a mountain or swim in an ocean? Whichever way the family votes, I'll have my sketchbook and pencils packed and ready to go.

Chapter 8

Test Writing: The Expository Essay

On written tests, you are often asked to write an expository essay. For example, you might be asked to write about your idea of friendship, or you might be asked to write about a valuable possession you have. This type of essay allows you to demonstrate your writing skills while explaining a topic you already know about. A test essay usually has to be written in a limited amount of time. Explaining a topic with which you are familiar means that you can use your knowledge and experience to come up with ideas and details quickly. Then you can use most of your test time to demonstrate the traits of good writing. The following table gives more information about these traits.

Six Traits of an Expository Test Essay

Ideas	The topic is narrowed to a specific subject to be explained. Each detail clearly relates to the topic.
Organization	Details are arranged with care, such as in order of importance, from general to specific, or order of steps in a sequence.
Voice	The writing style fits with the purpose and audience of the explanation.
Word Choice	Specific nouns and verbs help the reader understand what the writer is explaining or how a process is completed.
Sentence Fluency	Declarative sentences are used to give information. A variety of sentence types and structures creates a pleasing rhythm to the writing.
Conventions	Capitalization, spelling, punctuation, and grammar are correct.

Unit 2 • Expository Writing • 109

Ch. 8 **Test Writing: The Expository Essay**

Preparing to Write Your Test Essay

The first step in writing your test essay is to read the writing prompt carefully. The writing prompt usually gives you several types of information. This may include test-taking instructions, what type of essay to write (descriptive, explanatory, etc.), and what topic to write about. Here is an example of a prompt for an expository essay.

Instructions
You have 25 minutes to complete the written composition. Read the prompt below. Then use separate paper to plan and draft your composition. Only your draft will be scored.

Writing Prompt
Many people have a hero—someone whom they admire and try to be like. The hero may have accomplished great things, or the hero may simply exhibit certain personality traits. This person may be alive today, may have lived in the past, or may be an imaginary person in literature. Think about what qualities you think a hero should have. Then think of a person, real or imaginary, who fits these criteria. Write an essay explaining who your hero is and why.

---

1. Study the Prompt
Before you begin to write your essay, take a few moments to study the prompt. You can sort through the information in the prompt by answering the questions that follow.

Test Writing: The Expository Essay — Ch. 8

What is the purpose of the essay? Scan the prompt for key words that tell you what kind of essay to write.

Words That Signal an Expository Essay

explain, explaining

tell, telling

reasons

examples

What should you write about? Study the prompt to determine exactly what you must write. This information is usually stated in one key sentence, and it is often the last sentence of the writing prompt. In the Writing Prompt on page 110, the key sentence is this one:

Write an essay explaining who your hero is and why.

The other sentences in the prompt help you understand your purpose for writing, but this sentence tells you exactly what to write.

How much time do you have to write? According to the Instructions section of this prompt, you have 25 minutes to write the essay. If a prompt does not state a time limit, this information may be printed on another page in the test booklet, or your teacher may inform you of the time limit.

What other instructions are stated? Check the prompt for additional instructions. A prompt may include a reminder list of things to be sure to include in your essay.

2. Plan Your Time

After studying the prompt, make a quick plan for how to use your time. If you have 25 minutes to write the test, you could use your time as follows:

5–7 minutes: Study the prompt and complete the prewriting.

13–15 minutes: Write the essay.

5 minutes: Revise and edit the essay.

Unit 2 • Expository Writing • 111

3. Prewrite

During the time set aside for prewriting, you should gather ideas and details for your topic and organize the information.

Gather ideas and details. Use a few of your prewriting minutes to gather ideas and details.

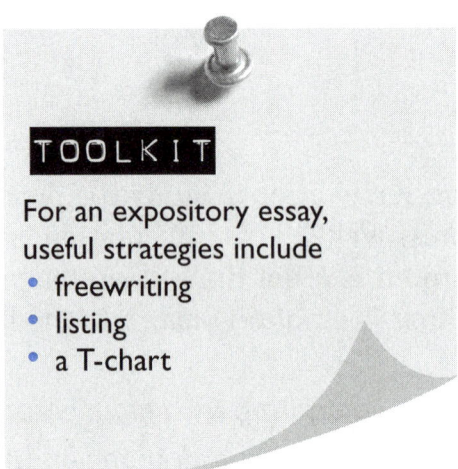

TOOLKIT

For an expository essay, useful strategies include
- freewriting
- listing
- a T-chart

Tip

During prewriting, it's easy to lose track of your goal and write down information that is off topic. To keep yourself on track, reread the writing prompt halfway through your prewriting session.

The lists below show how one writer gathered ideas for a topic and then listed reasons and examples to develop the topic.

possible heroes
a president--Abraham Lincoln
my granddad
Rosa Parks
the boy who survives in the wilderness in the book <u>Hatchet</u>

hero: my granddad--list of reasons why
hard worker (farmer)
cares about family (even the annoying preschoolers)
teaches me how to do jobs on the farm
respects nature (the land, the animals, the environment)

Organize the information. Use your remaining prewriting time to organize your information. During a 25-minute testing period, it is reasonable to plan for a 3- to 5-paragraph essay. To save time, use a simple outline such as the one on page 113 to group key points. Use your own ways of abbreviating words to save time.

Test Writing: The Expository Essay Ch. 8

beginning
--what a hero is: someone who puts others before him/herself
--my hero--my granddad

middle
--para. 1: hard worker
--para. 2: devoted to family
--para. 3: respects nature

end
--sum up heroic qualities
--you don't have to be famous to be a hero

Writing Your Test Essay

After studying the prompt, gathering ideas and details, and organizing your information, you are ready to write your essay. To keep yourself on track, follow the organizational plan you made during prewriting. Refer to it between paragraphs so that you don't go off track.

The model essay below follows the outline in the prewriting, above. It contains some errors in conventions that the writer will fix during the polishing stage.

My Hero: Granddad Lloyd

A hero is someone who puts other peopel and the enviroment before himself or herself. The best example, my Granddad. His name is Lloyd, and I call him Granddad Lloyd. A farmer who raises beef cattle and different kinds of crops. Granddad lloyd is a hero because he is a hard worker, he is devoted to family, and he respects the environment.

Granddad Lloyd is heroic because he is a hard worker. He doesn't always feel like getting up before dawn to set up irrigation pipes in his fields.

Unit 2 • Expository Writing • 113

Ch. 8 Test Writing: The Expository Essay

He doesn't always feel like going out in freezing, snowy weather to feed hay to the cows in the pasture. But he does these things. Because he values hard work. He always says, Something worth doing at all is worth doing well.

Granddad Lloyd is heroic because he is devoted to his family. One of the reasons he works so hard is that he wants to provide a good home for his wife (Grandmother June). Also, to earn enough money to help his grandkids a little bit. He paid for the after-school woodwork class that I took last semester. Granddad Lloyd also wants to show by example how you can make your life good through hard work.

Granddad lloyd is heroic because he respects the enviroment. He used to use toxic pesticides on his crops, but now he is trying to use organic ways to fix problems. He lets each field "rest" every seventh year. Helps the soil get back its nutrients. He doesn't dump used motor oil on the ground, and he doesn't spill diesel on the ground when he fills up his tractors from the storage tank. Respecting the environment takes extra time and extra money, but Granddad does it.

For all these reasons, Granddad Lloyd is a hero. He is living proof that you don't have to be famous, or dead, to be a hero.

Polishing Your Test Essay

During the last few minutes of your test period, review your essay to correct errors in capitalization, spelling, punctuation, and grammar. Mark your corrections directly on the copy to be scored and make all marks neatly and cleanly. You don't want to lose points because someone couldn't make out your words due to a sloppy correction!

Test Writing: The Expository Essay Ch. 8

The table below explains some commonly used editing marks.

Mark	Meaning	Example
≡	Capitalize a letter.	i have a dog. (i with ≡ under it)
/	Change a capital letter to lower-case.	My D/og is a beagle.
ℓ	Delete (remove).	My do*o*g is a beagle.
^	Insert here.	My dog ^ is a beagle. (Buster above)
⋀	Insert a comma here.	Buster is my best friend ⋀ and I love him.
¶	Start a new paragraph.	A dog is a wonderful pet. ¶ Cats are good pets, too I have a kitten named Roxy.
∽	Switch the order.	Sometimes Roxy tries to steal (toys Buster's).

In the following example, the writer corrects some errors in his introductory paragraph.

A hero is someone who puts other peop*l*e/ and the enviro^nment before himself or herself. The best example ⋀ my Granddad. His name is Lloyd, and I call him Granddad Lloyd. ^ A farmer who raises beef cattle and different kinds of crops. Granddad lloyd is a hero because he is a hard worker, he is devoted to family, and he respects the environment.

(that I can think of is)
(He is)

Unit 2 • Expository Writing • 115

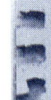

Ch. 8 **Test Writing: The Expository Essay**

Evaluating an Expository Test Essay

When teachers evaluate your test essay, they know that you planned and wrote the essay in a short amount of time. Consequently, they do not expect a perfect essay. At the same time, they do expect you to demonstrate your knowledge of the traits of writing. They will look to see

- how completely you respond to the prompt
- how well you support your ideas with reasons and examples
- how clearly you organize your essay
- how you use voice to make your writing interesting and enjoyable
- how correctly you write sentences
- how correctly you use the conventions of writing

The rubric on the next page shows guidelines for evaluating an expository test essay.

Test Writing: The Expository Essay — Ch. 8

Expository Test Essay Rubric

	4 **Strong**	3 **Effective**	2 **Developing**	1 **Beginning**
Ideas	The writer wrote to the prompt; reasons and examples are relevant.	The writer wrote to the prompt; most reasons and examples are relevant.	The writer included some relevant reasons and examples.	The writer did not write to the prompt. There are few reasons or examples.
Organization	Information is arranged logically.	Most information is arranged logically.	Organization of information is awkward.	Information is included in random order.
Voice	The writing style helps the reader connect to the explanation.	The writing style of some paragraphs draws the reader in.	The writing style of one or two sentences draws the reader in.	The writing is mechanical, making it hard for readers to connect.
Word Choice	Transitions and vivid words are used.	A few transitions and vivid words are used.	One or two transitions or vivid words are used.	No transitions or vivid words are used.
Sentence Fluency	Most sentences are complete.	A few sentences are incomplete.	Many sentences are incomplete.	Most sentences are incomplete.
Conventions	Few errors in capitalization, spelling, punctuation, or grammar are present.	Several errors in capitalization, spelling, punctuation, or grammar are present.	Errors in capitalization, spelling, punctuation, and grammar do not prevent understanding.	Errors in capitalization, spelling, punctuation, and grammar prevent understanding.

Unit 2 • Expository Writing

Ch. 8 **Test Writing: The Expository Essay**

Evaluate a Model Test Essay

Work with a partner to evaluate the following model essay. Reread the prompt on page 110 and use the rubric on page 117. Write your score here: _____. In a class discussion, explain the score that you gave.

My Hero, Granddad Lloyd

A hero is someone who puts other people and the environment before himself or herself. The best example I can think of is my granddad. His name is Lloyd, and I call him Granddad Lloyd. He's a farmer who raises beef cattle and different kinds of crops. Granddad Lloyd is a hero because he is a hard worker, he is devoted to family, and he respects the environment.

Granddad Lloyd is heroic because he is a hard worker. He doesn't always feel like getting up before dawn to set up irrigation pipes in his fields. He doesn't always feel like going out in freezing, snowy weather to feed hay to the cows in the pasture. But he does these things because he values hard work. He always says, "Something worth doing at all is worth doing well."

Granddad Lloyd is heroic because he is devoted to his family. One of the reasons he works so hard is that he wants to provide a good home for his wife (Grandmother June). Also, ^(he wants) to earn enough money to help his grandkids a little bit. ^(For example,) He paid for the after-school woodwork class that I took last semester. Granddad Lloyd also wants to show by example how you can make your life good through hard work.

Granddad Lloyd is heroic because he respects the environment. He used to use toxic pesticides on his crops, but now he is trying to use organic ways to fix problems. He lets each field "rest" every seventh year to help the soil get back its nutrients. He doesn't dump used motor oil on the ground, and he doesn't spill diesel on the ground when he fills up his tractors from the storage tank. Respecting the environment takes extra time and extra money, but Granddad does it.

For all these reasons, Granddad Lloyd is a hero. He is living proof that you don't have to be famous, or dead, to be a hero.

Test Writing: The Expository Essay Ch. 8

Write an Expository Test Essay

Practice what you have learned by completing the following task.

> **Instructions**
> You have 25 minutes to complete the written composition. Read the prompt below. Then use separate paper to plan and draft your composition. Only your draft will be scored.
>
> **Writing Prompt**
> Sooner or later, everyone gets angry at a friend. What are some useful strategies for dealing with anger with a friend? Write an essay in which you explain at least two useful ways of dealing with anger with a friend.

Unit 2 • Expository Writing • 119

Unit 2

Expository Writing Wrap-Up

The activities and information in these pages will help you continue to strengthen your expository writing skills. In You Be the Judge, use the Expository Writing Rubric to evaluate a student's work. The Ideas for Writing are additional expository writing prompts you can use for practice. And finally, in the Unit 2 Reflections, you can list important ideas you have learned in this unit and set goals for future learning.

You Be the Judge

Use what you've learned about the traits of expository writing to evaluate a student essay. First, review the traits of expository writing on page 63, in the unit opener. Next, read the student essay printed below. Finally, in the rubric that follows the essay, assign the essay a score for each writing trait. In the space provided, explain each score that you assign.

Sailing

by Katie M., Hull, MA

Some people imagine sailing is sitting in a boat and gliding slowly across the water—but that's not competitive racing.
  I compete in lots of regattas, or sailing races, and they are not easy. We race in teams of two in a 12-foot boat. These boats, called Club 420s, were built for speed. In even just a fair amount of wind, it is hard to keep the boat from capsizing. No time for relaxing, you need to be alert and ready to react.
  Last summer in the National Junior Olympics regatta, I was sailing with my partner, Ned. We weren't used to sailing in the open ocean where there is a lot more wind and waves. At first we managed to keep our boat upright and stay on

course. We were sailing against 50 other teams. Many boats were colliding because the wind was so strong.

In the last race, we were in second place with a substantial lead, but as we rounded the first marker, our boat capsized and threw us into the water. The sail went completely under.

As we struggled to get back up, we thought the other teams would laugh, but they didn't. They stopped to make sure we were all right. Some kept going because they wanted to win, but there were many nice people who helped us. We managed to right our boat and finish the race. It was an exciting finish because we still didn't come in last.

Through sailing I met lots of new people I know I will see again. Sailing is a great summer activity because you're on the water, getting stronger, being with your friends, and competing against others.

I have taken many of my friends out on my boat, and they love it. My friend Giovanna started two years ago, and now she competes and does well. As for me, this is my sixth year, and I have won many regattas and can't wait until this summer.

Unit 2

Expository Writing Rubric

	4 Strong	3 Effective	2 Developing	1 Beginning
Ideas Score____	explanation:			
Organization Score____	explanation:			
Voice Score____	explanation:			
Word Choice Score____	explanation:			
Sentence Fluency Score____	explanation:			
Conventions Score____	explanation:			

Ideas for Writing

The assignments on this page will give you additional practice with expository writing. Your teacher may choose one or let you pick one that's most interesting to you.

1. A radio station is searching for the best local break-out artist of the year. To nominate a musical artist or band, you must write an essay of 350–400 words explaining why this individual or band is the best break-out artist of the year. Essays will be evaluated by a team made up of two disc jockeys, a music teacher, an English teacher, and a record producer.

2. How do you bake a cake from scratch, train for a skateboard competition, or learn a foreign language? Choose something you know how to do and write an essay explaining how your classmates can do the same thing. Your essay should be approximately 350–400 words in length. With your teacher's permission, ask for a show of hands in class; then make copies of your essay to pass out to interested people.

3. Create a week's worth of daily entries for a blog called Welcome to My World. Each entry of 50–100 words should explain something important from your life or about yourself. *Note: Do not post personal information about yourself on the Internet except with a parent or guardian's permission. Safe sites for a blog include a school-sponsored Web site or other site that protects its users' personal information.* Alternatives to posting your blog on the Internet include e-mailing your blog to friends, day by day, and saving copies in your time capsule of written works.

4. With each generation, technology changes. What kinds of technology do you use today that your older relatives did not use? How does this technology make your life different from their lives a generation or two ago? Write an essay of 350–400 words in which you compare and contrast the effects of technology in your life and the life of an older relative. Share the final copy of your essay with family members.

Unit 2 Reflections

How are you different as a writer now that you have completed this unit on expository writing? What new knowledge do you have? How is your writing stronger? What kinds of things could you work on to become even stronger as an expository writer? Use the following space to reflect on your work in this unit and to set goals for the future.

Focus on Me: My Achievements as an Expository Writer

What I've learned about expository writing in this unit:
Ways my expository writing is stronger now:
Things I can do to practice my skills of expository writing:

Unit 3

Persuasive Writing

The Unit at a Glance
Get to Know the Genre 125
Ch. 9 Write an Editorial 131
Ch. 10 Write a Persuasive Essay 145
Ch. 11 Write a Review 159
Ch. 12 Test Writing: The Persuasive Essay 173
Persuasive Writing Wrap-Up 185

Get to Know the Genre: Persuasive Writing

From the time we are little kids, we have ways of persuading people to agree with us. As children, we might beg, cry, throw a fit, or nag. Unfortunately, these methods tend to annoy the other person, whether or not we're successful. As we get older, we develop more skill at persuading others to agree with us. For instance, think of a time when you wanted to see a movie, but your friend wanted to see a different movie. How did you try to persuade your friend to watch the movie of your choice?

Persuasive writing is much like spoken persuasion. In **persuasive writing**, the writer presents a case for or against a viewpoint

Unit 3

or an action. A thesis statement, supporting reasons, and a memorable conclusion are essential ingredients.

Give It a Try: Think About Prior Experience

Think of a time when you defended an opinion or viewpoint to someone who disagreed with you. What was the issue in question? Jot down your memories of who said what in the following graphic organizer.

The opinion or viewpoint that I defended was	
I said	*and the other person said*
I said	*and the other person said*
I said	*and the other person said*
I brought the discussion to a close by saying	

> Find a subject you care about … It is this genuine caring, not your games with language, which will be the most compelling and seductive element in your style.
> —KURT VONNEGUT (American author, 1922–2007)

126 • The Writer's Studio   Level A

In this book, you have been learning about different forms of writing and the traits of writing. The table below explains more about the traits of persuasive writing.

Six Traits of Persuasive Writing

Ideas	The topic is narrowed to a specific position to be defended. Reasons and examples support the position.
organization	The introduction states the writer's position. Body paragraphs give supporting reasons and respond to objections. The conclusion restates the position.
voice	The writer's voice shows his or her concern or enthusiasm, balanced with a sense of trustworthiness.
word choice	Words are accurate. Descriptive words are fair.
sentence fluency	Sentences are complete. A variety of structures creates a pleasing rhythm.
conventions	Capitalization, spelling, punctuation, and grammar are correct.

Real-World Example

Persuasive writing tries to convince readers to agree with an opinion or to take a particular action. In the following persuasive paragraph, the writer, Larry West, tries to convince readers to recycle.

Unit 3

Ideas: West identifies his main idea.

Voice: West connects with the reader by using the second-person point of view.

Ideas: West responds to the possible objection that a reader doesn't have a place to recycle things.

Organization: West ends with his strongest supporting detail.

Do your part to reduce waste by choosing reusable products instead of disposables. Buying products with minimal packaging (including the economy size when that makes sense for you) will help to reduce waste. And whenever you can, recycle paper, plastic, newspaper, glass and aluminum cans. If there isn't a recycling program at your workplace, school, or in your community, ask about starting one. By recycling half of your household waste, you can save 2,400 pounds of carbon dioxide [from entering the atmosphere] annually.

—from "Top 10 Things You Can Do to Reduce Global Warming" by Larry West, About.com

Conventions: Parentheses enclose a related, yet less important, detail.

Organization: West organizes the paragraph by listing ways to recycle.

Sentence fluency: This sentence begins with an introductory phrase.

Give It a Try: Examine the Real-World Example

Can you find additional examples of the six traits of good writing in the model paragraph above? On separate paper, list three traits of good writing. For each one, quote or describe an example from the model.

Get Ready to Write

Now that you've explored the qualities of persuasive writing, you're ready to create some persuasive pieces of your own. In the chapters that follow, you'll write an editorial about a hot topic at your school, a persuasive essay about a class you'd like to see started, a review of something you've read, and a persuasive essay about homework. You'll use the stages of the writing process—prewriting, drafting, revising, editing, and publishing—and you'll be presented with models and mini-lessons along the way.

As you work through these chapters, you can enrich your understanding by trying the suggestions below. These tips will help you connect what you're learning in this unit to your own life and the world around you.

LEARNING TIPS

- Read the editorial or opinion column in your local newspaper or school newspaper. What topics do the writers cover? What tones do they use? How do they organize their articles?

- Read posters hanging at school, in public buildings, and in other places. Often, a poster uses very few words, along with an image, to persuade readers.

- Practice your persuasive skills in daily life. Persuade a parent to raise your allowance, to let you eat dessert first, or to read a book you like. Send persuasive text messages or e-mails to friends and watch to see how effective you were.

- Share your opinions in conversations with friends. Practice giving convincing reasons why your opinion should be taken seriously. Pay attention to how your listeners respond.

Chapter 9

Write an Editorial

Your opinions matter. In your school, in your community, and in your country, there are issues on which people disagree. These issues are sometimes called hot topics, hot-button issues, pro-con debates, or debatable issues. You probably have opinions about many of them. Writing an **editorial** is a great way to express your opinions on a specific issue. Most editorials are published in newspapers and magazines, either in print or online. Other editorials are published online as blog entries.

Why should you write an editorial? Besides writing to express your opinions, you can write to inform people of facts on an issue and to help people figure out what *their* opinions are. In this chapter, you'll write an editorial on an issue in your school.

Six Traits of an **Editorial**

Ideas	The topic is narrowed to the writer's position on an issue in the school or community. Reasons and examples are convincing.
Organization	The introduction states the writer's position. Body paragraphs give convincing reasons and respond to objections. The conclusion restates the position.
Voice	The writer demonstrates concern or enthusiasm, balanced with a sense of trustworthiness.
Word Choice	Words are accurate. Descriptive words show the writer's opinions, yet they are fair.
Sentence Fluency	Sentences are complete. A variety of structures creates a pleasing rhythm.
Conventions	Capitalization, spelling, punctuation, and grammar are correct.

Unit 3 • Persuasive Writing • 131

Ch. 9 **Write an Editorial**

The following is the introductory paragraph of an editorial. In it, the writer identifies a debatable issue and states her position on the issue.

> In his first month on the job, Library Director Jim Garris has made a bold proposal. He wants to build a soundproof computer recreation room in the southeast corner of the school library. Some staff, parents, and students argue that this space is needed for the study tables that are already there. Others argue that our library should "get with the times" and provide a computer room where students can play games and do homework. In this debate, the wise decision for the welfare of our students is to build the computer recreation room.

Give It a Try: Examine the Model Paragraph

Working with a partner, use the model paragraph above to answer the following questions. Write your answers on separate paper.

1. **Ideas.**
   a. What is the issue that people are debating?
   b. What is the writer's position on the issue?
2. **Organization.** Does the writer state her position in the beginning or at the end of the paragraph? Why do you think she chooses this location?
3. **Voice and word choice.** Choose one sentence that uses an especially vivid or expressive word or phrase. Copy the sentence, underlining the vivid word or phrase. Then explain what the underlined word(s) tell you about the writer's voice.
4. **Sentence fluency.** What is one strategy that the writer uses to create sentence variety?

5. **Conventions.** Read this first part of a sentence from the paragraph.

    Others argue that our library should "get with the times" and . . .

    What noun or nouns are referred to by the pronoun *Others*?

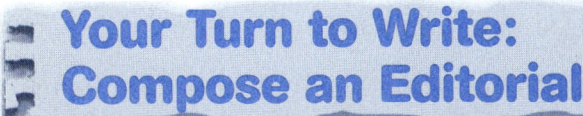

Your Turn to Write: Compose an Editorial

Now you'll write your own editorial. Read the assignment carefully and follow the strategies and instructions for each stage of the writing process.

Assignment

What are some of the hot topics at your school? Choose a debatable issue that relates to your school and write a 300-word editorial that
- identifies the issue
- states your position on the issue
- gives at least two reasons to support your opinion
- responds to one objection to your position
- concludes by restating your position

Your editorial should be suitable for publication in a school newspaper.

Prewrite

Analyze the Prompt. What does the prompt tell you about your goals for this assignment? Reread the assignment above and answer the questions on the next page. Write your answers on separate paper.

Unit 3 • **Persuasive Writing** • **133**

Ch. 9   **Write an Editorial**

1. What is the purpose of this editorial?
2. Who is the audience for this editorial?
3. How long does the editorial need to be?

Choose a Topic. Follow these two steps:
1. In a class discussion, make a list of at least five hot-topic issues at your school. Write them on notebook paper.
2. Decide which of the topics on the lists interests you the most and circle it. This will be your topic for your editorial.

Gather Ideas and Details. As your teacher instructs you, form a group with classmates who have chosen the same topic. As a group, identify two positions on the issue. Then brainstorm for reasons that support each position. Create a T-chart like the one that follows to organize your work.

Topic: _____

Position A:	Position B:
Supporting reasons:	Supporting reasons:
•	•
•	•
•	•
•	•
•	•

134 • The Writer's Studio   Level A

Write an Editorial   Ch. 9

Here is how the writer of the model paragraph gathered ideas and details for the editorial.

Topic: building a computer recreation room in the southeast corner of the library

Position A: support the plan	Position B: oppose the plan
Supporting reasons: • some students don't own comp. • place to hang out with friends • public library doesn't have games • get homework done during lunch • everyone should know how to use a computer	Supporting reasons: • too expensive • library is for studying, not playing • public library has some computers, so use those • use a friend's computer • school library already has 3 computers

Organize Ideas and Details. Create an outline like the one below to gather and organize ideas for your editorial.

The issue: _____

My position on the issue: _____

My thesis statement: _____

Body paragraph 1: my first supporting reason: _____

_____

Body paragraph 2: my second supporting reason: _____

_____

Body paragraph 3: my response to an opposing reason: _____

_____

Unit 3 • **Persuasive Writing** • **135**

Ch. 9 **Write an Editorial**

Note: You could include your response to an opposing reason in your first or second body paragraph. In this case, you don't need a third body paragraph.

In the model paragraph below, the writer included a reason supporting her position *and* she responded to an opposing reason.

> It is wise to build a computer room in the library because unfortunately, many students do not have computers at home. By staying after school, using a study hall, or using lunch period, they can have access to a computer. Some people may object to this reasoning. They may point out that the library already has three computers in the front area. However, three computers are not enough for a student body of 500 students.

supporting reason
objection
response to objection

Draft

Word choices are always important in a piece of writing, but they are especially important in persuasive writing. Your words can influence how your reader responds to your position. Using vivid, expressive words while remaining fair and polite will help you connect to your readers. On the other hand, using unfair descriptions or making fun of your opposition makes you seem overly emotional and unreliable.

Use Expressive yet Balanced Words. The following lists offer some ideas for choosing expressive yet balanced words. As you work on the rough draft of your editorial, add more words to the three lists.

136 • The Writer's Studio   Level A

Write an Editorial Ch. 9

When you want to defend an idea, use words such as:

fair	clear	obvious
wise	beneficial	

When you want to criticize or find fault, use words such as:

shameful	unfounded	unlikely
doubtful	questionable	

When you want to signal a contrast in ideas, use words such as:

in the other hand	in spite of	despite that
in contrast	however	

Write Your Editorial. Using your prewriting and planning notes, write the rough draft of your editorial. Express your opinions forcefully and confidently. If you can use fair, balanced words now, great! If some words are overly emotional or unfair, you can replace them with balanced, fair words during the revision stage.

The model below shows how the writer made some changes to add fair, balanced words.

> In his first month on the job, Library Director Jim Garris has made a ~~shocking~~ *bold* proposal. He wants to build a soundproof computer recreation room in the southeast corner of the school library. Some staff, parents, and students ~~are griping~~ *argue* that this space is needed for the study tables that are already there. Others ~~lash out~~ *argue* that our library should "get with the times" and provide a computer room where students can play games and do homework. In this debate, the wise decision for the welfare of our students is to build the computer recreation room.

Unit 3 • **Persuasive Writing** • 137

Ch. 9 **Write an Editorial**

Revise

When you revise the rough draft of your editorial, pay attention to pronouns. These plain little words usually go unnoticed by a reader. However, if used incorrectly, pronouns can confuse or misinform your reader. The following mini-lesson explains more about this grammar issue.

Mini-Lesson: Using Pronouns Correctly

Using pronouns correctly helps you to express your ideas accurately. It also helps you to avoid confusing your reader. As a result, your reader's attention remains focused on your key ideas and details. In contrast, a confusing or misused pronoun can bring your ideas to a screeching halt, at least from your reader's perspective. Instead of focusing on your ideas, the reader stumbles. *Who is "he"?* the reader may ask. *What does "this" refer to?*

➡ A **pronoun** is a word that takes the place of a noun in a sentence.

➡ An **antecedent** is the word or word group to which a pronoun refers.

A pronoun should **agree in number** with its antecedent. *Number* refers to whether a word names one or more than one person or thing. For example, a singular noun such as *teacher* needs a singular pronoun like *he* or *she*. A plural noun like *students* needs a plural pronoun like *they* or *their*.

singular: My teacher talked about the plan for a new computer room, and she listed reasons to supports the plan.

plural: Students are eager to find out what kinds of games they can play on the computers.

138 • The Writer's Studio   Level A

Write an Editorial   Ch. 9

Besides agreeing in number, a pronoun should **agree in gender** with its antecedent. *Gender* refers to whether the word names a male, a female, or something that is not male or female.

male: Jim Garris described his vision of a fun, supportive space for students.

female: Principal Victoria Morales said that she is concerned about costs.

neutral: Does this computer have any game software installed on it?

Plural pronouns do not indicate a gender.

plural: The girls discussed their questions about the computer room.

plural: Meanwhile, the boys planned an editorial to express their views.

plural: The computers don't have to be costly if they are donated or pre-owned.

In the model below, the writer has made edits so that pronouns and antecedents agree. She chose to change subjects, but she could have changed pronouns instead.

There is another reason to build the computer room, even more important than making computers easily available. This reason is that ~~each~~ students need~~s~~ a fun, safe place to play games on computers. Even if they went to a public library to use a computer, they would not be allowed to play games. Those computers only have word-processing software and limited Internet access. Since school is such a vital part of a student's lives, they ~~we~~ should be able to work as well as play here.

Unit 3 • **Persuasive Writing** • 139

Ch. 9   **Write an Editorial**

> **Give It a Try: Revise Your Editorial for Correct Pronoun Reference**
>
> Revise your work for correct pronoun reference. Read your editorial, circling each pronoun. Draw an arrow from the pronoun to its antecedent. Then check to see if they agree in gender and number. Make revisions, as necessary.

Revise Your Editorial. Use the following checklist to revise the rough draft of your editorial. The Editorial Rubric that follows the checklist will help you determine how strong your article is and where to make revisions.

Ideas
- ❑ Place a check mark next to the sentence(s) where you state a clear position on the issue. If your position is not clear, revise it.
- ❑ Underline three of your most convincing reasons and examples. Do you need to add more? Cross out any reasons that are weak or unconvincing.

Organization
- ❑ Does your editorial have a beginning, a middle, and an end? Label these three parts.

Voice
- ❑ Underline words/phrases that show you're concerned or enthusiastic about your position on the issue while remaining fair and balanced. Write *voice* above these words/phrases.

Word choice
- ❑ Circle three transitions that show contrasts.
- ❑ Circle three vivid, expressive words.

Sentence fluency
- ❑ Do you use complete sentences? Revise any incomplete ones.
- ❑ Check for sentence variety. If you have too many sentences of the same length or that begin the same way, revise them.

Write an Editorial — Ch. 9

Editorial Rubric

	4 Strong	3 Effective	2 Developing	1 Beginning
Ideas	A clear position is supported with convincing reasons.	A clear position is stated, but reasons are not fully explained.	A position is stated, and one reason is included.	The position is not clear. No specific reasons are included.
Organization	Information is arranged logically, with a strong beginning, middle, and end.	Most information is arranged logically.	Organization of information is awkward.	Information is included in random order.
Voice	The writer uses a confident, balanced tone.	The writer's tone is mostly confident and balanced.	The writer uses a confident, balanced tone in one or two paragraphs.	The writer's tone is preachy or otherwise unbalanced.
Word Choice	Words accurately and fairly help to express opinions.	A few words are inaccurate or unfair.	Many words are inaccurate or unfair.	Words do not accurately or fairly support an opinion.
Sentence Fluency	Sentences are complete, and a variety of structures are used.	Sentences are mostly complete; some variety is used.	Most sentences are complete, but there is little variety.	Sentences are mostly incomplete or short and simple.
Conventions	Few errors in capitalization, spelling, punctuation, or grammar are present.	Several errors in capitalization, spelling, punctuation, or grammar are present.	Errors in capitalization, spelling, punctuation, and grammar do not prevent understanding.	Errors in capitalization, spelling, punctuation, and grammar prevent understanding.

Unit 3 • Persuasive Writing

Ch. 9   **Write an Editorial**

 Edit

Now that you have revised your editorial, you are almost ready to publish it. One final step remains: editing the piece to correct mistakes in capitalization, spelling, punctuation, or grammar.

Edit Your Editorial. Edit the revised copy of your editorial. The following questions will help you decide what to change, remove, or leave in place.

Conventions
- ❑ Did you use correct pronoun references?
- ❑ Did you use a comma when you joined sentences with a coordinating conjunction?
- ❑ Did you use a comma when you began a sentence with a subordinate clause?
- ❑ Did you correct spelling mistakes, either with a friend's help or by using a dictionary?

PUBLISH

Presentation. Prepare your editorial for publication by writing or typing the final, edited copy.

Publish Your Editorial. Here are ideas for publishing your work.
- ❑ Submit the editorial to your school newspaper.
- ❑ If your school has a Web page where students can post opinion pieces, post your editorial there.
- ❑ If you have a blog, post the editorial as today's entry.
- ❑ Give a copy of your editorial to someone who shares your interest in the issue. This person could be a classmate, a teacher, or even a family member.

142 • The Writer's Studio   Level A

Write an Editorial Ch. 9

Evaluate Your Editorial

Your teacher will either assess your editorial, ask you to self-assess your editorial, or ask you to switch with a partner and assess each other's work.

Evaluate the Model Editorial

Work with a partner to evaluate the model editorial that follows. Use the rubric on page 141 and write your score here: _____. In a class discussion, explain the score that you gave.

A Bold Idea

In his first month on the job, Library Director Jim Garris has made a bold proposal. He wants to build a soundproof computer recreation room in the southeast corner of the school library. Some staff, parents, and students argue that this space is needed for the study tables that are already there. Others argue that our library should "get with the times" and provide a computer room where students can play games and do homework. In this debate, the wise decision for the welfare of our students is to build the computer recreation room.

It is wise to build a computer room in the library because unfortunately, many students do not have computers at home. By staying after school, using a study hall, or using lunch period, they can have access to a computer. Some people may object to this reasoning. They may point out that the library already has three computers in the front area. However, three computers are not enough for a student body of 500 students.

Unit 3 • Persuasive Writing • 143

Ch. 9 **Write an Editorial**

There is another reason to build the computer room, even more important than making computers easily available. This reason is that students need a fun, safe place to play games on computers. Even if they went to a public library to use a computer, they would not be allowed to play games. Those computers only have word-processing software and limited Internet access. Since school is such a vital part of students' lives, they should be able to work as well as play here.

In spite of the loud opposition to building a computer recreation room, the choice is clear. Building the computer room would make computers available to students who don't have them, and it would provide a safe place to play computer games. Jim Garris's plan is solid and sensible.

Chapter 10
Write a Persuasive Essay

In the previous chapter, you learned about the editorial. In this chapter, you'll learn about the persuasive essay. Both types of writing share a single purpose: to persuade readers to agree with the writer's opinions or to take a certain action. But the two types of persuasive writing are different, too.

Editorials are written about a current hot topic, of interest to newspaper or magazine readers. Persuasive essays, on the other hand, may be written about a broader selection of topics, and they have many different types of audiences.

As you work through the process of writing a persuasive essay, you will build upon what you learned about writing editorials, but you'll consider different audiences and new issues.

Six Traits of a Persuasive Essay

Ideas	The writer has a specific persuasive purpose (reason for writing). Reasons and examples support the purpose.
Organization	The introduction states the writer's purpose. Body paragraphs give supporting reasons. The conclusion restates the purpose.
Voice	The writer's enthusiasm or concern for the topic causes the reader to consider the persuasive purpose carefully.
Word Choice	Subject-area words or terms are used accurately and help to achieve the purpose for writing.
Sentence Fluency	Sentences are complete. A variety of structures creates a pleasing rhythm.
Conventions	Capitalization, spelling, punctuation, and grammar are correct.

Ch. 10 **Write a Persuasive Essay**

In the persuasive paragraph below, the writer tries to convince his teacher to take the class on a field trip to a monster truck rally.

Field trips are supposed to teach students something from the real world, and the new information must relate to class content. With these requirements in mind, I propose that our math class take a field trip to a monster truck rally. While we are there, we can do activities like these: Use stopwatches to time trucks and compare their speeds; draw diagrams of the obstacle course and measure the angles; learn to measure the diameter, radius, and circumference of a tire; copy down the prices of hot dogs and sodas and calculate how much cheaper the same foods are at a grocery store; and much more. With these fun activities, every student in class will see how math relates to the real world.

Give It a Try: Examine the Model Paragraph

Use the model paragraph above to answer the following questions. Write your answers on separate paper.

1. **Ideas.** Copy the sentence that expresses the writer's main idea.
2. **Organization.** Which sentence forms the conclusion of the paragraph? Copy that sentence.
3. **Voice and word choice.** List the math terms that the writer uses.
4. **Sentence fluency.** Which sentence is a compound sentence? Copy it and circle the comma and coordinating conjunction.
5. **Conventions.**
    a. Why does the writer use a colon in the third sentence?
    b. Why does the writer use semicolons to separate the items in the list?

146 • The Writer's Studio   Level A

Write a Persuasive Essay   Ch. 10

Your Turn to Write: Compose a Persuasive Essay

Now you'll write your own persuasive essay. Read the assignment carefully and follow the strategies and instructions for each stage of the writing process.

Assignment

The parent association at your school has announced that parents will be offering after-school hobby classes. Their ideas for classes include woodworking, fashion design, engine repair, building a collection (of stamps, etc.), a book club, cooking, and calligraphy. They need your input to decide which classes to offer. Write an essay of 350 words in which you persuade the parent association to offer the hobby class of your choice. This class can be one from the list above, or another one that you prefer.

Prewrite

Analyze the Prompt. Read the assignment closely to find answers to the following questions. Write your answers on separate paper.

1. What is the purpose of this essay?
2. Who is the audience for this essay?
3. How long does the essay need to be?

Unit 3 • Persuasive Writing • 147

Ch. 10 Write a Persuasive Essay

Choose a Topic. On your paper, complete the following sentences to choose a topic.

1. Two hobbies that I know a lot about are these...

   a. I like the first one because...

   b. I like the second one because...

2. A hobby that I am curious about is...
   This hobby seems as if it would be fun to learn because...

3. Of these three hobbies, the one that I most want to write about is...

Gather Ideas and Details. With your teacher's permission, gather in a small group. Discuss the kinds of ideas and details that should be included in your persuasive essay. During the discussion, jot down useful information. To get the discussion going, use these sentence starters:

Basically, this hobby requires you to . . .

Parents would enjoy teaching this hobby because . . .

Students would enjoy doing this hobby because . . .

Some of the benefits of this hobby are . . .

A question I have about this hobby is . . .

A good experience with this hobby was the time when . . .

This hobby is *not* . . .

Organize Ideas and Details. You can use a persuasive map to record your purpose for writing and the supporting reasons and details. Review the information you collected during the group discussion and fill in the persuasive map that follows.

148 • The Writer's Studio   Level A

Write a Persuasive Essay — Ch. 10

My purpose for writing is to

↓

Reason 1:		
Detail:	Detail:	Detail:

↓

Reason 2:		
Detail:	Detail:	Detail:

↓

Reason 3:		
Detail:	Detail:	Detail:

Ch. 10 Write a Persuasive Essay

In the following model, the writer has organized ideas about a fashion design hobby class. Notice that the support for Reason 2 is weak—only one supporting detail.

My purpose for writing is to convince the parent association to offer a hobby class in fashion design.

Reason 1: Fashion design is creative.

| Detail: matching colors | Detail: sketching designs | Detail: using a sewing machine |

Reason 2: Fashion design would give students a reason to make costumes for the school drama department.

| Detail: learn about costume design | Detail: | Detail: |

Reason 3: Fashion design would help students save money by making their own clothes.

| Detail: save money by making own clothes | Detail: save money by altering thrift-store clothes | Detail: |

150 • The Writer's Studio   Level A

Write a Persuasive Essay Ch. 10

 Draft

As you know, a strong introductory paragraph contains a thesis statement. (You can review the mini-lesson on thesis statements on page 85.) In a persuasive essay, the thesis declares exactly what the writer wants the reader to agree to, believe, or do.

Here are examples of thesis statements.

With these requirements in mind, I propose that our math class take a field trip to a monster truck rally.

(This thesis statement identifies a clear persuasive purpose for writing the paragraph.)

When the parent association considers which hobby classes to teach after school, they should consider fashion design.

(This thesis statement would be stronger if the writer stated directly that the parent association should *teach* the class, instead of using two clauses about *considering* classes.)

Write a Thesis Statement. On separate paper, write a thesis statement for your persuasive essay.

Just as the introductory paragraph needs a strong thesis statement, other paragraphs need strong topic sentences. The following mini-lesson will help you write topic sentences.

Mini-Lesson: Writing Topic Sentences

Each paragraph in an essay develops one main idea. The sentence that expresses the main idea of a paragraph is a *topic sentence*.

A **topic sentence** expresses the main idea of a paragraph.

The other sentences in the paragraph give details, examples, facts, or other support.

Unit 3 • Persuasive Writing • **151**

Ch. 10 Write a Persuasive Essay

In the following model paragraph, the topic sentence is underlined. The remaining sentences give supporting details.

<u>A fashion design class would help students save money.</u> How? By designing and making their own clothes. Sewing shirts, skirts, pajama sets, and shorts from fabric costs less than buying these things at the mall. What's more, the fashion designer can choose the fabric that he or she likes best. In addition, learning how to alter previously used clothes, such as those from thrift shops, would save money. Fashion design just makes sense!

Each topic sentence in an essay expresses a key reason or idea of the essay. In a persuasive essay, a topic sentence expresses one reason why the reader should agree with the thesis statement.

Give It a Try: Write a Topic Sentence

The paragraph below is missing a topic sentence. On the line provided, write a topic sentence that expresses the main idea of the paragraph.

_____

_____ Most of a student's day is taken up with traditional studies in math, science, English, and social studies. When do students get to be creative? Who is going to teach them to think creatively and develop skills in matching colors, sketching designs, using a sewing machine, following how-to sewing instructions, and more? Students who take a fashion design hobby class from the parent association would learn all these creative skills.

Write a Persuasive Essay

Ch. 10

Give It a Try: Write Topic Sentences for Your Paragraphs

Look at the persuasive map that you created on page 149. Each block of a Reason plus Details represents one paragraph in the body of your essay. Use the information in each Reason box to write a topic sentence that expresses the main idea of that paragraph. Write your topic sentences on separate paper.

Write Your Persuasive Essay. It's time to write the rough draft of your persuasive essay. Use your persuasive map, your thesis statement, and your topic sentences to compose a well-organized and well-supported essay.

T!p

Remember to stick to *one* position in your essay. Don't try to take both sides, or your arguments will lose their power and credibility.

Revise

You have put a lot of planning, organization, and written work into the creation of your essay. You have written a complete draft of the essay. Now step back and look at the big picture by getting some gut-level responses from fellow writers.

Get Peer Feedback. Gather in a circle of 4 to 5 people, as your teacher directs. Pass a clean copy of your rough draft to the person sitting on your left. Each person should read silently. Then take turns sharing reactions to one another's writing. Use the following sentence starters.

Something I liked about this essay is . . .

Something that I wanted to know more about is . . .

I think the target audience would be persuaded because . . .

One reason that wasn't clear is…

One detail that could be stronger is…

I loved it when you wrote…

Unit 3 • **Persuasive Writing** • **153**

Ch. 10 Write a Persuasive Essay

As you listen to feedback on your essay, take notes. Do you need to explain a reason in greater detail? Add a supporting detail?

Revise Your Persuasive Essay. Make necessary revisions to the content or organization of your essay. Use your notes on the peer feedback you received, along with the following checklist. The Persuasive Writing Rubric that follows the checklist will help you determine how strong your article is and where to make revisions.

Ideas
- ❏ Place a check mark next to the sentence(s) where you state a clear persuasive purpose for writing. If your purpose is not clear, revise these sentences.
- ❏ Underline three of your most convincing reasons and examples. Do you need to add more? If any examples are weak and unconvincing, cross them out.

Organization
- ❏ Does your essay have a beginning, a middle, and an end? Add any missing part(s).
- ❏ Does each paragraph have a topic sentence? Write *T* next to the topic sentence of each paragraph.
- ❏ Have you removed any ideas or details that stray from the topic of each paragraph? Cross out any irrelevant details.

Voice
- ❏ Underline words or phrases that show your enthusiasm for your topic. Write *voice* above these words.
- ❏ Underline words where your attitude toward the topic engages, or draws in, your reader. Write *voice* above these words.

Word choice
- ❏ Circle any specialized words or terms in your essay. Are these words spelled and used correctly?

Sentence fluency
- ❏ Revise any incomplete sentences.
- ❏ Do you use sentence variety? Revise some sentences if necessary.

Write a Persuasive Essay Ch. 10

Persuasive Essay Rubric

	4 Strong	**3** Effective	**2** Developing	**1** Beginning
Ideas	The essay has a clear persuasive purpose and convincing reasons.	A clear purpose is stated, but reasons are not fully explained.	The purpose or the reasons may be unfocused or only loosely connected.	The purpose is not clear. No specific reasons are included.
Organization	Information is arranged logically, with a strong beginning, middle, and end.	Most information is arranged logically.	Organization of information is awkward.	Information is included in random order.
Voice	The writer uses a confident, engaging tone.	The writer's tone is mostly confident and engaging.	The writer uses a confident, engaging tone in one or two paragraphs.	The writer's tone is flat, dull, or uncaring.
Word Choice	Words are accurate and fair.	Most words are accurate and fair.	Many words are used incorrectly or express unfair ideas.	The incorrect use of words makes ideas hard to understand.
Sentence Fluency	Sentences are complete, and a variety of structures are used.	Sentences are mostly complete; some variety is used.	Most sentences are complete, but there is little variety.	Sentences are mostly incomplete or short and simple.
Conventions	Few errors in capitalization, spelling, punctuation, or grammar are present.	Several errors in capitalization, spelling, punctuation, or grammar are present.	Errors in capitalization, spelling, punctuation, and grammar do not prevent understanding.	Errors in capitalization, spelling, punctuation, and grammar prevent understanding.

Unit 3 • **Persuasive Writing** • 155

Ch. 10 Write a Persuasive Essay

Edit Your Persuasive Essay. Edit the revised copy of your persuasive essay. The following questions will help you decide what to change, remove, or leave in place.

Conventions
- ❑ Did you use semicolons to separate items in a series if one or more items include a comma?
- ❑ If you used a colon, did you use it to announce a list or idea, in conjunction with a phrase like *as follows* or *like this*?
- ❑ Did you use a comma when you joined sentences with a coordinating conjunction?
- ❑ Did you use a comma when you began a sentence with a subordinate clause?
- ❑ Did you correct spelling mistakes, either with a friend's help or by using a dictionary?

PUBLISH

Presentation. Prepare your persuasive essay for publication by writing or typing the final, edited copy.

Publish Your Persuasive Essay. Here are ideas for publishing your work.
- ❑ Share your essay with someone who may be able to teach you the hobby that you wrote about, or who would enjoy forming a hobby club with you.
- ❑ Write a letter to your principal, persuading him or her to approve after-school hobby clubs. Include a copy of your essay to demonstrate what you have in mind.
- ❑ Share your essay with a friend who knows very little about the hobby you wrote about. Then answer any questions he or she has about the hobby.

Write a Persuasive Essay Ch. 10

Evaluate Your Persuasive Essay

Your teacher will either assess your essay, ask you to self-assess your essay, or ask you to switch with a partner and assess each other's work.

Evaluate the Model Persuasive Essay

Work with a partner to evaluate the following model essay. Use the rubric on page 155 and write your score here: _____. In a class discussion, explain the score that you gave.

Three Cheers for a Fashion Design Class

Fashion design is a fun hobby, but it is also one of the most useful life skills that a young person can have. When the parent association considers which hobby classes to teach after school, they should consider fashion design. Fashion design encourages creativity, it's useful to the drama department, and it teaches money-saving skills. For these reasons, fashion design is a must when it comes to after-school hobby classes.

Most of a student's day is taken up with traditional studies in math, science, English, and social studies. When do students get to be creative? Who is going to teach them to think creatively and develop skills in matching colors, sketching designs, using a sewing machine, following how-to sewing instructions, and more? Students who take a fashion design hobby class from the parent association would learn all these creative skills.

A fashion design class would not only teach students to be creative but would also be useful to the school drama

Ch. 10 **Write a Persuasive Essay**

department. By making costumes in the hobby club, students could learn about costume design.

A fashion design class would help students save money. How? By designing and making their own clothes. Sewing shirts, skirts, pajama sets, and shorts from fabric costs less than buying these things at the mall. What's more, the fashion designer can choose the fabric that he or she likes best. In addition, learning how to alter previously used clothes, such as those from thrift shops, would save money. Fashion design just makes sense!

Not every student will be interested in taking a fashion design class, but many will. These students will have the opportunity to learn creativity, costume and clothing design, and money-saving skills. For these reasons, the parent association should include fashion design in its lists of after-school hobby classes.

Write a Review

What is your opinion of the last book that you read? Would you recommend it to a friend?

When was the last time you tried a new food because a friend convinced you to do so? What did the friend say to convince you?

What is the most recent music purchase you have made? Did you read reviews of the album before you downloaded it?

In all of these situations, you made decisions about something because of its strengths and weaknesses, its appealing points and unappealing points. Either you or someone else pointed out these qualities.

Similarly, the writer of a review expresses opinions about an item such as a book, a food, or a music album. The review can influence readers to try the item or to avoid it altogether. In this chapter, you'll share your opinions in a review of a story, book, or poem.

Six Traits of a Review

Ideas	The writer gives opinions about a specific item using convincing reasons and examples.
Organization	The review has a beginning, a middle, and an end.
Voice	The writer's tone is confident and knowledgeable.
Word Choice	Nouns, adjectives, adverbs, and verbs are specific and lively. Sensory details bring life to sights, sounds, textures, smells, and/or tastes.
Sentence Fluency	Specific, accurate adjectives help to make the writer's opinions clear.
Conventions	Titles are written correctly. Capitalization, spelling, punctuation, and grammar are correct.

Unit 3 • Persuasive Writing • 159

Ch. 11 Write a Review

In the following book review, the writer gives his opinions about the main character, plot, and message in a short story.

A Drive in the Country by Michael J. Rosen is a picture storybook that will appeal to teenagers as well as children. Readers can relate to the likable main character, a boy who tells about his family's Sunday drive in the country. First, they gather drinks, snacks, maps, and joke books. Then the boy, his brother and sister, his parents, and the family dog pile into the car. On their drive, they make stops to pick wild berries, shop at a little country store, and feed horses. They sing songs, struggle with the map, and watch the countryside. The boy's simple descriptions of each experience help the reader feel his delight. As darkness falls, the boy falls asleep. When he wakes up, he is home again. He leaves the reader with a heartwarming thought: It doesn't matter whether the family drives everywhere or nowhere, as long as they drive there together.

Give It a Try: Examine the Model Paragraph

Answer the following questions about six traits in the model paragraph. Write your answers on separate paper.

1. **Ideas.**
    a. What book is the writer reviewing?
    b. Who is the author of the book?
2. **Organization.** Does the writer place his thesis (main opinion) about the book at the beginning or end of the review? Why do you think he chose this placement?
3. **Voice and word choice.** List three words that help to express the writer's opinions.

Write a Review   Ch. 11

4. **Sentence fluency.**
   a. Copy the paragraph's shortest sentence.
   b. How does a short sentence help to create a pleasing rhythm in the paragraph?
5. **Conventions.** Where and why does the writer use italic type?

Your Turn to Write: Compose a Review

Now you'll write your own review. Read the assignment carefully and follow the strategies and instructions for each stage of the writing process.

Assignment

Choose a story, book, or poem to review for your classmates. Write a 250-word review in which you
- give the title and author of the work
- give a thesis about the work
- support your thesis with reasons and examples
- leave your reader with a memorable thought about the work

Prewrite

Analyze the Prompt. What does the prompt tell you about your goals for this assignment? Read the assignment closely to find answers to the following questions. Write your answers on separate paper.
1. What is the purpose of this review?
2. Who is the audience for this review?
3. How long does the review need to be?

Choose a Topic. To choose a subject for your review, create a graphic organizer like the one that follows. In the three columns at the top, list works that you have read. Below that, write answers to the questions.

Unit 3 • Persuasive Writing • **161**

Ch. 11 **Write a Review**

Stories	Books	Poems

1. Which work do you remember most vividly? Explain.

2. Which work do you have the strongest opinions about? Explain.

3. Which work would your classmates most likely want to know about? Explain.

4. Based on your responses in items 1–3, which work is the best choice for this assignment?

162 • **The Writer's Studio**   Level A

Write a Review   Ch. 11

Gather Ideas and Details. You can use an idea web to organize ideas and details for your review. Here is an example:

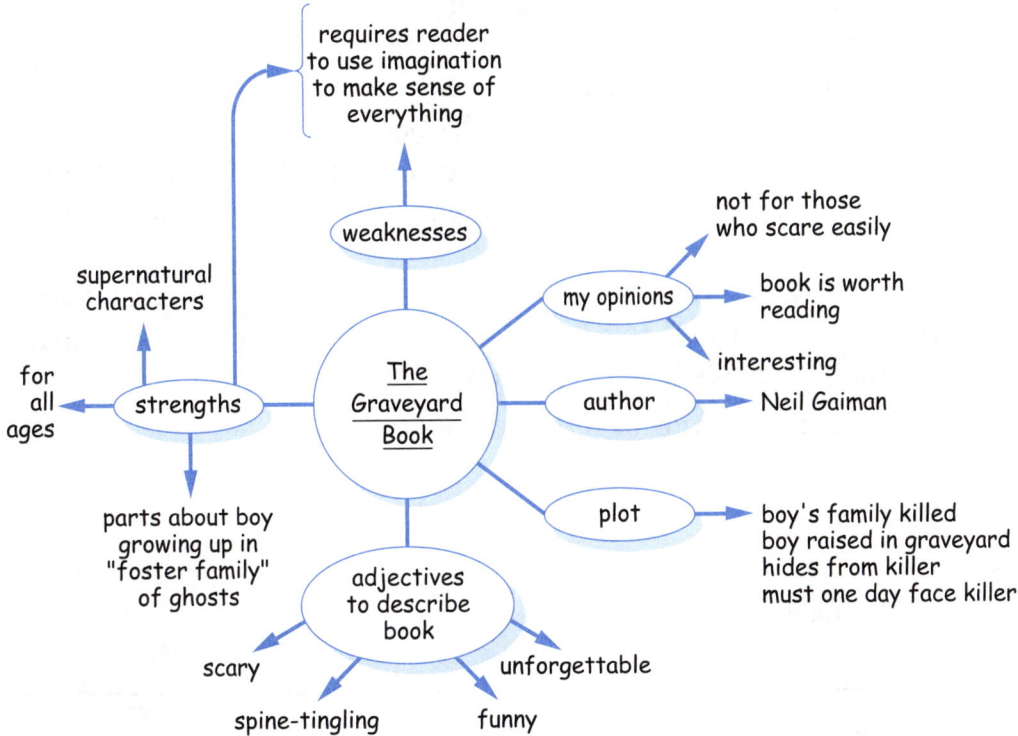

On a separate sheet of paper, create your own web. Write the name of the work you chose in the center and add links to categories such as those shown in the example. Fill in ideas and details related to each category.

Organize Ideas and Details. Reread your writing assignment on page 161. The bullet list of items to include in your review can help you organize the ideas and details. Look at this example:

A. The title and author of the work.
   - The Graveyard Book
   - by Neil Gaiman
B. My thesis.
   This novel is spine-tingling, funny, and unforgettable.

Unit 3 • **Persuasive Writing** • 163

Ch. 11 **Write a Review**

  C. Supporting reasons and examples.
   - scary scene in which toddler escapes killer
   - taken in by ghosts, who name him Nobody
   - mysterious Silas provides supplies
   - learns secrets of graveyard
   - will have to face his enemy
  D. A memorable thought about the book.
   This is a story about learning to face fears with the help of your own support system, however odd or wacky it may be.

Organize Your Ideas and Details. Use the information that you wrote in your idea web to fill in the blank outline below. Add ideas and details, as needed, to complete the outline.

  A. The title and author of the work.

   - _____
   - _____

  B. My thesis.

   _____

  C. Supporting reasons and examples.

   - _____
   - _____
   - _____
   - _____

  D. A memorable thought about the book.

   _____
   _____

164 • **The Writer's Studio**   Level A

Write a Review Ch. 11

Draft

The following guidelines will help you create a strong review. Keep them in mind as you write.

- State a definite opinion. Don't be uncertain or hesitant.

  uncertain: kind of scary

  strong: spine-tingling

- Offer your opinions clearly and directly. Remember, this is more than a plot summary.
- Double-check your facts, such as the spelling of the author's name and characters' names, plot details, and so on.
- A positive or a negative review of the work is acceptable. But be sure to support that evaluation with reasons or examples.

In the example sentences below, the writer has made changes to make his opinions strong and clear.

The book opens with ~~an interesting~~ *the scariest* scene *of the story*. A toddler escapes as his family is killed by a man named Jack. He toddles to a nearby graveyard, where he is taken in by the ghosts there. Then, *in a comical conversation,* the ghosts decide that the boy looks like nobody else in the cemetery, and they name him Nobody.

Write Your Review. Write your review using your outline, your idea web, and the bulleted list above to guide you.

Revise

The revision stage of your writing process offers the opportunity to make a good review even stronger. At this stage, you may want

Unit 3 • **Persuasive Writing** • **165**

Ch. 11 Write a Review

to break a long paragraph into two shorter ones, adding topic sentences for each. You may want to make your thesis stronger, or write a new closing sentence. You may want to cut out a detail that doesn't relate, or add a detail that does relate.

Revise Your Review. Use the following checklist to revise the rough draft of your review. The Review Rubric that follows the checklist will help you determine how strong your review is and where to make revisions.

Ideas
- ❏ Place a star next to the sentence where you identify one *specific* story, book, or poem.
- ❏ Underline three of your most convincing supporting reasons and examples. Do you need more? Cross out any weak or unconvincing reasons.

Organization
- ❏ Does the review have a beginning that states a thesis, a middle that gives supporting reasons, and an ending that leaves the reader with a memorable opinion? If you're missing any of these parts, add them.

Voice
- ❏ Look for places where you state your opinions with confidence. Write *voice* above these words/sentences. Revise any places where you seem unconfident or unsure.

Word choice
- ❏ Circle at least three vivid, accurate adjectives you used to make your opinions clear.

Sentence fluency
- ❏ Do you use a mix of long and short sentences? If you have too many of one or the other, revise your sentence lengths.

Write a Review Ch. 11

Rubric for a Review

	4 Strong	**3 Effective**	**2 Developing**	**1 Beginning**
Ideas	The writer focuses on one persuasive point. Reasons are convincing.	The writer focuses on one persuasive point, but details need to be stronger.	The writer focuses on one topic, but ideas are not convincing.	A persuasive point is not clear. Details seem unrelated.
Organization	Reasons are arranged from least to most convincing.	The most convincing reason is clear but not placed last.	The reasons do not have a clear sequence of least to most convincing.	Reasons, if present, are included in no particular order.
Voice	The writer uses tone or point of view to connect to the reader.	The writer's use of tone or point of view is not consistent.	The writer's tone or point of view connects with the reader in one sentence.	The tone is bored, bossy, argumentative, or otherwise unpleasant.
Word Choice	Words are accurate and fair.	Most words are accurate and fair.	Many words are used incorrectly or express unfair ideas.	The incorrect use of words makes ideas hard to understand.
Sentence Fluency	A variety of sentence types is used in a pleasing rhythm.	A variety of sentence types is used, but some may be awkward.	Sentences are complete but are mostly short and simple.	Sentences are mostly of one type or are incomplete.
Conventions	Few errors in capitalization, spelling, punctuation, or grammar are present.	Several errors in capitalization, spelling, punctuation, or grammar are present.	Errors in capitalization, spelling, punctuation, and grammar do not prevent understanding.	Errors in capitalization, spelling, punctuation, and grammar prevent understanding.

Ch. 11 **Write a Review**

 **Edit**

Check that your review clearly states the title of the work you are reviewing. Then learn about the conventions of punctuation and capitalization in titles in the mini-lesson that follows.

Mini-Lesson: Writing Titles

As you edit your review, make sure that you follow the conventions for writing titles.

Underline the titles of long works, including novels, picture storybooks, plays, magazines, and newspapers. If you are working on a computer, you can use *italic type* instead of underlining.

<u>The Graveyard Book</u>

A Drive in the Country

Place quotation marks around the titles of short works, including short stories, poems, newspaper articles, magazine articles, and songs.

"The Boscombe Valley Mystery"

"The Raven"

Capitalize the first and last words of a title, plus any major words in the title. The articles *a*, *an*, and *the* and prepositions in the middle of a title are not capitalized.

"The Raven"

<u>Penny from Heaven</u>

<u>The House of the Scorpion</u>

Give It a Try: Write Titles Correctly

As a class, determine the correct way to write the titles of the works being reviewed. Begin the activity by stating the name of

168 • The Writer's Studio   Level A

Write a Review Ch. 11

the work that you have reviewed. Then show the class how to write the title correctly by writing it on the board.

Edit Your Review. Edit the revised copy of your review. The following questions will help you decide what to change, remove, or leave in place.

Conventions
- ❏ Did you use the correct conventions for writing titles?
- ❏ Did you capitalize proper nouns?
- ❏ Did you use semicolons to separate items in a series if one or more items include a comma?
- ❏ If you used a colon, did you use it to announce a list or idea, in conjunction with a phrase like *as follows* or *like this*?
- ❏ Did you use a comma when joining sentences with a coordinating conjunction?
- ❏ Did you use a comma when beginning a sentence with a subordinate clause?
- ❏ Did you correct spelling mistakes, either with a friend's help or by using a dictionary?

PUBLISH

Presentation. Prepare your review for publication by writing or typing the final, edited copy.

Publish Your Review. Here are ideas for publishing your work.
- ❏ Display a copy of your review in your classroom.
- ❏ Check to see if an online bookseller sells the book you reviewed. If so, use the Web site's tool for reviewing books to type in a copy of your review.
- ❏ With a group of classmates, or with the entire class, collect your reviews into a booklet. Distribute a copy to each person who is published in the booklet.
- ❏ Give a copy of your review to a person you think would enjoy reading the book or story you reviewed. Even better, lend the person a copy of the book or story, too.

Ch. 11 **Write a Review**

Evaluate Your Review

Your teacher will either assess your review, ask you to self-assess your review, or ask you to switch with a partner and assess each other's work.

Evaluate the Model Review

Work with a partner to evaluate the following model review. Use the rubric on page 167 and write your score here: _____. In a class discussion, explain the score that you gave.

The Graveyard Book: Spooky Yet Funny

The Graveyard Book is the Newbery Award-winning book by Neil Gaiman, published in 2008. This novel is spine-tingling, funny, and unforgettable.

The book opens with the scariest scene of the entire story. A toddler escapes as his family is killed by a man named Jack. He toddles to a nearby graveyard, where he is taken in by the ghosts there. Then, in a comical conversation, the ghosts decide that the boy looks like nobody else in the cemetery, and they name him Nobody. They decide to raise him themselves, to keep him safe from Jack. A fun buzz of mystery is added by Silas, a man who brings food and other necessities to Nobody. Is Silas alive or dead? The really interesting part of the story is how, year by year, Nobody gets older while living in the cemetery and meeting supernatural creatures. He learns the secrets of the graveyard. But Nobody cannot hide forever.

170 • The Writer's Studio   Level A

Write a Review Ch. 11

Eventually, he will have to face his enemy, and readers will be curious about how he'll handle this.

The plot and the main character, Nobody, will appeal to readers of all ages, even adults. Some readers may be frustrated by Gaiman's writing style. It is like poetry, not because it rhymes, but because readers must use their imaginations to make sense of everything. For me, this is a strength, but for others, it could be a stumbling point. Overall, this is an unforgettable story about learning to face fears with the help of your own support system, however odd or wacky it may be.

Unit 3 • **Persuasive Writing** • 171

Chapter 12

Test Writing: The Persuasive Essay

Writing a persuasive essay test is an excellent chance to show off your writing and thinking skills. As with any writing assignment, a persuasive essay allows you to show how well you can use the traits of writing. In addition, to write a persuasive essay you must take a stand on an issue. You must form a firm opinion, and you must support your opinion with reasons and examples. By doing these things, you demonstrate your *critical thinking* skills—your ability to use reason and logic. This chapter will help you prepare to show off your writing and thinking skills on a written test. On the following pages, you'll analyze a sample prompt, and you'll write a persuasive essay in a testlike situation. First, look at the six traits below.

Six Traits of a Persuasive Test Essay

Ideas	The topic is narrowed to a specific position to be defended. Reasons and examples support the position.
Organization	The introduction states the writer's position. Body paragraphs give supporting reasons and respond to objections. The conclusion restates the position.
Voice	The writer's voice shows his or her concern or enthusiasm, balanced with a sense of trustworthiness.
Word Choice	Words are accurate. Descriptive words are fair.
Sentence Fluency	Sentences are complete. A variety of structures creates a pleasing rhythm.
Conventions	Capitalization, spelling, punctuation, and grammar are correct.

Unit 3 • **Persuasive Writing** • 173

Ch. 12   **Test Writing: The Persuasive Essay**

Preparing to Write Your Test Essay

A persuasive writing prompt will give you a topic and ask you to take a side or express an opinion. Here is an example:

> **Instructions**
> You have 55 minutes to complete the written composition. Read the prompt below. Then use separate paper to plan and draft your composition. Only your draft will be scored.
>
> **Writing Prompt**
> Your school board is considering the idea that students should help clean school classrooms and restrooms at the end of each school day. Before making its final decision, the board would like to hear what students have to say. Do you agree or disagree with the idea of helping to clean your own classroom and restroom? Write an essay for your school board to read. Explain whether or not you think that students should help clean classrooms and restrooms at the end of each school day.
>
> **Remember to**
> - write about the assigned topic
> - state a clear opinion on the topic
> - use convincing reasons and examples
> - respond to at least one objection to your viewpoint
> - edit your writing for conventions

1. Study the Prompt

Before you begin to write your essay, take a few moments to study the prompt. Answer these important questions:

What is the purpose of the essay? Scan the prompt for key words that tell you what kind of essay to write.

174 • The Writer's Studio   Level A

Words That Signal a Persuasive Essay

opinion	whether or not
point of view	reasons
perspective	agree/disagree

What should you write about? A writing prompt includes two or three main parts. The context, or setup, gives you the background information on the topic. In the prompt on page 174, the setup is the beginning of the second paragraph.

A writing prompt also includes a specific, focused writing assignment. In the prompt on page 174, the writing task is this:

Write an essay for your school board to read. Explain whether or not you think that students should help clean classrooms and restrooms at school each day.

A writing prompt often—but not always—includes reminders about what to include. In the prompt on page 174, the reminders are included last, in a bullet list. Don't skip over this section! Read the list carefully to learn what teachers will look for when they score your essay test.

How much time do you have to write? The prompt states that students have 55 minutes to write their essays. If a prompt does not state a time limit, look for the information on another page in your test booklet or ask your teacher.

2. Plan Your Time

After studying the prompt, make a quick plan for how to use your time. If you have 55 minutes in which to write the test, you could use your time as follows:

15 minutes:	Study the prompt and complete the prewriting.
25 minutes:	Write the essay.
10 minutes:	Revise the essay. Make "big" changes now, such as adding or removing sentences, moving sentences, and clarifying sentences.
5 minutes:	Edit the essay. Fix mistakes in capitalization, spelling, punctuation, and grammar.

Ch. 12   Test Writing: The Persuasive Essay

TOOLKIT

For a persuasive essay, useful prewriting strategies include
- T-chart
- pro-con chart
- listing
- freewriting

3. Prewrite

During the time set aside for prewriting, decide your opinion on the topic, gather ideas and details, and organize the information.

Take a stand on the issue. Remember that there is no "correct" opinion to have. Rather, your essay will be scored on how well you support the opinion you express. Use a few minutes of prewriting time to decide which point of view you can best support. A T-chart or pro-con chart, like the one below, can help.

Gather ideas and details. A T-chart or pro-con chart not only helps you decide your opinion on the issue but also helps you gather supporting reasons, examples, and facts. Take a look at the pro-con chart below. Based on the ideas listed in each side, which side of the issue would you take?

students cleaning the school

pros	cons
responsibility for our daily environment	time: cleaning won't fit into school day
respect for school property	not the student's responsibility
appreciation for the work it takes to keep a school clean	most students won't clean things well
school spirit	school is for learning in class, not doing manual labor
sense of community with other students	no easy way to enforce this
might keep students from being so messy	a few students would end up doing all the work
saves the school money	

176 • The Writer's Studio   Level A

Test Writing: The Persuasive Essay — Ch. 12

Organize the information. Use your remaining prewriting time to plan the arrangement of information in your essay. During a 55-minute testing period, it is reasonable to plan for a four- to six-paragraph essay. Use a simple strategy to organize the introduction, body, and conclusion of the essay.

In a persuasive essay, it works well to arrange your reasons from least to most important. That way, you end on a strong note. Include your response to an objection in the paragraph about one of your reasons, or in a separate paragraph before your final, strongest reason.

In the example outline below, the writer used formal Roman numerals to number the paragraphs. However, she used informal bullets to list supporting details for each paragraph. She underlined key organizational phrases. This method made the most sense to her. Similarly, you should use a method that makes sense to you.

> **TOOLKIT**
>
> For a persuasive essay, useful organizing strategies include
> - a beginning-middle-end chart
> - an opinion-and-reasons chart
> - an informal outline

Tip: Include all pieces of information required by the writing prompt. For instance, the prompt on page 174 reminds you to respond to at least one objection to your viewpoint. Refer to your T-chart or pro-con chart to find objections.

I. <u>My opinion</u>: Students should be required to help clean school classrooms and restrooms at the end of each school day.

II. <u>Reason 1</u>: responsibility for our school environment
   - teaches students that the care of our world is in our hands
   - gives us a chance to learn about nontoxic cleaners and recycling

III. <u>Reason 2</u>: respect for school property
   - keeping something clean makes you appreciate it more

Unit 3 • **Persuasive Writing** • 177

- in contrast, having something "magically" cleaned for you makes you take it for granted
IV. <u>Objection</u>: no easy way to enforce this.
<u>My response</u>: Use detention and/or a grading system to enforce the rule.
V. <u>Reason 3</u>: sense of community with other students
- working as a team builds team spirit
- can compare this to household chores at home; sharing the work helps you bond with other people and care about them
VI. <u>My conclusion</u>: Responsibility, respect, and community enrich our lives and are worth the effort to create.

Writing Your Test Essay

Now it's time to begin writing your essay. This is the part of your test that will be scored, so be sure to use your best handwriting, spell out all words instead of using abbreviations, and follow your outline carefully.

For many students, the hardest part of writing an essay test is getting started. The blank page stares up at you, reminding you that each sentence you write will be carefully evaluated. Don't let this kind of thinking take over. A quick and simple way to get started is to (1) write a sentence that identifies the topic and (2) write a sentence stating your opinion about the topic. Before you know it, your first paragraph is done.

Test Writing: The Persuasive Essay Ch. 12

> The school board is considering whether to require students to help clean classrooms and restrooms at the end of each school day. This task, however inconvenient it may be, would teach students responsibility for our environment, respect for school property, and how to build a sense of community.

Once you've written the introduction, you need only to support the opinion you stated. Your outline will tell you exactly what to write, and in what order. Focus on getting your ideas down on paper in clear sentences. You can correct spelling and other mistakes later.

Polishing Your Test Essay

In a 55-minute test period, plan to use the final 15 minutes to revise and edit your essay. A useful guideline is to use around 10 minutes to make larger changes (revisions) and 5 minutes to make smaller changes (edits). Use these minutes as you best need them.

Look at this paragraph from a model essay. During the writer's revision process, she added a supporting example and a transition. She also removed two sentences.

> Most important of all, helping to clean the school would help students build a sense of ~~School~~ community. *For example, we build a community at home by helping to keep our home clean.* We bond with the people we work with to meet our daily needs. ~~I have chores at home including cleaning the bathroom once a month.~~ *Similarly,* Seeing our friends work to keep the school clean lets us see them in a new light. We appreciate there effort, and we want to give back the same effort. As a result, we see ourselves as one team, and we root for our team. ~~A sense of community is one of the good things in life.~~

Unit 3 • Persuasive Writing • 179

Ch. 12 **Test Writing: The Persuasive Essay**

After revising the essay, the writer corrected mistakes in capitalization, punctuation, and spelling. Here is how the same paragraph looks now.

> Most important of all, helping to clean the school would help students build a sense of ~~S~~chool community. *For example, we build a community at home by helping to keep our home clean.* We bond with the people we work with to meet our daily needs. ~~I have chores at home including cleaning the bathroom once a month.~~ *Similarly,* Seeing our friends work to keep the school clean lets us see them in a new light. We appreciate ~~there~~ *their* effort, and we want to give back the same effort. As a result, we see ourselves as one team, and we root for our team. ~~A sense of community is one of the good things in life.~~

Evaluating a Persuasive Test Essay

Teachers will evaluate your test essay using a rubric like the one they use for non-test essays. They will take into account the fact that you wrote this test in one sitting, in a limited amount of time. The rubric on the next page shows a typical set of guidelines for evaluating a persuasive test essay.

Test Writing: The Persuasive Essay — Ch. 12

Persuasive Test Essay Rubric

	4 Strong	3 Effective	2 Developing	1 Beginning
Ideas	The writer wrote to the prompt. Reasons are convincing.	The writer wrote to the prompt but included a few unrelated details.	The main idea relates to the prompt, but many details are unrelated.	The writer did not write to the prompt. Reasons are unconvincing or absent.
Organization	Reasons are arranged from least to most important.	The most important reason is clear but not placed last.	The reasons do not have a clear sequence of least to most important.	Reasons, if present, are included in no particular order.
Voice	The voice shows concern or enthusiasm balanced with trustworthiness.	Several paragraphs show concern, enthusiasm, and/or trustworthiness.	A few sentences show concern, enthusiasm, or trustworthiness	Writing is mechanical, with no sense of a reliable writer behind the words.
Word Choice	Words are accurate and fair.	Most words are accurate and fair.	Many words are used incorrectly or express unfair ideas.	The incorrect use of words is confusing or misleading.
Sentence Fluency	A variety of sentence types is used in a pleasing rhythm.	A variety of sentence types is used, but some may be awkward.	Sentences are complete but are mostly short and simple.	Sentences are mostly of one type or are incomplete.
Conventions	Few errors in capitalization, spelling, punctuation, or grammar are present.	Several errors in capitalization, spelling, punctuation, or grammar are present.	Errors in capitalization, spelling, punctuation, and grammar do not prevent understanding.	Errors in capitalization, spelling, punctuation, and grammar prevent understanding.

Unit 3 • Persuasive Writing

Ch. 12   **Test Writing: The Persuasive Essay**

Evaluate a Model Test Essay

Work with a partner to evaluate the following model composition. Reread the prompt on page 174 and use the rubric on page 181. Write your score here: _____. In a class discussion, explain the score that you gave.

> The school board is considering whether to require students to help clean classrooms and restrooms at the end of each school day. This task, however inconvenient it may be, would teach students responsibility for our environment, respect for school property, and how to build a sense of community.
>
> In school, students are already learning about the importance of protecting the environment. One part of our environment is our school. by taking care of our school, we care for our environment. If we use nontoxic cleaning supplies, we help to protect and preserve our environment. We take charge to make sure that things are done the safe way.
>
> Cleaning classrooms and restrooms would help students develop respect for school property. if students have to work to keep their school clean, they will be more likely to respect school property. For example, If you know you have to clean the bathroom walls, you will be less likely to write on them. In contrast, having something "magically" cleaned for you makes you take it for granted.
>
> Some people will say that there is no easy way to enforce a rule of having students clean the school, the truth is, the school can enforce this rule just like other rules. They can assign detention to students who ~~brake~~ break the rule. Or the school board could add a new line to the report card for

Test Writing: The Persuasive Essay Ch. 12

"Citizenship" or "Community Service." Teachers could assign a participation grade to this category, for cleaning.

Most important of all, helping to clean the school would help students build a sense of ~~S~~chool community. We bond ^For example, we build a community at home by helping to keep our home clean.^ with the people we work with to meet our daily needs. ~~I have chores at home including cleaning the bathroom once a month.~~ ^Similarly,^ ~~S~~eeing our friends work to keep the school clean lets us see them in a new light. We appreciate ^their^ ~~there~~ effort, and we want to give back the same effort. As a result, we see ourselves as one team, and we root for our team. ~~A sense of community is one of the good things in life.~~

With all these benefits‚ responsibility, respect, and community‚ our lives will be enriched by the policy of having students help to clean the school. These benefits are worth the ^it takes^ effort to create ^them^.

Write a Persuasive Test Essay

Practice what you have learned by completing the following assignment. Use separate paper for prewriting and drafting. Only your draft will be scored.

Instructions
You have 55 minutes to complete the written composition. Read the prompt below. Then use separate paper to plan and draft your composition. Only your draft will be scored.

Unit 3 • **Persuasive Writing** • 183

Ch. 12　**Test Writing: The Persuasive Essay**

Writing Prompt
Your teachers are considering the idea of homework-free weekends and holidays. They would give you the normal amount of homework to complete on Monday through Thursday nights. However, they would not give homework assignments to complete on Friday nights, weekends, or holidays. What is your opinion of this idea? Write an essay for your teachers to read. Explain whether or not you think they should announce homework-free weekends and holidays.

Persuasive Writing Wrap-Up

The activities and information in these pages will help you continue to strengthen your persuasive writing skills. In You Be the Judge, use the Persuasive Writing Rubric to evaluate a student's work. The Ideas for Writing are additional persuasive writing prompts you can use for practice. And finally, in the Unit 3 Reflections, you can list important ideas you have learned in this unit and set goals for future learning.

You Be the Judge

Use what you've learned about the traits of persuasive writing to evaluate a student essay. First, review the traits of persuasive writing on page 127. Next, read the student essay below. Finally, in the rubric that follows the essay, assign the essay a score for each writing trait. In the space provided, explain each score that you assign.

No Gym
by Matt S., Pittsburgh, PA

Dear Editor:

Everybody loves sports, especially high school sports, but nobody likes gym class. If you are an in season athlete, physical education just seems a waste of time.

Some people may say Phys. Ed. is what the students need to prepare themselves for future habits. I veto this opinion and say that athletes already know excellent ways to stay healthy later on in life. Robert Steinbeck of Pittsburgh McNaugher, shared that he tries to teach his students responsibility and ways to keep healthy but also mentioned that the athletes he coaches learn ways to stay fit by doing the workouts with their team.

Being an athlete myself, when I have gym I'm always scared of getting hurt. Gym teachers always try to push the students to work their hardest, but on a game day for an athlete they could be tired or even get hurt in class. It would be safer for the athletes if they just did not have to put themselves in that position.

The recommended amount of physical activity is around 60 minutes a day. The football team at North Allegheny High School practices around two and a half hours a day, varying on the day of the week. Phys. Ed. is 42 minutes every other day that extra 42 minutes can make athletes weak from 20 minute runs or trying hard in a team activity.

A lot of athletes have the attitude "I don't need to try, I play a sport." And get nothing out of gym class anyways. Athletes could focus more on academics not having to participate in gym. They could have a study hall to do their school work, which they do not have as much time for after school because of their after school sport.

Athletes who already know ways to better their future should not have to put themselves at risk of injury by participating in Phys. Ed. Athletes can prepare themselves and learn life lessons from coaches and important figures in their sport. Inspiration would not be needed from Phys. Ed. for Athletes.

Sincerely,

Matt S.

Persuasive Writing Rubric

	4 Strong	3 Effective	2 Developing	1 Beginning
Ideas Score_____	*explanation:*			
Organization Score_____	*explanation:*			
Voice Score_____	*explanation:*			
Word Choice Score_____	*explanation:*			
Sentence Fluency Score_____	*explanation:*			
Conventions Score_____	*explanation:*			

Ideas for Writing

The assignments that follow will give you additional practice with persuasive writing. Your teacher may choose one or let you pick one that's most interesting to you.

1. Your school's principal has formed a committee to revise the school handbook. The committee has invited students to submit essays either supporting or opposing a school rule. The committee will consider each essay carefully when deciding to keep, revise, or remove rules from the handbook. Write a persuasive

essay of 350–400 words for the committee, either supporting or opposing a school rule.

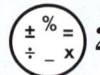 2. What is a hot-button topic at your school? Perhaps it's a big issue, such as school closures or busing. Perhaps it's a smaller issue, such as a dress code. Choose a topic that people are buzzing about and write a 200-word editorial for your school paper in which you

- take a position on the topic
- use statistics (numbers) to support your position. (For instance, interview 20 students and report the percentage of students who agree with you.)

3. Your school Web site has a page called From Me to You. On this page, students can post reviews of books, music, or products (anything from shampoo to dirt bikes). Only students at your school can log on and read this site. For the site, write a 100-word review in which you present the pros and cons of an item. Conclude by offering your opinion of whether this item is worth the purchase.

4. What is the one thing in your life that most needs to change, yet the change depends on someone else? Perhaps you want to eat vegetarian meals, yet your mom or dad always cooks meat-based meals. Perhaps you need your friend's help to fix your bicycle, yet he never has time to help you. Write a persuasive e-mail of 150–200 words in which you convince someone to do something helpful for you.

Unit 3 Reflections

How are you different as a writer now that you have completed this unit on persuasive writing? What new knowledge do you have? How is your writing stronger? What kinds of things could you work on to become even stronger as a persuasive writer? Use the following space to reflect on your work in this unit and to set goals for the future.

Focus on Me: My Achievements as a Persuasive Writer

What I've learned about persuasive writing in this unit:

Ways my persuasive writing is stronger now:

Things I can do to practice my skills of persuasive writing:

Unit 4

Literary Writing

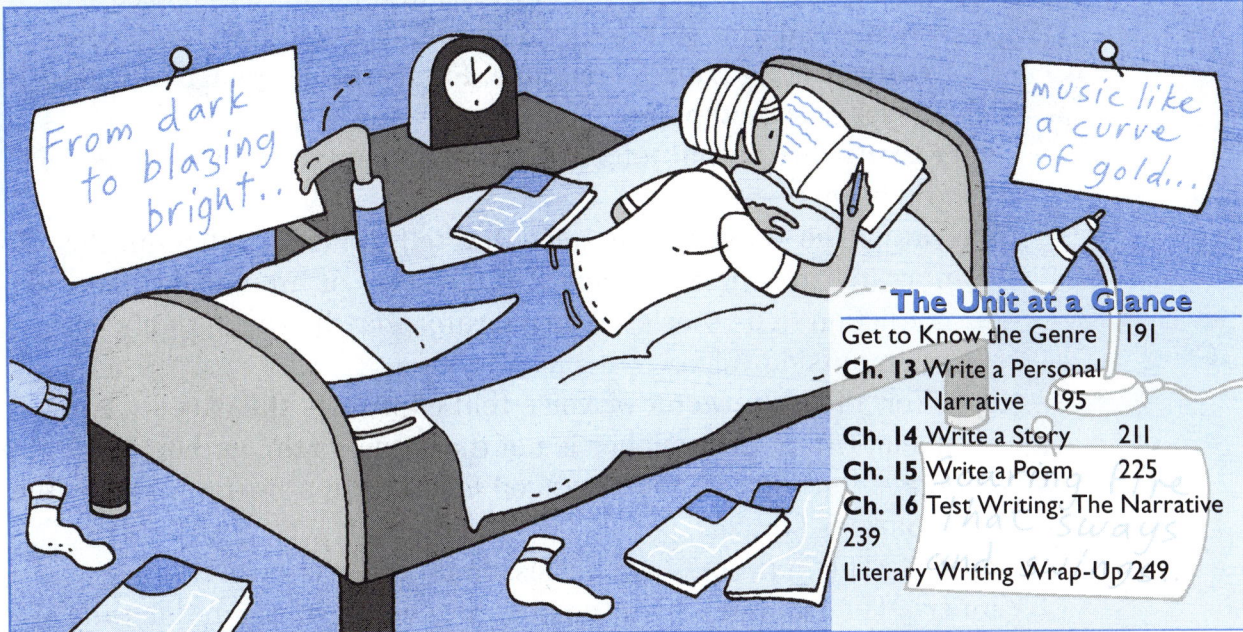

The Unit at a Glance
Get to Know the Genre   191
Ch. 13 Write a Personal Narrative   195
Ch. 14 Write a Story   211
Ch. 15 Write a Poem   225
Ch. 16 Test Writing: The Narrative   239
Literary Writing Wrap-Up 249

Get to Know the Genre: Literary Writing

Literary writing is a huge and delightful category. It includes all kinds of creative writing, such as plays, novels, biographies, and poetry. Some literary works, such as the personal narrative, tell about real people and events. Others, such as short stories, tell about imaginary people and events. Poetry expresses ideas and emotions in the form of lines and stanzas.

When we talk about literary writing, we use special terms. Some of the terms you need to know are explained in the following mini-glossary.

Unit 4

Mini-Glossary: Literary Terms

dialogue The conversation between characters in a story. A character's spoken words.

figurative language The use of words and phrases in a creative way instead of a literal way. The reader must use imagination to interpret figurative language. Figurative language includes similes and metaphors.

narrative A work that tells a story about real or imaginary people and events.

narrator The character or voice that tells a story. In fiction, the narrator may be a character in the story or an outside voice. In nonfiction (true stories), the narrator may be the author's voice or an outside voice.

speaker The character or voice that expresses the ideas in a poem. Often, the speaker is not the same as the author.

stanza A group of lines arranged together in a poem. A blank line separates stanzas.

theme The main message or lesson of a literary work.

unity The state in which the actions, events, ideas, and details of a work all support one theme.

Remember: what lasts in the reader's mind is not the phrase but the effect the phrase created: laughter, tears, pain, joy.
—Isaac Asimov
(American author, 1920–1992)

Many people write literary works for the enjoyment it brings them. In school, you may sometimes be asked to write a story or poem. This is an opportunity to show what you know about these types of writing. This unit will guide you through the process of writing three types of literary works: a personal narrative, a short story, and a poem. Finally, you'll learn how to respond to a literary writing prompt on a test.

Literary writing includes the same six traits as the other forms of writing you have studied. The following table explains how these traits help to make literary writing strong.

192 • The Writer's Studio   Level A

Six Traits of Literary Writing

Ideas	The work is unified by one theme.
Organization	Narratives have a beginning, a middle, and an end, with a clear sequence of events. Poems are arranged in lines and stanzas.
Voice	The writer or main character shines through as a real person with an interesting attitude toward the subject of the work.
Word Choice	Words and figurative language create vivid pictures and emotions for the reader.
Sentence Fluency	Narratives use a variety of sentence types and sentence beginnings. Poems have a rhythm to the lines.
Conventions	Quotation marks enclose spoken words. Spelling and capitalization are correct.

Real-World Example

The following paragraphs begin a funny story about a cowboy named Gus in *Gullible Gus*, by Maxine Rose Schur.

Organization: The beginning of the story introduces the main character and his problem.

Word choice: These words help to create an informal tone.

Sentence fluency: The writer uses a mix of short and long sentences.

Cowboy Gus believed everything people told him. Everything! The other cowboys at the ranch fed him the biggest lies, and he swallowed them whole.

"Watch out, Gus!" Billy Bones once hollered. "It's going to rain nails!" And before he could add, "Just kidding," Gus ran to the barn and stuck a bucket on his head. Another time, Judd Mudd told Gus, "Tonight the hens will sing lullabies," and Gus slept in the chicken coop so he wouldn't miss the music.

Poor Gus! People just loved to tease and trick him. But their jokes made him sadder than dry soup. Finally, he couldn't take it anymore. He rode into town to see Doc Hickory.

Voice: Phrases like this one make the narrator's voice playful and interesting.

Conventions: Quotation marks enclose a character's spoken words.

Ideas: This story is unified by the theme gullibility, or being too believing.

Unit 4 • Literary Writing • 193

Unit 4

Give It a Try: Examine the Real-World Example

Find additional examples of the traits of good writing in the model you just read. On separate paper, list three traits of good writing. For each one, quote or describe an example from the model.

Get Ready to Write

Now that you've explored the qualities of literary writing, you're ready to create some literary pieces of your own. In the chapters that follow, you'll write a personal narrative about something that surprised you, a short story about imaginary events, a poem about a strong emotion, and a narrative about a situation you resolved. You'll use the stages of the writing process, and you'll be presented with models and mini-lessons along the way.

As you work through these chapters, you can enrich your understanding by trying the suggestions below. These tips will help you connect what you're learning in this unit to your own life and the world around you.

LEARNING TIPS

- Practice using literary writing to make your notes and e-mails to friends more interesting.

- Browse literary writing at a library. Find out what kinds of literary writing that you like and check out one or two books to read.

- Form a literary club with friends, even if it meets only once or twice this year. Share your own literary writing or read aloud from published works.

- Ask a teacher if you can create a Literary Bulletin Board, where students can hang examples of their work, share tips, suggest useful Web sites, and so on.

- Create a poster that explains figurative language, and hang it in the classroom or explain it in an oral presentation.

194 • The Writer's Studio   Level A

Chapter 13
Write a Personal Narrative

This chapter is all about YOU. As you work through the process of writing a personal narrative, you will think and write about yourself. You can be completely honest or you can make up details and conversations to fit the purpose of your story. But ultimately, your story will reveal something about yourself to your reader.

In a personal narrative, the writer shares a sequence of events that show how he or she resolved a conflict or confronted a truth. For example, the story may be about how the writer overcame challenges to win a spot on the basketball team. The purpose of writing a personal narrative is to draw in readers and make them feel as if they are right there, experiencing the events of the story. Just as the events of the narrative had an effect on you, the events can affect your readers, too.

Six Traits of a Personal Narrative

Ideas	The writer focuses on one main conflict to be resolved. Each scene and dialogue relates to this conflict.
Organization	The order of events is clear.
Voice	The writer uses the first-person point of view. The tone fits with how the writer wants the reader to feel after reading the narrative: amused, sad, triumphant, or something else.
Word Choice	The writer balances realistic, everyday language with word choices that keep the reader interested.
Sentence Fluency	Sentences in dialogue show realistic speech patterns. Narrative sentences are complete.
Conventions	Quotation marks are used to begin and end a character's words. Proper nouns are capitalized. The present tense or past tense is used consistently. Spelling is correct.

Unit 4 • Literary Writing

Ch. 13   **Write a Personal Narrative**

In the narrative below, the writer tells how he used his skateboarding talent to get a girl to notice him.

My Flawless Landing

Looking down the street, I see Caitlin and Raneese coming my way. I grin at Marcos, standing nearby. "They don't call me Burly for nothing," I say. I hitch up my pants and cinch the leather belt tighter. I plant my left foot on my board and push with my right. The skateboard accelerates. "Watch this!" I call out.

Ahead on the street, I had set up a homemade flatbar. On my board, I fly toward it. Just before reaching the flatbar, I do an ollie, popping the board up in the air. Coming down on the rail, I complete a flawless railslide. Unfortunately, I don't stick the landing, and the trick ends in a slam. "Ouch!" I laugh, picking myself up off the pavement.

Caitlin and Raneese are closer now. "Watch this!" I say loudly to Marcos. I speed toward the flatbar again, do an ollie, and finish with a railslide. I stick the landing! Gliding up to the two girls, I grin. "Hello, ladies. See anything you like?"

"Nothing I wasn't doing when I was a grommet," Caitlin says, laughing. "Face it. Little kids can do ollies and railslides." But she is smiling. She is interested. Success!

Give It a Try: Examine the Model Narrative

Answer the following questions about six traits in the personal narrative. Write your answers on separate paper.

1. **Ideas.** What main thing does the narrator want?
2. **Organization.** List three different things the narrator does, in the order in which he does them.
3. **Voice and word choice.** List words the narrator uses that help to define him as a character or make him memorable.

4. **Sentence fluency.** Are the narrator's spoken words (the sentences in quotation marks) mainly short sentences or long sentences? Why do you think this is?

5. **Conventions.** Copy three different lines of dialogue, including the punctuation and quotation marks. Notice whether the end punctuation mark (comma, exclamation mark, question mark) is inside or outside the quotation mark.

Your Turn to Write: Compose a Personal Narrative

Now you'll write a personal narrative. Read the assignment carefully and follow the strategies and instructions for each stage of the writing process.

Assignment

Write a 400-word personal narrative for your classmates to read, telling about a time that you were surprised by a person, an event, or a truth. To help your readers feel as though they are sharing your experience, be sure to
- focus on one specific time you were surprised
- make the order of events clear
- use words and dialogue that sound natural and interesting
- show how things ended or were resolved
- use a consistent tone, or attitude, toward the event, such as fear, delight, sadness, anger, or amusement. Help your reader feel this emotional response along with you.

Prewrite

Analyze the Prompt. What does the prompt tell you about your goals for this assignment? Read the assignment closely to answer the following questions. Use separate paper.

Ch. 13 Write a Personal Narrative

1. What is the purpose of this personal narrative?
2. Who is the audience for this personal narrative?
3. How long does the personal narrative need to be?

Choose a Topic. Which surprise in your life would you like to tell about in a personal narrative? Use one of the following strategies to choose a topic for your story.

1. **Listing.** When was the last time you were surprised by a person, an event, or a truth? Write a phrase or sentence that identifies that experience. Then think of another time you were surprised and list that experience below the first one. Continue listing times you were surprised until you have five or six. Finally, review your list and circle the time that you would most like to write about.

> Surprises
>
> --when I found out Jamie was moving away
>
> --when my parents gave me a surprise party
>
> --when the Trevinos gave me some baby rabbits
>
> --the time I realized that Gabby was not a good friend
>
> --when I found out that Darnell likes me

2. **T-chart.** Label one side of the chart Happy Surprises and the other side Unpleasant Surprises. Search your memory and list times when you were surprised in happy ways or unpleasant ways. Finally, review your lists and circle the example you would like to write about.

198 • The Writer's Studio   Level A

Write a Personal Narrative   Ch. 13

Happy Surprises	Unpleasant Surprises
when I found five dollars	when I got kicked off the soccer team
when my parents gave me a surprise party	when I found out Jamie was moving away
(when the Trevinos gave me some baby rabbits)	the time I realized that Gabby was not a good friend
when I found out that Darnell likes me	

Gather Ideas and Details. In the following table, fill in details to answer each question about the time you were surprised.

5 Ws Plus H

Who?	
What?	
When?	
Where?	
Why?	
How?	

Unit 4 • Literary Writing • 199

Organize Ideas and Details. Create a **timeline** to organize the events of your personal narrative. Begin with the first important action, conversation, or thought that leads to the surprise. Then continue listing actions, conversations, or thoughts in order, leading up to the surprise. You can organize your timeline by listing things in one of these ways

- by day of the week
- by time of day
- by simple sequence (first, second, third, etc.), as in the example below.

1. We go for a drive.
2. We arrive at the Trevinos' farm.
3. Mom says to come with her and winks at me.
4. Mrs. Trevino welcomes us and smiles at me.
5. Mr. Trevino brings out a banana box.
6. I discover my gift, five baby rabbits.
7. I respond with thanks and joy.

Draft

Since your personal narrative is about something that happened to you, you'll write your story using the first-person point of view. You are the central character of your story. You will tell about actions and conversations from your own point of view. What did *you* see? What did *you* hear? What did *you* think, suspect, say, or do? Use first-person pronouns such as *I, me, my, myself, we, our,* and *us* to write your sentences.

Here is the first paragraph from the story about the narrator who receives a gift of baby rabbits. The first-person pronouns are underlined, to help you study the first-person point of view.

On a sunny, cool autumn day, my parents took me and my brother and sister for a ride. It wasn't

Write a Personal Narrative   Ch. 13

unusual for <u>us</u> to go visit friends, so <u>I</u> didn't suspect anything. Little did <u>I</u> know, this trip was all about <u>me</u>.

Besides paying attention to the narrative point of view, you need to think about the story's *tense*. You can choose to tell your story in the present tense or the past tense. The following mini-lesson explains more about these choices.

Mini-Lesson: Using a Consistent Tense

As you know, a verb's *tense* shows whether the action or state of being occurs in the past, the present, or the future.

→ Verbs in the **past tense** show action or state of being that has already happened.

    I <u>rode</u> my skateboard to the park.

    I <u>felt</u> nervous about the competition.

→ Verbs in the **present tense** show action or state of being that is currently happening.

    I <u>ride</u> my skateboard to the park.

    I <u>feel</u> nervous about the competition.

→ Verbs in the **future tense** show action or state of being that will (or might) happen.

    I <u>will ride</u> my skateboard to the park.

    I <u>might feel</u> nervous about the competition.

Unit 4 • Literary Writing

Ch. 13 Write a Personal Narrative

This table shows examples of verbs in the past, the present, and the future tenses.

Past Tense	Present Tense	Future Tense
asked	ask	will ask
ate	eat	will eat
felt	feel	will feel
got	get	will get
went	go	will go
heard	hear	will hear
laughed	laugh	will laugh
listened	listen	will listen
rode	ride	will ride
ran	run	will run
said	say	will say
screamed	scream	will scream
seemed	seem	will seem
thought	think	will think
whispered	whisper	will whisper

When writing your personal narrative, be sure to use a consistent tense to tell your story. For this story, choose to use either the *past tense* or the *present tense*.

Write a Personal Narrative   Ch. 13

The story about the skateboarder, at the beginning of this chapter, uses the present tense consistently. Here is the first paragraph from that story, with the present-tense verbs underlined.

Looking down the street, I <u>see</u> Caitlin and Raneese coming my way. I <u>grin</u> at Marcos, standing nearby. "They don't <u>call</u> me Burly for nothing," I <u>say</u>. I <u>hitch</u> up my pants and <u>cinch</u> the leather belt tighter. I <u>plant</u> my left foot on my board and <u>push</u> with my right. The skateboard <u>accelerates</u>. "Watch this!" I <u>call</u> out.

Following is a paragraph from the story about the surprise gift from the Trevinos. It uses the past tense, and the writer has made changes to create a consistent past tense.

We kids sat in the back of our van as we drove along the mountain road. I look^ed out at cactuses, scrub brush, a brilliant blue sky, and puffs of clouds. Soon enough we got to the Trevinos' farm. We park^ed under a huge oak tree, and we kids start^ed trotting toward the barn where we normally played. But my mom called, "Nora, you come with me." And she winked at me.

Give It a Try: Decide Which Tense to Use in Your Narrative

Which tense do you want to use to tell your personal story: past tense or present tense? To get a feel for how each tense would sound, complete the following sentences. First, use the past tense. In the second set of sentences, use the present tense. Use separate paper.

Ch. 13 **Write a Personal Narrative**

> **1. Use the past tense.** I was surprised when . . . . The strongest emotion I felt was . . . .. In the end, I thought . . . .
>
> **2. Use the present tense.** I am surprised when . . . . The strongest emotion I feel is . . . . In the end, I think . . . .
>
> Which tense do you think would work better for telling your story: past or present?

Write Your Personal Narrative. Using the timeline that you created, write your personal narrative. Make sure that your story has a beginning, a middle, and an end.

- The **beginning** sets the stage for the story. Hook your reader's interest by creating curiosity about the surprise. You can do this by showing your own curiosity or suspense as the main character.
- The **middle** of the story leads up to and includes the surprise. Keep the story moving by telling what people say and do. Brief descriptions to help your reader create a mental picture are great. However, don't give long descriptions that bring the story to a standstill.
- The **end** brings the story quickly to a close. Tell how you responded to the surprise, how it changed you, or some other personal response. Just as it was memorable for you, you can help it be memorable for your reader.

 Revise

You have a complete draft of your personal narrative. It uses the first-person point of view, and it uses a consistent verb tense. It tells who, what, when, where, why, and how about the time you were surprised. It ends by giving your response to the surprise. This is a strong start, and you should feel a well-deserved sense of accomplishment.

204 • The Writer's Studio   Level A

Write a Personal Narrative   Ch. 13

Now, during the revision stage, focus on making each part of your story stronger. This is the time to clarify actions, statements, or thoughts. This is the time to cut out details or sentences that do not move the plot forward.

Revise Your Personal Narrative. Use the following checklist to revise the rough draft of your story. The Personal Narrative Rubric that follows the checklist will help you determine how strong your story is and where to make revisions.

Ideas
- ❏ Underline the sentence in which you identify the main conflict you faced. In this narrative, the conflict is your suspense or curiosity about the coming surprise.

Organization
- ❏ Number each main event, action, conversation, and thought that helps to move the story forward. If an event or action goes off track, cross it out.

Voice
- ❏ Do you use the first-person point of view consistently? Make revisions if needed.
- ❏ Do you use a tone that fits with your attitude toward the events of the story? Write *voice* over two words or phrases that demonstrate your tone and attitude.

Word choice
- ❏ Circle two vivid or interesting words that help keep your reader's interest.

Sentence fluency
- ❏ Check that you've used complete sentences to tell about actions and events.
- ❏ Have you used realistic speech patterns in dialogue? (For instance, since people do not always speak in complete sentences, the dialogue in your story may contain realistic-sounding sentence fragments.) Find a realistic-sounding line of dialogue and write *realistic* above it.

Unit 4 • Literary Writing • **205**

Ch. 13 **Write a Personal Narrative**

Personal Narrative Rubric

	4 **Strong**	**3** **Effective**	**2** **Developing**	**1** **Beginning**
Ideas	One conflict is resolved through relevant actions and dialogue.	One conflict is resolved. Most actions and dialogue clearly relate.	Actions and dialogue are only loosely related to the conflict.	The conflict is not clear. Actions and dialogue do not seem related.
organization	The story has a beginning, a middle, and an end. Order of events is clear.	The story has a beginning, a middle, and an end. Order of events is mostly clear.	The beginning or end of the story is unclear. Order of events is sometimes unclear.	The story needs structure. Events are included in no particular order.
voice	The writer uses first-person point of view consistently. Tone fits with the conflict.	The writer uses first-person point of view in most sentences. Tone mostly fits with the conflict.	The writer uses first-person point of view but not consistently. Tone is not consistent.	The writer does not use the first-person point of view. Tone does not fit with the conflict.
word choice	Realistic words are balanced with interesting word choices.	Realistic words are balanced with several interesting word choices.	Realistic words are balanced with one or two interesting word choices.	Word choices are basic. Interesting words are needed.
sentence fluency	Most sentences are complete. Sentence fragments make dialogue sound real.	Two or three sentence fragments are used outside of dialogue.	Sentence fragments are distracting and difficult to understand.	Many sentence fragments are used, making it hard to understand the story.
conventions	Quotation marks, capitalization, and verb tense are used correctly.	There are two or three mistakes in the use of quotation marks, capitalization, or verb tense.	There are many mistakes in the use of quotation marks, capitalization, or verb tense.	Mistakes in the use of quotation marks, capitalization, and verb tense make the story hard to understand.

The Writer's Studio   Level A

Write a Personal Narrative Ch. 13

Edit

During the editing stage of your writing process, check that you have used quotation marks correctly.

- Use quotation marks to enclose a character's spoken words.

- At the end of the quoted words, a comma or a period goes inside the closing quotation mark.

- At the end of the quoted words, a question mark or exclamation mark goes inside the closing quotation mark if it is part of the character's spoken sentence.

Look closely at the quotation marks and punctuation in the following model paragraph.

"Come in this house right now!" she bossed us playfully. "Sit down right there on the blue sofa. Just push Tiger Lily out of the way." I sat on the couch and pulled the cat into my lap instead of pushing her away. I couldn't resist asking, "What's up?"

Edit Your Personal Narrative. Edit the revised copy of your story. The following questions will help you decide what to change, remove, or leave in place.

Conventions
❑ Did you capitalize the names of people, pets, towns, and other proper nouns?
❑ Did you enclose a character's spoken words in quotation marks?
❑ Did you use the first-person point of view consistently?
❑ Did you use either the present tense or the past tense consistently?
❑ Did you correct spelling mistakes, either with a friend's help or by using a dictionary?

Unit 4 • Literary Writing • **207**

Ch. 13   **Write a Personal Narrative**

PUBLISH

T!p

Give your story a title that will grab your reader's interest. Choose a title that hints at the surprise in the story or that uses an interesting word or phrase from the story.

Here are ideas for publishing your personal narrative.
- ❏ Read your story aloud to the class.
- ❏ Display your story on a bulletin board in class.
- ❏ Read your story to your family before or after dinner tonight.
- ❏ Post a copy of your story to your personal Web page.
- ❏ Mail a copy of your story to a distant friend or family member.
- ❏ Create a podcast of your story.
- ❏ Place a copy of your story in the personal time capsule that you are creating during this school year.

Evaluate Your Personal Narrative

Your teacher will either assess your narrative, ask you to self-assess your narrative, or ask you to switch with a partner and assess each other's work.

Evaluate the Model Personal Narrative

Work with a partner to evaluate the following model personal narrative. Use the rubric on page 206 and write your score here: _____. In a class discussion, explain the score that you gave.

Surprise in a Banana Box

On a sunny, cool autumn day, my parents took me and my brother and sister for a ride. It wasn't unusual for us to go visit friends, so I didn't suspect anything. Little did I know, this trip was all about me.

We kids sat in the back of our van as we drove along the mountain road. I looked out at cactuses, scrub brush, a brilliant blue sky, and puffs of clouds. Soon enough we got to the Trevinos' farm. We parked under a huge oak

208 • The Writer's Studio   Level A

tree, and we kids started trotting toward the barn where we normally played. But my mom called, "Nora, you come with me." And she winked at me.

Full of curiosity, I went up onto the front porch. I noticed that the blue paint on the porch needed a new coat. Then the front door opened. Mrs. Trevino is an old, old lady with smile wrinkles all over her face. Today, her smile beamed right at me like a spotlight. I could barely contain my curiosity.

"Come in this house right now!" she bossed us playfully. "Sit down right there on the blue sofa. Just push Tiger Lily out of the way." I sat on the couch and pulled the cat into my lap instead of pushing her away. I couldn't resist asking, "What's up?"

Just then, Mr. Trevino came out of the kitchen carrying one of those large, strong boxes that bananas are shipped in. It has drawings of bananas done in red ink all over the sides. Was he about to give me a box of bananas? Mr. Trevino set the big box next to me on the sofa and then scooped up Tiger Lily.

I gasped. I may have skipped a breath or two. There in the banana box was a bunch of baby rabbits. They looked exactly like white puffs of clouds, only they had delicate ears sticking up. They weren't scared of me at all. They sniffed around the box, making little hopping movements to get around. I counted five bunnies.

"These are for you," said Mrs. Trevino. "We noticed that your brother has a dog, and your sister has a cat. We thought you needed your own pet. We'll help you build a rabbit hutch and teach you how to care for them. What do you think?"

I had never been so surprised in all my life. I felt singled out and special. And of course I loved my new pets. "I love them!" I said. I would show the Trevinos my gratitude later, by repainting their front porch. But right now, I had five bunnies to name.

Chapter 14

Write a Story

You are already a storyteller. In daily life, you tell your friends about funny events, a friend's weird behavior, or a disappointing experience. Telling stories about your life helps you make sense of it and helps you bond with other people. You can use your skills of spoken storytelling to help you tell stories in writing. In fact, you have already done this. In Chapter 13, you wrote a personal narrative about real events and people. Now you'll build on your skills of storytelling by writing a story about imaginary people and events. Compare the six traits of a story with the traits of a personal narrative

Six Traits of a Story

Ideas	The writer focuses on one main conflict to be resolved. Each scene and dialogue relates to this conflict.
Organization	The order of events is clear.
Voice	The writer uses a consistent narrative point of view. The tone fits with how the writer wants the reader to feel after reading the narrative: amused, sad, triumphant, or something else.
Word Choice	The writer uses vivid words to help show action, feelings, thoughts, and so on.
Sentence Fluency	Sentences in dialogue show realistic speech patterns. Narrative sentences are complete.
Conventions	Quotation marks are used to begin and end a character's words. Proper nouns are capitalized. The present tense or past tense is used consistently. Spelling is correct.

Unit 4 • Literary Writing • 211

Ch. 14 Write a Story

In the following story, the narrator tells how one girl overcame her jealousy of a classmate who seemed to have a perfect life.

Jealousy

Bethany was the kind of girl who lights up a room. Everybody wanted to know her, and this fact made Daisy narrow her eyes with jealousy. Why was it so easy for some people? Daisy wondered. Every day, Bethany did something that made people laugh with her, admire her, or follow her around like a puppy. Daisy, for one, was sick of it.

Then, one Friday after school, Daisy trudged out to the curb to wait for her mom. She noticed a hunched figure sitting on the curb, pressed up next to the bushes. Looking closely, Daisy saw that it was Bethany, and she was crying.

Suddenly, Daisy's mom pulled up in her car and called out, "Daisy! It's pizza night, and I'm hungry enough to eat an elephant!"

Daisy froze as Bethany looked up at her.

Bethany said, "You're so lucky, Daisy. My mom just called to say she's running late *again*, and I have to walk home and fix my own dinner. I wish she wanted to spend time with me, like your mom."

Daisy stood absolutely still for a moment. Then, recovering her voice, she said, "Why don't you call your mom and ask if you can come home with me for pizza night?"

And that was the beginning of a new friendship.

Write a Story   Ch. 14

Give It a Try: Examine the Model Story

Answer the following questions about six traits in the model story you just read. Write your answers on separate paper. When you are finished, share your answers with your peers in a class discussion.

1. **Ideas.** What is Daisy's main problem?
2. **Organization.**
   a. Which paragraph introduces Daisy's main problem?
   b. Which paragraph shows how Daisy solves her problem?
   c. Which paragraph tells how things turned out between the two girls?
3. **Voice and word choice.** List three words or phrases that you think are vivid or interesting.
4. **Sentence fluency.** Copy one sentence that helps to create a pleasing flow by using an introductory element, an interrupting phrase, or something else.
5. **Conventions.** In the story, circle the word *mom* each time it is used. Why didn't the writer capitalize this word?

Your Turn to Write: Compose a Story

Now you'll write your own story. Read the assignment carefully and follow the strategies and instructions for each stage of the writing process.

Assignment

A local author wants to encourage students to write fiction. He has invited students in your class to write a story about an embarrassing moment. This author has promised to read and give feedback on each story that students send him.

Unit 4 • Literary Writing • 213

Ch. 14 Write a Story

He asks only that the story
- be between 250 and 300 words
- be of interest to readers aged 19 or younger
- be about people and events that you make up

Write a story to send to the author and follow his guidelines.

 **Prewrite**

Analyze the Prompt. What does the prompt tell you about your goals for this assignment? Read the assignment closely to find answers to the following questions. Use separate paper.

1. What is the purpose of this story?
2. Who is the audience for this story?
3. How long does the story need to be?

Choose a Topic. With your teacher's permission, gather in a small group and share ideas about embarrassing moments. The following sentence starters may help.

The thing that would embarrass me most is . . .

I felt so bad for this person when I saw . . .

Parents can embarrass you when they . . .

Older (younger) brothers or sisters can embarrass you when . . .

A friend can embarrass you when . . .

Something you don't normally think of as embarrassing is . . .

After each person has spoken, complete the following sentence:

The embarrassing moment that I will write about is _____

_____

214 • **The Writer's Studio**   Level A

Write a Story Ch. 14

Gather and Organize Ideas and Details. You can use a story map to plan your story. Following is an example of how one writer planned a story about an embarrassing moment.

Beginning

Who is the main character?
DeShawn

What problem or conflict does he or she face?
He likes a girl and wants her to notice him.

Setting:
school, mostly cafeteria

List of Characters:
DeShawn
Marcos
Raneese

Middle

What happens that is embarrassing?
DeShawn laughs and accidentally blows pudding out of his nose. A glob of it lands on Raneese.

Main Event 1
Raneese insults Marcos.

Main Event 2
DeShawn laughs and sprays pudding.

End

Does the main character solve the problem or conflict? How?
No--he doesn't get her to notice him in a good way!

How does the main character feel about this solution?
horrified and embarrassed

Unit 4 • Literary Writing • 215

Ch. 14 **Write a Story**

Here is a blank version of the story map you just studied. Copy it into your notebook and use it to plan your own story.

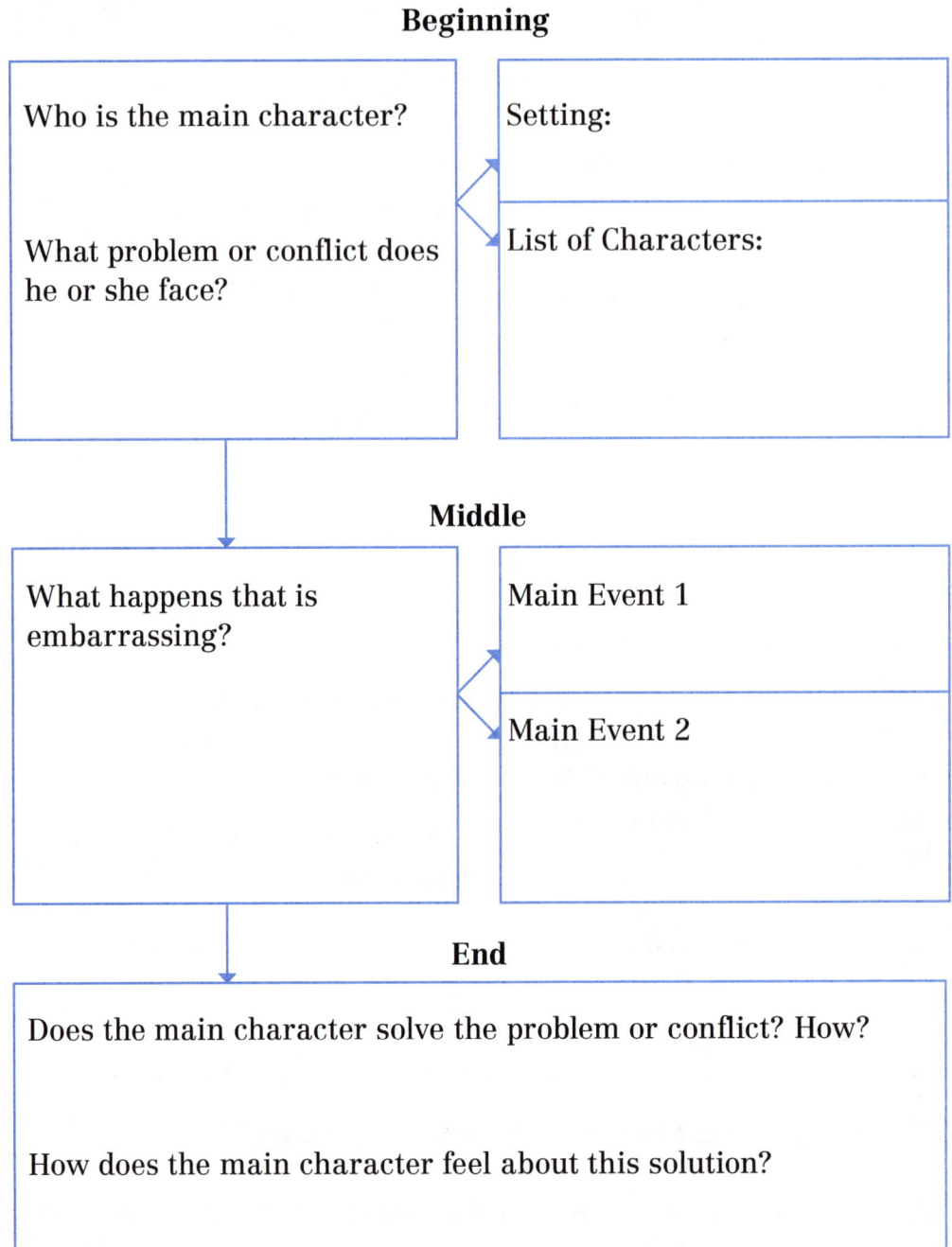

Write a Story Ch. 14

Draft

As you know, each paragraph in an essay focuses on one main idea. The paragraph has a topic sentence that expresses the main idea, and it has supporting sentences that develop the main idea. But what about paragraphs in a story? How do you know what makes a paragraph complete and when to start a new paragraph? The following mini-lesson will answer such questions.

Mini-Lesson: Forming Paragraphs in a Story

The main purpose of paragraphs in a story is to organize actions and dialogue. In a story, you'll use paragraphs to

- create "chunks" of related actions
- create a slow or fast pace of action
- organize character's spoken words

Think of your story as a timeline. Each paragraph should move the story forward along this line. To do this, each paragraph should focus on one "chunk" of action in the story. This chunk may be one key action that requires a lot of detail to make clear. Or it may be a series of smaller actions that, together, move the story forward.

Paragraphs in stories may be short or long. In fact, it's good to include a mix of short and long paragraphs. As with a variety of sentence lengths, a variety of paragraph lengths creates a pleasing rhythm. Long paragraphs cause the reader to slow down and pay attention. Short paragraphs causes the pace of the story to speed up, since the reader can read them quickly. If you want to create a sense of speed or urgency, use shorter paragraphs. If you want to create a slower pace, use longer paragraphs.

Besides using paragraphs to create chunks of action and to give your story a rhythm, you use paragraphs to organize dialogue. Start a new paragraph each time a character begins

Unit 4 • Literary Writing • 217

Ch. 14 Write a Story

speaking. In that paragraph, include only that character's spoken words. Begin a new paragraph for the next character's words.

The following paragraphs are taken from the story about DeShawn's embarrassing moment. Notice how the writer has formed paragraphs.

"Today's the day," said DeShawn. "I'm gonna sit at Raneese's table at lunch."	This paragraph gives DeShawn's words.
Marcos laughed. "Raneese doesn't know you exist. You're gonna sit there, eat your bologna sandwich, and then the bell will ring. And Raneese *still* won't know you exist."	A new paragraph begins when Marcos responds to DeShawn.
"Today's the day," repeated DeShawn stubbornly.	A new paragraph begins when DeShawn responds to Marcos.
At last lunchtime arrived. In the cafeteria, DeShawn casually approached Raneese's table. He slid into an empty chair. No one gave him a glance. He rattled his brown paper bag, pulling out a sandwich, a cup of chocolate pudding, a plastic spoon, and an orange. Raneese and her friends remained deep in conversation.	This paragraph includes the chunk of actions related to DeShawn's sitting down but not being noticed.

Give It a Try: Mark Paragraph Breaks in a Story

Following is another portion of the story about DeShawn. Read the sentences and then decide how to organize them into paragraphs. Write a paragraph symbol ¶ to show where each new paragraph should begin. When you're done, discuss your results with a classmate.

218 • The Writer's Studio   Level A

Write a Story Ch. 14

> Marcos dropped into the remaining empty seat. "What's up, DeShawn?" he said loudly. DeShawn glared at him and picked up the pudding. He pulled the plastic top off, paying more attention to Raneese than to his food. Raneese was saying, "And then I saw my sister holding hands with some goofball from our class, I think his name is Marcos. I mean, how embarrassing is that? I would just *die*." Marcos's mouth fell open and his face flushed red.

Write Your Story. Using your story map, write a rough draft of your story. Here are some things to consider at this stage of the process:

- **Ideas.** As you write, keep your theme (an embarrassing situation) in mind.
- **Organization.** Tell about actions and/or thoughts in the order in which they happened.
- **Voice.** Decide if you want the voice in your paragraph to be *yours* (the writer's), or the voice of a character.
- **Word choice.** Use words that show the narrator's attitude toward the sequence of events. Since your reader will share the narrator's attitude, ask yourself, "How do I want my reader to feel about this embarrassing situation? Alarmed? Amused? Pitying?"

Revise

Revise Your Story. Use the following checklist to revise the rough draft of your story. The Story Rubric that follows the checklist will help you determine how strong your story is and where to make revisions.

Unit 4 • Literary Writing • 219

Ch. 14 **Write a Story**

Ideas
- ❑ Underline the sentence that makes your topic clear.

Organization
- ❑ Does the narrative have a beginning, a middle, and an end?
- ❑ Is the order of the events and characters' thoughts clear?
- ❑ Have you used paragraphs to organize dialogue and chunks of action?

Voice
- ❑ Is the narrator's voice consistent?
- ❑ Do you use either the first-person point of view or the third-person point of view consistently? Cross out and revise any areas that are inconsistent.

Word choice
- ❑ Find two plain, vague, or overused words. Cross out each one and replace it with a more vivid, expressive, or interesting word. Use a thesaurus if necessary.

Sentence fluency
- ❑ Do you use a mix of short and long sentences?
- ❑ Have you used complete sentences to tell about actions and events?
- ❑ Find a realistic-sounding line of dialogue, and write *realistic* above it.

Write a Story Ch. 14

Story Rubric

	4 Strong	3 Effective	2 Developing	1 Beginning
Ideas	The work is unified by one theme.	The theme is clear, but some details do not relate.	The writer is beginning to make the theme clear.	The theme is not clear. Most details seem unrelated.
Organization	The order of actions/thoughts is clear.	Most details follow a logical order.	Organization of details is awkward.	Actions or thoughts are in random order.
Voice	The narrator's attitude toward the theme is clear.	The narrator's attitude toward the theme can be figured out.	The narrator's attitude toward the theme is hard to figure out.	The narrator doesn't show any particular attitude toward the theme.
Word Choice	Vivid words are used throughout the story.	Most paragraphs use vivid words.	One or two paragraphs use vivid words.	Words are plain and basic.
Sentence Fluency	Sentences are varied. Dialogue is realistic.	Most paragraphs have varied sentences. Dialogue is mostly realistic.	The writer has made a few attempts to vary sentences and write realistic dialogue.	All sentences are of one length. Dialogue doesn't seem realistic.
Conventions	Quotation marks enclose spoken words. Spelling, punctuation, and capitalization are correct.	There are a couple of mistakes in punctuation, spelling, or capitalization.	There are a many mistakes in punctuation, spelling, and capitalization.	Mistakes in conventions make the writing hard to understand.

Unit 4 • Literary Writing • 221

Ch. 14 **Write a Story**

 Edit

Edit Your Story. Edit the revised copy of your story. The following questions will help you decide what to change, remove, or leave in place.

Conventions
- ❏ Did you capitalize proper nouns?
- ❏ Did you enclose characters' spoken words in quotation marks?
- ❏ Did you use either the present tense or the past tense consistently?
- ❏ Did you use apostrophes correctly to form contractions?
- ❏ Did you use a comma when joining sentences with a coordinating conjunction?
- ❏ Did you use a comma when beginning a sentence with an introductory element?
- ❏ Did you correct spelling mistakes, either with a friend's help or by using a dictionary?

PUBLISH

Presentation. Prepare your descriptive paragraph for publication by writing or typing the final, edited copy.

Publish Your Story. Here are ideas for publishing your work.
- ❏ Submit your story to a magazine or Web site that publishes the writing of young people.
- ❏ Work with classmates to create a self-published collection of stories.
- ❏ Read your story aloud to the class.
- ❏ Display your story on a bulletin board in class.
- ❏ Read your story to an elderly person who would enjoy a visit from you.
- ❏ Post a copy of your story to your personal Web page.
- ❏ Create a podcast of your story.

222 • **The Writer's Studio**   Level A

Write a Story Ch. 14

Evaluate Your Story

Your teacher will either assess your story, ask you to self-assess your story, or ask you to switch with a partner and assess each other's work.

Evaluate the Model Story

Work with a partner to evaluate the following model story. Use the rubric on page 221 and write your score here: _____. In a class discussion, explain the score that you gave.

Today is the Day

"Today's the day," said DeShawn. "I'm gonna sit at Raneese's table at lunch."

Marcos laughed. "Raneese doesn't know you exist. You're gonna sit there, eat your bologna sandwich, and then the bell will ring. And Raneese *still* won't know you exist."

"Today's the day," repeated DeShawn stubbornly.

At last lunchtime arrived. In the cafeteria, DeShawn casually approached Raneese's table. He slid into an empty chair. No one gave him a glance. He rattled his brown paper bag, pulling out a sandwich, a cup of chocolate pudding, a plastic spoon, and an orange. Raneese and her friends remained deep in conversation.

Marcos dropped into the remaining empty seat. "What's up, DeShawn?" he said loudly.

DeShawn glared at him and picked up the pudding. He pulled the plastic top off, paying more attention to Raneese than to his food.

Unit 4 • Literary Writing • 223

Ch. 14 Write a Story

Raneese was saying, "And then I saw my sister holding hands with some goofball from our class, I think his name is Marcos. I mean, how embarrassing is that? I would just *die*."

Marcos's mouth fell open and his face flushed red.

DeShawn clamped his mouth shut, but laughter escaped as a loud snorting sound through his nose. Not only that, but chocolate pudding spewed out of his nose along with the snorting laughter. It sprayed across the lunch table.

With horror, DeShawn looked at Raneese. She was staring at him, her eyes narrowed into slits. A glob of chocolate pudding rested on the tip of her nose.

"Today *is* the day, man!" Marcos said brightly to DeShawn. "Raneese finally knows you exist!"

Chapter 15

Write a Poem

Poems have the power to tap into our emotions quickly and often surprisingly. Because poems can be so powerful, many people assume that they cannot write poetry. They think it takes a special talent or a lot of training. But the truth is, anyone can write a poem if he or she has something to express. Putting thoughts and feelings into lines and stanzas, instead of into sentences and paragraphs, is easier than you might think. This chapter will show you how. You'll study a model poem about fear, and you'll write a poem about an emotion of your choice. First, read the six traits of an effective poem. How are these traits different from the ones you studied in Chapter 14, Write a Story?

Six Traits of a Poem

Ideas	The poem is unified by one theme.
Organization	The words or sentences are arranged in lines and stanzas.
Voice	The writer or main character shines through as a real person with an interesting attitude toward the theme.
Word Choice	Words and figurative language create vivid pictures and emotions for the reader.
Sentence Fluency	Lines and stanzas of the poem have a rhythm that draws in the reader.
Conventions	The writer's use of capitalization, punctuation, and spelling is consistent.

Unit 4 • Literary Writing • 225

Ch. 15 Write a Poem

In the following poem, the writer uses figurative language to express emotions of fear and triumph.

> Night Fright
>
> Darker than a shadow, quiet as a whisper,
> it came.
> The floorboard cried out to warn me.
> My heart was a jackhammer.
> Like a soldier in panic, I grabbed my weapon.
> I pushed the button and . . . light
> from my flashlight filled the room.
> The night fright was banished.

Give It a Try: Examine the Model Poem

Answer the following questions about six traits in the model poem above. Write your answers on separate paper. Then discuss your responses with classmates.

1. **Ideas.** What word or phrase would you choose to express the theme of the poem?

2. **Organization.**
   a. How many stanzas does this poem have?
   b. How many lines does this poem have?

3. **Voice and word choice.** List three examples of figurative language used in the poem.

4. **Sentence fluency.** The writer uses only short sentences in the poem. Do you think this strategy creates a smooth or a choppy rhythm? Explain.

5. **Conventions.** List two rules of capitalization that the writer follows.

226 • The Writer's Studio   Level A

Write a Poem Ch. 15

Your Turn to Write: Compose a Poem

Now you'll write your own poem. Read the assignment carefully and follow the strategies and instructions for each stage of the writing process.

Assignment

The fund-raising committee at your school is putting together a poetry booklet to sell to school families. The booklet will be called *Tsunami of Emotion*, and it will contain poems written by students. The poems will be illustrated with sketches and photographs, also by students. For the booklet, write a poem of around 15 lines in which you

- express a strong emotion about a subject of your choice
- use at least three examples of figurative language
- use rhyming or nonrhyming lines, as you choose

Prewrite

Analyze the Prompt. What does the prompt tell you about your goals for this assignment? Read the assignment closely to find answers to the following questions. Write your answers on separate paper.

1. What is the purpose of this poem?
2. Who is the audience for this poem?
3. How long does the poem need to be?

Choose a Topic and Gather Ideas. What emotion will you choose for the theme of your poem? Explore different emotions while completing the following table about figures of speech. By the time you've completed the table, you'll have at least one great idea for a poem.

Unit 4 • Literary Writing • **227**

Ch. 15 **Write a Poem**

Similes

A simile makes a comparison by using the word *like*, *as*, or *than*.

Like a frightened cat, she dug her nails into my arm.
His mood was **as** dark **as** a thundercloud.
To me, you are more valuable **than** diamonds.

Write two similes of your own to express how you (or someone else) feels or shows emotions. 1. 2.	3. List ideas for poems that could use one or more of these similes. Example: *a poem about being afraid*

Metaphors

A metaphor makes a comparison indirectly by saying that one thing *is* the other thing.

That puppy **was** the sun coming into my world.
Your voice **is** music to my heart.
I **am** a *T.rex*; hear me roar!

Write two metaphors of your own to express emotions. 4. 5.	6. List ideas for poems that could use one or more of these metaphors. Example: *a poem about how much I love my puppy*

228 • The Writer's Studio   Level A

Write a Poem   Ch. 15

Personification

Personification is a figure of speech in which nonhuman things are given human qualities.

> The night **wind sang** me a soothing lullaby.
> The soccer **ball jumped** out of the closet and **shouted**, "Let's play!"
> The silent **phone stared** at me, **mocking** my loneliness.

Write two sentences that use personification to express an emotion.

7.

8.

9. List ideas for poems that could use personification. Example: *a poem about feeling lonely before I met my best friend*

Organize Ideas and Details. You can organize ideas and thoughts about your theme by writing a paragraph. Doing this allows you to get ideas down on paper without worrying about the form of the poem yet. Here is an example of one writer's paragraph about anger. He used the first-person point of view and spoke directly to the person who angered him.

> I was mad when you hung up the phone and wouldn't talk to me. I felt rejected. I felt unloved. I felt unimportant. That night, it rained really hard. I felt like the sky was expressing my emotions. The next morning, I woke up to hear birds singing. They sounded so bright and cheerful. They sounded like sunlight, if that had a sound. I realized that nature was expressing my emotions again. I am bright and sunny today.

Unit 4 • Literary Writing • 229

Ch. 15 **Write a Poem**

Write a Paragraph. Now you try it. Write a paragraph to express a strong emotion. Be sure to use a few examples of figurative language.

 Draft

At this point, you have chosen a theme for your poem: one of the emotions from the table on figurative language. You have gathered ideas to express in the poem by writing a paragraph. Now you're ready to arrange your words and sentences in lines and stanzas.

You can start by taking the sentences from your paragraph and writing them as a list, like this:

> I was mad when you hung up the phone and wouldn't talk to me.
> I felt rejected.
> I felt unloved.
> I felt unimportant.
> That night, it rained really hard.
> I felt like the sky was expressing my emotions.
> The next morning, I woke up to hear birds singing.
> They sounded so bright and cheerful.
> They sounded like sunlight, if that had a sound.
> I realized that nature was expressing my emotions again.
> I am bright and sunny today.

As you can see, this work is beginning to look and sound more like a poem already.

230 • The Writer's Studio   Level A

Write a Poem   Ch. 15

Arrange Your Ideas in Lines and Stanzas. Now it's your turn. Arrange the sentences in your paragraph in a list like the one on the previous page.

Revise

To revise your poem, you'll need to strip away unnecessary words, leaving the bare bones of your ideas. You may need to shift some words onto different lines or change line breaks. You may want to add words or group lines into stanzas.

Here is how the writer of the poem about anger revised his work. The circled words are instructions to himself.

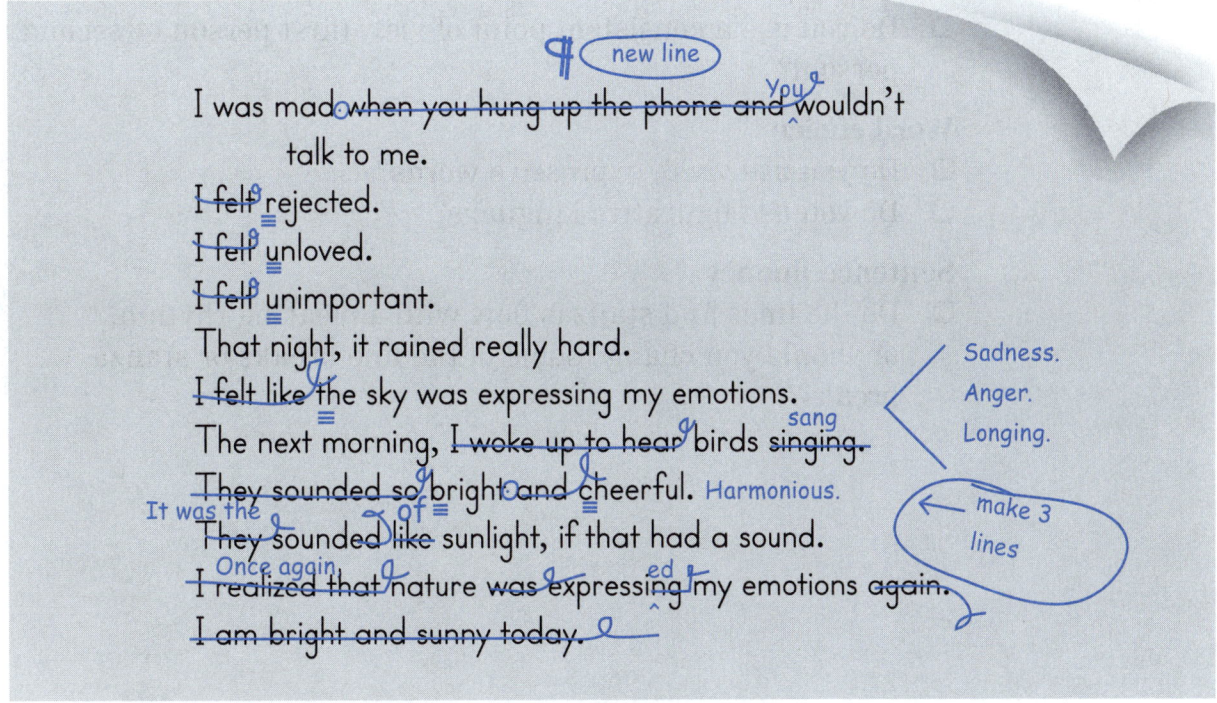

To see the final version of the poem without the revision marks to distract you, turn to page 237.

Unit 4 • Literary Writing • 231

Ch. 15 **Write a Poem**

Strengthen Your Poem. Make your poem stronger by cutting unnecessary words, adding new or vivid word choices, and making line breaks and stanzas, as you choose. The work you are doing now will help your poem shine as an example of expressive poetry.

Revise Your Poem. Revise your poem again, this time using the checklist below. In addition, the Poem Rubric that follows the checklist will help you judge the strength of your poem.

Ideas
- ❑ Is the poem unified by one theme?
- ❑ Does the poem have a title that hints at the theme?

Organization
- ❑ Are the words and sentences arranged in lines and stanzas?

Voice
- ❑ Is the speaker's voice interesting and expressive?
- ❑ Do you use a consistent point of view (first person or second person)?

Word choice
- ❑ Do you use vivid, expressive words?
- ❑ Do you use figurative language?

Sentence fluency
- ❑ Do the lines and stanzas flow with a pleasing rhythm, or should you change some of the line breaks or stanza breaks?

Poem Rubric

	4 Strong	3 Effective	2 Developing	1 Beginning
Ideas	The poem is unified by one theme.	The theme is clear, but some details do not relate.	The writer is beginning to make the theme clear.	The theme is not clear. Most details seem unrelated.
Organization	The words are effectively arranged in lines and stanzas.	The words are arranged in lines and stanzas; some line breaks are awkward.	The words are arranged in lines and stanzas, but the effect is awkward.	The words are arranged in a paragraph.
Voice	The speaker's emotions are clear and interesting.	The speaker's emotions are clear but don't consistently draw in the reader.	The emotions are weak; they don't consistently draw in the reader.	No clear emotions are expressed, making it hard to connect to the poem.
Word Choice	Vivid words and figurative language help the reader feel the emotions.	Vivid words and figurative language help the reader feel some of the emotions.	One or two vivid words and examples of figurative language are used.	Words are plain and basic. No figurative language is used.
Sentence Fluency	Lines and stanzas have a rhythm that draws in the reader.	Lines and stanzas have a rhythm, but a few breaks are awkward.	Lines and stanzas have many awkward breaks.	There is no clear pattern or rhythm.
Conventions	Capitalization is consistent. Punctuation and spelling are correct.	There are a few mistakes in capitalization, punctuation, or spelling.	There are many mistakes in capitalization, punctuation, and spelling.	Mistakes in conventions make the poem hard to understand.

Write a Poem Ch. 15

Ch. 15 **Write a Poem**

 **Edit**

You may have heard that poetry breaks the conventions of writing. Poems don't always use complete sentences, for example. Poets may choose to capitalize words that are not normally capitalized—or not to use capitalization at all.

It is true that some poems don't follow all the conventions of writing. However, writing poetry is not an excuse for breaking all the rules. To help your reader understand your work, it's best to use the conventions of writing. If you do break a rule, do so for a reason.

The following mini-lesson explains some rules of capitalization and how these rules apply to writing poetry.

Mini-Lesson: Capitalization in Poetry

When you write a poem, it's safe to follow the basic rules of capitalization, including these:

➡ Capitalize proper nouns and proper adjectives.
   examples: Paul Revere, Friday, French accent

➡ Capitalize the first word of a sentence.
   example: I was mad. You wouldn't talk to me.

➡ Capitalize the first word in a direct quotation.
   example: The sun said, "Good morning!"

➡ Capitalize the pronoun *I*.
   example: Like a soldier in panic, I grabbed my weapon.

In addition, you may choose to follow this guideline:

→ Capitalize the first word in a line of poetry.

   example: **I** was mad.
                You wouldn't talk to me.
                Rejected
                Unloved
                Unimportant

Give It a Try: Add Capitalization to a Poem

The following poem uses the same words as the model poem on page 226, but all capitalization has been removed. In addition, this version has different line breaks. How would you capitalize this version of the poem?

Use editing marks to show which words you would capitalize. Then explain your choices in a class discussion.

    darker than a shadow,
    quiet as a whisper.
    it came.
    the floorboard cried out
    to warn me.
    my heart was a jackhammer.
    like a soldier in panic,
    i grabbed my weapon.
    i pushed the button and . . .
    light from my flashlight
    filled the room.
    the night fright
    was banished.

Give It a Try: Edit Your Poem for Capitalization

Review your poem, paying close attention to capitalization. Add or change capital letters, as you choose. Then, in a class discussion, explain your choices.

Ch. 15 **Write a Poem**

Edit Your Poem. Edit the revised copy of your poem. The following questions will help you decide what to change, remove, or leave in place.

Conventions
- ❏ Did you follow the basic rules of capitalization?
- ❏ Did you enclose characters' spoken words in quotation marks?
- ❏ Did you use apostrophes correctly to form contractions?
- ❏ Did you correct spelling mistakes, either with a friend's help or by using a dictionary?

PUBLISH

Presentation. Prepare your descriptive paragraph for publication by writing or typing the final, edited copy.

Publish Your Poem. Here are ideas for publishing your work.
- ❏ Work with friends to create a poetry booklet. Enhance the themes of the poems by adding drawings and photographs. Finally, make copies for each person who is published in the booklet. Make additional copies for other friends and family members.
- ❏ Create a Web site where you and your friends can post your poetry for a public audience. Follow safety precautions for dealing with the public, which include not revealing your address or phone number.
- ❏ Plan a stand-up poetry night where you and others can stand before a friendly audience and read your poems aloud.
- ❏ Ask a friend to film you while you read your poem. Send a copy of the recording to a distant family member, post it to a safe Web site, or place a copy of it in your time capsule for this school year.

Evaluate Your Poem

Your teacher will either assess your poem, ask you to self-assess your poem, or ask you to switch with a partner and assess each other's work.

Write a Poem   Ch. 15

Evaluate the Model Poem

Work with a partner to evaluate the following model poem. Use the rubric on page 233 and write your score here: _____. In a class discussion, explain the score that you gave.

Full Circle

I was mad.
You wouldn't talk to me.
    Rejected
    Unloved
    Unimportant
That night, it rained really hard.
The sky was expressing my emotions.
    Sadness
    Anger
    Longing
The next morning, birds sang.
    Bright
    Cheerful
    Harmonious
It was the sound of sunlight.
Once again, nature expressed my emotions.

Chapter 16

Test Writing: The Narrative

Writing stories can be so much fun and so creative that you may wonder, "Why would a teacher ask me to write a narrative on a test?" As with other forms of writing, the narrative can be a showcase for your skills of using the traits of writing. In addition, you can write a narrative to show your understanding of, or your point of view on, a particular theme. For instance, after reading a story about characters who celebrate a cultural holiday, you may be asked to write a story that shows why cultural holidays are important. In this way, you share your knowledge and opinions through fiction instead of nonfiction.

The following table explains how the traits of writing relate to writing a narrative on a test.

Six Traits of a Narrative Test Essay

Ideas	The writer focuses on one main conflict to be resolved. Each scene and dialogue relates to this conflict.
Organization	The order of events is clear.
Voice	The writer uses a consistent narrative point of view. The tone fits with how the writer wants the reader to feel after reading the narrative.
Word Choice	The writer uses vivid words to help show action, feelings, thoughts, and so on.
Sentence Fluency	Sentences in dialogue show realistic speech patterns. Narrative sentences are complete.
Conventions	Quotation marks are used to begin and end a character's words. Proper nouns are capitalized. The present tense or past tense is used consistently. Spelling is correct.

Unit 4 • Literary Writing • 239

Ch. 16 **Test Writing: The Narrative**

Preparing to Write Your Test Essay

On a test, a narrative writing prompt may be linked to a passage that you read. For example, you may read about how Johnny Appleseed planted trees to help American pioneers live off the land. Then, the prompt may ask you to write a story about a time you did something to protect nature.

Another type of narrative prompt may stand alone instead of referring to a reading passage. The prompt in the box below is a stand-alone prompt.

Instructions
You have 45 minutes to complete the written composition. Read the prompt below. Then use separate paper to plan and draft your composition. Only your draft will be scored.

Writing Prompt
What kinds of family traditions do you or your friends have? Some traditions are built around food—pizza Friday or pancake Saturday. Other traditions are built around activities—collecting donations for charity or having a family reunion. Write a story that shows why family traditions are important. You can write about real or imaginary characters.

---

1. Study the Prompt
Take a few moments to study the prompt before you begin to write your response. Answer these important questions:

What is the purpose of the writing assignment? Scan the prompt for key words that tell you what kind of response to write.

Words That Signal a Narrative Response
narrative
story
characters

240 • The Writer's Studio   Level A

What should you write about? Study the prompt to determine exactly what you must write. As with other types of writing prompts, look for an *imperative sentence.* In the prompt on page 240, the imperative sentence is this one:

Write a story that shows why family traditions are an important part of life.

This sentence is your assignment in a nutshell. See if other sentences give you additional information about what to write. The imperative sentence above is followed by this sentence, which gives important information:

You can write about real or imaginary characters.

How much time do you have to write? The prompt on the previous page states that you have 45 minutes to write the narrative. If a prompt does not state a time limit, your teacher will tell you how long this testing period will last.

2. Plan Your Time

After studying the prompt, make a quick plan for how to use your time. If you have 45 minutes to write the test, you could use your time as follows:

10 minutes:	Study the prompt and do prewriting.
25 minutes:	Write the story.
10 minutes:	Revise and edit the story.

3. Prewrite

On a narrative test, you may be tempted to start writing the story and just make it up as you go along. However, the prewriting stage is too important to skip. By planning exactly what events to include in your story, and in what order, you give yourself many advantages. You save time. You are able to create a story with a clear beginning, middle, and end. You don't waste time writing scenes that don't move the story along. And you allow yourself time to revise and edit the story.

Ch. 16   **Test Writing: The Narrative**

 Within the limits of the assignment, choose a topic you care about. Your concern and enthusiasm for the topic will shine through. For instance, in choosing a family tradition, don't assume that it has to be a "normal" tradition. It could be offbeat, such as painting each other's toenails or doing yard work together.

Choose a topic. The writing prompt tells you to write about a family tradition, but it doesn't specify what tradition. Therefore, your first task is to choose a tradition to write about. Here is a three-step approach to choosing a topic:

1. Jot down a list of three to five traditions you know about.

2. Ask yourself, "Which tradition would best help me show the importance of family traditions in life?"

3. Circle the tradition that best answers the question in step 2. This is your topic.

Family Traditions

birthday—special meal, birthday cake, a new privilege each year

(family councils—monthly family night with pizza, to make decisions and plan things)

New Year's Eve—staying up until midnight and then taking a family photo at midnight

summer at the farm—all the cousins stay with Grandmother and Granddad at their farm during the first week of July

TOOLKIT

For planning a narrative, useful strategies include
- a timeline
- a beginning-middle-end table
- a story map (see page 216)

242 • The Writer's Studio   Level A

Test Writing: The Narrative — Ch. 16

Gather ideas and details. Next, select a strategy for choosing and organizing the characters and events of your story.

Beginning

<u>Setting</u>: Anya's house

<u>Characters</u>: Mom, Dad, Anya, Aaron

<u>What happens/the problem</u>: Anya wants to attend her friend's birthday party sleepover instead of staying home for the monthly family council.

Middle

<u>Main Event 1</u>: Anya decides to skip this month's family council.

<u>Main Event 2</u>: Anya gets ready to go to the party while the family gets ready for the family council.

<u>Main Event</u> 3: Anya realizes that the family council is her chance to have a say in what her family does, and to have her parents' undivided attention. She is not sure she wants to give this up.

End

<u>How Anya solves her problem</u>: She decides to stay home for family council night, and she'll plan her own sleepover for another time.

Writing Your Narrative Test Essay

Write the story and keep yourself on track by referring to your timeline, table, or story map. Your main goal is to get the story

Unit 4 • Literary Writing • **243**

Ch. 16 Test Writing: The Narrative

down on paper. However, since you won't have time to recopy the story neatly, use your best handwriting now. Leave margins around the sides of the paper, where you can write revisions.

Here are the opening paragraphs of the story about Anya and her family tradition. Notice that the writer
- follows her story map closely
- sets up the theme and conflict of the story right away
- uses dialogue to help move the story along
- makes a few mistakes in spelling, punctuation, and capitalization that she will fix later

> Anya's family tradition
>
> Anya walked slowly into the kichen where her mom was making a batch of brownies. She said, "Mom, I'm not comeing to the family council tonight."
>
> "What? her Mom said. It's a tradition that we have a family council on the third Friday night of every month. We order pizza, I make a really gooey dessert. And we all talk about the family decisions, *together*."
>
> "I know, Mom, but Maddys birthday-slumber party is tonight. I'm going to that instead. Its just down the street, so I don't need a ride." And Anya walked out of the kitchen to get ready for the party.

Polishing Your Narrative Test Essay

Use the final minutes of the test period to correct mistakes in capitalization, spelling, punctuation, and grammar. You might be tempted to skip this part of the writing process, especially when time is limited. However, polishing your draft helps your reader

244 • The Writer's Studio   Level A

Test Writing: The Narrative   Ch. 16

focus on your story instead of stumbling over misspelled words, incomplete sentences, or dialogue that gets lost because there are no quotation marks.

Here is how the writer corrected her opening paragraphs.

> Anya's family tradition
>
> Anya walked slowly into the kitchen where her mom was making a batch of brownies. She said, "Mom, I'm not coming to the family council tonight."
>
> "What?" her Mom said. "It's a tradition that we have a family council on the third Friday night of every month. We order pizza, I make a really gooey dessert. And we all talk about the family decisions, *together*."
>
> "I know, Mom, but Maddy's birthday-slumber party is tonight. I'm going to that instead. It's just down the street, so I don't need a ride." And Anya walked out of the kitchen to get ready for the party.

Evaluating a Narrative Test Essay

When teachers evaluate a narrative test, they will be looking to see if you
- wrote to the prompt
- included only relevant details in an organized manner
- followed conventions of capitalization, spelling, punctuation, and grammar

Unit 4 • Literary Writing • **245**

Ch. 16 Test Writing: The Narrative

The following rubric shows guidelines for evaluating a narrative written for a test.

Narrative Test Essay Rubric

	4 Strong	**3 Effective**	**2 Developing**	**1 Beginning**
Ideas	The work is unified by one theme.	The theme is clear, but some details do not relate.	The writer is beginning to make the theme clear.	The theme is not clear. Most details seem unrelated.
Organization	The order of actions/thoughts is clear.	Most details follow a logical order.	Organization of details is awkward.	Actions or thoughts are in random order.
Voice	The narrator's attitude toward the theme is clear.	The narrator's attitude toward the theme can be figured out.	The narrator's attitude toward the theme is hard to figure out.	The narrator doesn't show any particular attitude toward the theme.
Word Choice	Many vivid words are used.	A few vivid words are used.	One or two vivid words are used.	Words are plain and basic.
Sentence Fluency	Sentences are varied. Dialogue is realistic.	Most paragraphs have varied sentences. Dialogue is mostly realistic.	The writer has made a few attempts to vary sentences and write realistic dialogue.	All sentences are of one length. Dialogue doesn't seem realistic.
Conventions	Quotation marks enclose spoken words. Spelling and capitalization are correct.	There are a couple of mistakes in punctuation, spelling, or capitalization.	There are a many mistakes in punctuation, spelling, and capitalization.	Mistakes in conventions make the writing hard to understand.

Evaluate a Model Narrative Test Essay

Work with a partner to evaluate the following model narrative. Reread the prompt on page 240 and use the rubric above. Write your

Test Writing: The Narrative   Ch. 16

score here: _____. In a class discussion, explain the score that you gave.

Anya's family tradition

Anya walked slowly into the kitchen where her mom was making a batch of brownies. She said, "Mom, I'm not coming to the family council tonight."

"What?" her Mom said. "It's a tradition that we have a family council on the third Friday night of every month. We order pizza, I make a really gooey dessert. And we all talk about the family decisions, *together*.

"I know, Mom, but Maddy's birthday-slumber party is tonight. I'm going to that instead. It's just down the street, so I don't need a ride." And Anya walked out of the kitchen to get ready for the party.

When Aaron got home from baseball practice he shouted, "Hey, everybody! I say we get pepperoni pizza tonight!" Anya continued brushing her hair. When her dad got home he called out, "Hey, everybody! Wait till you hear about this idea I have for a weekend family trip." Anya continued applying her lip gloss. Her lips were bright, but her heart was heavy.

When Anya was ready to leave for the party, she stepped out of her room. No one had come to check on her, and no one had tried to convince her to stay for the family council. She felt disappointed. She looked into the living room. Her family was gathered already, without her. There were plates and cups and brownies set out. Dad was flipping through some colorful travel brochures. Aaron was sorting

Unit 4 • **Literary Writing** • 247

Ch. 16 Test Writing: The Narrative

pizza coupons. Mom was opening up the calendar where they wrote down all their family plans.

Suddenly, Anya wanted to be part of the scene in the living room more than anything else in the world. Maddy was a good friend, but this was her family. She loved the feeling of belonging that she felt during family traditions like this one. Tonight, that was more important than a party.

Anya walk~~s~~ed quickly into the room and ~~sits~~ sat down on the big floor pillow where she always ~~sits~~ sat. She opened her mouth to explain things to Mom, but Mom just smiled broadly and said, "Tonight is Anya's night to open the family council. Anya, take it away!"

Write a Narrative Test Essay

Are you ready to write your own narrative in a testlike situation? Practice what you have learned by completing the following assignment.

Instructions
You have 45 minutes to complete the written composition. Read the prompt below. Then use separate paper to plan and draft your composition. Only your draft will be scored.

Writing Prompt
Each of us experiences unfair treatment, but what matters is how we handle the situation. Write a story about a time when you were treated unfairly and how you reacted. Be sure that your story has a beginning, a middle, and an end.

Literary Writing Wrap-Up

The activities and information in these pages will help you continue to strengthen your literary writing skills. In You Be the Judge, use the Literary Writing Rubric to evaluate a student's work. The Ideas for Writing are additional literary writing prompts you can use for practice. And finally, in the Unit 4 Reflections, list important ideas you have learned in this unit and set goals for future learning.

You Be the Judge

Use what you've learned about the traits of literary writing to evaluate a student's work. First, review the traits of literary writing on page 193. Next, read the student's work printed below. Finally, in the rubric that follows, assign the work a score for each writing trait. In the space provided, explain each score that you assign.

At Attention
by Elizabeth D., Palm Bay, FL

As I boarded the plane, a thousand thoughts spun crazily through my head. My brother was leaving. He would never again look normal on a swing acting just plain stupid with me, make silly faces when my mom was lecturing, or tell me about his school crush. He was entering a new phase of his life, and it seemed I wouldn't share in it as I did now. That bothered me. This fact was so foreign it made me want to freeze time and stay his little sister forever.

He had always been my source of strength. Who is my brother, really? Is he the political nut that everyone calls him at school, or the guy who snuck to the roof to watch sunsets with me? He represents strength, never-ending love, and especially faith. I was so proud of him and so excited about where he was going, but part of me wished I could go with him.

When my dad and I arrived for the swearing-in ceremony, the auditorium was enormous, the stage was filled with flags representing different military branches, and in the middle was the largest of all: the American flag in its full glory. It stood rigidly, blazing red, white, and blue.

My brother looked different, confident. I wasn't even looking into his face; I was observing the way he stood and marched into the auditorium, with his back straight and chin up, with a newly acquired sense of purpose and direction. His shaved head made him look different, but his uniform was spiffy. The moment I saw him I wanted to run and give him the biggest hug and kiss, but I was restrained by my dad. I contented myself by looking at the lines of identical men raising their right hands and signing over the next five years of their lives in service to their country. I wondered if they were scared and uncertain and if they knew what they were doing.

After what seemed like forever, the swearing-in ended and the officer in front yelled a blood-curdling "At ease." My dad had his head turned, probably to hide tears. I raced out of my seat and hugged my brother. When I finally let him go, I noticed a difference in his face. Yes, on the surface he was out of breath from my suffocating hug, but he looked gruff and very military. And if you looked even deeper, his brown eyes quivered and moved with excitement.

I was getting it slowly; he knew who he was and where he was going. His future was uncertain, but he had taken the first steps. And those steps carried him past the double doors and yelling officers, past childhood, into the Navy, and then—who knows—the rest of his life.

Literary Writing Rubric

	4 Strong	3 Effective	2 Developing	1 Beginning
Ideas Score _____	*explanation:*			
organization Score _____	*explanation:*			
voice Score _____	*explanation:*			
word choice Score _____	*explanation:*			
sentence fluency Score _____	*explanation:*			
conventions Score _____	*explanation:*			

Unit 4

Ideas for Writing

The assignments on this page will give you additional practice with literary writing. Your teacher may choose one or let you pick one that's most interesting to you.

1. From time to time, most people learn surprising truths about themselves. They may realize that they are an outstanding athlete, or that they have a serious character flaw. They may suddenly see themselves through another person's eyes—and not like what they see. Write a personal narrative of around 400 words in which you tell the story of how you learned a surprising truth about yourself.

2. Campfire stories—tales told around a campfire—can be funny or scary, but they always keep people interested. Write a 300-word story that you could tell to your friends around a campfire. Be sure to use a consistent voice to help your readers feel like laughing in delight or screaming in fright.

3. Combine your skills of storytelling and writing poetry by writing a narrative poem. Like a story, a narrative poem tells a series of events involving characters and conflict. It can contain dialogue, too. Unlike a story, a narrative poem is arranged in lines and stanzas. The poem, like the poem you write in Chapter 15, expresses ideas vividly, without unnecessary words. It may use rhyming words, or it may not. Using this information, write a poem that tells the story of an important event in your life.

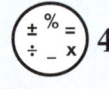 4. A science fiction story uses the ideas of science to tell about events or places that could exist, but don't (a moon colony, for example, or robot babysitters). Use ideas that you are learning in science class to write a science fiction story for your classmates. Be sure to unify the story around one conflict that must be solved, and use interesting characters and dialogue. Your story should be approximately 400 words long.

252 • The Writer's Studio   Level A

Unit 4 Reflections

How are you different as a writer now that you have completed this unit on literary writing? What new knowledge do you have? How is your writing stronger? What kinds of things could you work on to become even stronger as a literary writer? Use the following space to reflect on your work in this unit and to set goals for the future.

Focus on Me: My Achievements as a Literary Writer

What I've learned about literary writing in this unit:

Ways my literary writing is stronger now:

Things I can do to practice my skills of literary writing:

Unit 5

Response to Literature

The Unit at a Glance
Get to Know the Genre 255
Ch. 17 Respond to a Narrative 259
Ch. 18 Respond to a Poem 273
Ch. 19 Respond to a Document-Based Question 285
Ch. 20 Test Writing: The Critical-Lens Essay 299
Response to Literature Wrap-Up 308

Get to Know the Genre: Response to Literature

One of the most common forms of writing assigned to students is the response to literature. A **response to literature** examines a character, a theme, the plot, or another part of a story, novel, or poem. The purpose of writing a response to literature is to explain key ideas that you have about the work. Writing about literature also helps you understand the work better, because as you explore ideas on paper, you learn to think about the work in different ways.

To write an effective response to literature, pay close attention to the six traits of writing. These are the characteristics that make your writing strong and help your reader understand and feel interested in your ideas about literature.

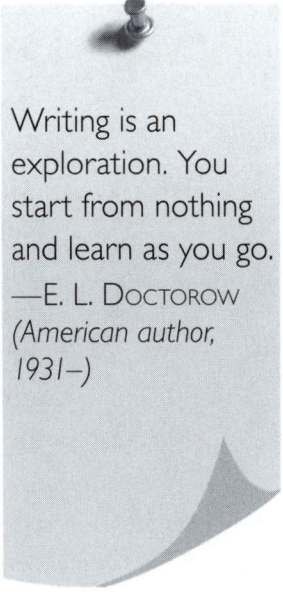

Writing is an exploration. You start from nothing and learn as you go.
—E. L. DOCTOROW
(American author, 1931–)

Unit 5

Six Traits of a Response to Literature

Ideas	The topic is narrowed to a specific character, theme, or other aspect of the literary work. Each detail clearly relates.
Organization	The response has a beginning, a middle, and an end. Details follow a logical order.
Voice	The writer uses an objective, knowledgeable tone.
Word Choice	Vivid, accurate words are used.
Sentence Fluency	A variety of sentence types and structures creates a pleasing rhythm to the writing.
Conventions	Capitalization, spelling, punctuation, and grammar are correct.

Real-World Example

Many responses to literature are written for a class or a test in school. Other responses are written for publication in magazines, journals, newspapers, Web sites, and other public sources. The character sketch on the next page is taken from the chapter "Modern Fantasy" in a book about literature for young people. In the character sketch, the writer explains how the main character of a novel changes over time.

Ideas: the title and author of the book

Ideas: the subject of this character sketch

Word choice: vivid noun

Sentence fluency: transition

Organization: chronological order of events that shape the character

Conventions: Tricky words are spelled correctly.

Voice: The writer uses the third-person point of view.

Organization: A closing sentence summarizes the character.

In chronicling the year-long survival of a mouse on an island, William Steig firmly establishes himself as a superb author as well as illustrator. *Abel's Island* details the survival of Abel, a very Victorian mouse, who is trapped on an island after being caught in a torrential rainstorm. Left on his own, this rodent Crusoe finds a hollow log and learns to feed off the land. In addition to battling physical elements, he overcomes the psychological fears of loneliness and overwhelming despair. Finally, after almost a year of foraging for himself, Abel is able, and easily swims the distance to shore. Creating more than a mouse melodrama, Steig shows us what qualities help a mouse or person survive. Abel relies on his resourcefulness, but he is kept alive by his love for his wife Amanda, his art, his friendship with a forgetful frog, and his joy of life.

Give It a Try: Examine the Real-World Example

Can you find additional examples of the traits of good writing in the model character sketch above? On separate paper, list three traits of good writing. For each one, quote or describe an example from the model.

Get Ready to Write

Now that you've explored the qualities of literary-response writing, you're ready to write some responses of your own. In the chapters that follow, you'll respond to a story, a poem, and a group of historical documents, and you'll also write about literature by examining a meaningful quotation. You'll use the stages of the writing process—prewriting, drafting, revising, editing, and publishing—and you'll be presented with models and mini-lessons along the way.

As you work through these chapters, you can enrich your understanding by trying the suggestions below. These tips will help you connect what you're learning in this unit to your own life and the world around you.

LEARNING TIPS

- Collect interesting and inspiring quotations from songs, movies, friends, speeches, and literature. Choose your favorites and write personal responses to them.

- After watching a movie with friends, have a discussion in which you explain your responses to a character or theme.

- Watch for assignments in other classes that ask for your written response. For example, a history assignment may ask you to write a response to a speech by Abraham Lincoln. A science assignment may ask you to respond to a biography of Albert Einstein or to the story of an invention.

Chapter 17

Respond to a Narrative

Have you ever tried to describe your best friend to someone who hasn't met this friend? Perhaps you described the friend's character traits or what it's like to hang out with him or her. In doing this, you were creating a character sketch. In that case, you were responding to a real live person. In a similar way, you can respond to characters in fiction. You might explain how they change during a narrative, how they relate to other people, or what their personality is like. A well-developed essay might do all three of these things. A paragraph-length response focuses on just one aspect of the character.

Why write a response to a literary character? For one thing, you share your conclusions about the character, based on details you see in the story. In addition, you may help readers understand the story better or learn from the story. Key traits of a well-written response are explained in the table below.

Six Traits of a Response to a Narrative

Ideas	The topic is narrowed to a specific character, theme, or other part of the literary work. Each detail clearly relates.
Organization	The response has a beginning, a middle, and an end. Details follow a logical order.
Voice	The writer uses an objective, knowledgeable tone.
Word Choice	Vivid, accurate words are used.
Sentence Fluency	A variety of sentence types and structures creates a pleasing rhythm to the writing.
Conventions	Capitalization, spelling, punctuation, and grammar are correct.

Unit 5 • Response to Literature • **259**

Ch. 17 Respond to a Narrative

In the response to literature below, the writer focuses on Sahara, a character in a novel. The writer's goal is to show how Sahara's actions and choices reveal her personality.

> In *Sahara Special*, Esmé Raji Codell tells the story of the spirited yet self-conscious Sahara Jones. After a heartbreak, Sahara must decide whether to hide from life or to find her own inner strength. Sahara devours books and loves to write, yet she refuses to do her schoolwork. She is in a world of her own, trying to cope with her dad's abandonment. Sahara ends up in a special-education program, and other kids call her Sahara Special. But Sahara is a survivor. When her mom gets her moved back to a regular classroom, Sahara is thrilled. But she is too afraid and self-conscious to speak out or participate in class. Instead, she watches and listens to the unusual teacher, Miss Pointy. Sahara soaks up new words, new ideas, and new courage. With new bravery, Sahara uses her writing and imagination to break free of her cocoon of self-protection.

Give It a Try: Examine the Model Paragraph

Answer the following questions about six traits in the model paragraph. Write your answers on separate paper. Then, in a class discussion, explain your answers.

1. **Ideas.**

    a. What is the title of the work of literature?

    b. Who is the author of the work of literature?

    c. Who is the subject of this character sketch?

260 • The Writer's Studio   Level A

Respond to a Narrative Ch. 17

2. **Organization.** Explain the writer's method of organizing the paragraph.

3. **Voice and word choice.** List three word choices that stand out as vivid or interesting.

4. **Sentence fluency.** Copy the introductory elements of three different sentences.

5. **Conventions.** Write the base word in each of the following words from the paragraph.

   a. abandonment

   b. education

   c. survivor

Your Turn to Write: Respond to a Narrative

Now you'll write your own response to a narrative. Read the assignment carefully and follow the strategies and instructions for each stage of the writing process.

Assignment

Choose a character from a story or novel that you think your classmates would want to know about. Write a character sketch of 100–150 words in which you explain the character's personality *or* explain the character's relationship with others. Be sure to include

- the title of the work of literature
- the author of the work of literature
- the name of the character you are examining
- supporting examples from the narrative

Unit 5 • Response to Literature • **261**

Ch. 17 Respond to a Narrative

Prewrite

Analyze the Prompt. What does the prompt tell you about your goals for this assignment? Read the assignment closely to find answers to the following questions. Write your answers on separate paper.

1. What is the purpose of this response to literature?
2. Who is the audience for this response to literature?
3. How long does the response need to be?

Choose a Topic. Make a list of stories and novels that you have enjoyed reading. Next to each title, write the name of a memorable character from that narrative. Which character has a personality that you would like to explain? Which character has an interesting way of relating to other characters?

Circle the name of the character who will be the focus of your character sketch.

Gather Ideas and Details. Create a character map like the one below to gather ideas and details for your character sketch.

Character's name	
Title and author of work in which he/she/it appears	
Human or animal? Briefly describe.	
Age	

262 • The Writer's Studio   Level A

Respond to a Narrative   Ch. 17

Personality	
Strengths	
Weaknesses	
Problems	
Other details	

Organize Ideas and Details. Use a beginning-middle-end table to organize the information to include in your character sketch. In the example table on the next page, the writer has organized details for a paragraph about a character named Jonathan.

Unit 5 • Response to Literature • **263**

Ch. 17 **Respond to a Narrative**

Beginning

character: Jonathan

title: "The Writer in the Family"

author: E. L. Doctorow

topic sentence: Jonathan relates to others by trying to please them.

Middle

Example 1: Jonathan agrees to write letters from his dead father.

Example 2: Jonathan is dishonest to please Aunt Frances.

Example 3: Jonathan realizes that he is trying to please others for no good reason.

End

Final thought: Jonathan decides to stop being dishonest and be true to himself instead.

 Draft

When writing a response to literature, let your interest in the topic shine through. At the same time, use an objective, knowledgeable tone. A few strategies will help you do this.

- Use vivid yet accurate nouns and verbs. For example, write "rat" instead of "rodent."

Respond to a Narrative　　Ch. 17

- Use specific names rather than descriptions. For example, write "Miss Pointy" instead of "her teacher."
- Use the third-person point of view.

Write Your Response to Literature. Write your character sketch, using the beginning-middle-end table to guide you. For reference, examine the sample rough draft below. The writer has jotted a few notes about revisions to do in the next stage of writing.

Jonathan, the main character in "The Writer in the Family" by E. L. Doctorow, relates to other people by trying to please them. In the end, he realizes that this is not the best way to live life. In the beginning of the story, Jonathan's father has just died. The family doesn't want to tell the father's mother that he died, because she is so old and fragile. So they tell the old woman that Jonathan's father has moved to Arizona for his health. Then, Jonathan's aunt asks him to write letters to the grandmother, pretending to be his father. Eager to please, Jonathan writes a few letters. As he tries to come up with stuff to write about, he starts to understand his father better. He comes to realize that his father lived his life trying to please others, and everyone took him for granted. Jonathan decides that he is done with trying to please others when they don't appreciate it. To show his new way of relating to people, he writes a letter to the grandmother (pretending to be his father) saying that he is dying. This will be the last letter. Jonathan's aunt is angry with him for this letter, but Jonathan knows that he was true to himself.

Focus on relationship to others, *not on a change in character.*

Delete details that just retell the plot. Give details only about relationship to others.

Use the aunt's name, not just "aunt."

Unit 5 • Response to Literature • **265**

Ch. 17 **Respond to a Narrative**

 **Revise**

At this point, you have the rough draft of your character sketch. You may have jotted down some notes about things that need to be revised. Now it's time to make changes—large or small—to make the paragraph as strong as possible. For example, add sentence variety by combining sentences or adding introductory elements. Remove details that distract the reader from your purpose for writing. The checklist and rubric below will help you decide what changes to make to strengthen your character sketch.

Revise Your Response to Literature. Use this checklist and the Response to Literature Rubric to revise your paragraph.

Ideas
- ❏ Does the paragraph focus on *one* of these: the character's personality or the character's manner of relating to others?
- ❏ Do you express your main idea in a topic sentence?
- ❏ Does each detail help to explain your main idea?

Organization
- ❏ Do you arrange the details in a logical order, such as time order or order of importance?

Voice
- ❏ Find two examples of third-person pronouns. Write *third person* above each one.
- ❏ Look for first-person pronouns (such as *I* and *me*). If you find any, revise them to the third-person point of view instead.

Word choice
- ❏ Circle two vivid, accurate words that clarify your ideas.

Sentence fluency
- ❏ Have you used a few different kinds of sentence openers?
- ❏ Have you used a few different sentence types (simple, compound, complex)?

Respond to a Narrative Ch. 17

Response to Literature Rubric

	4 Strong	3 Effective	2 Developing	1 Beginning
Ideas	One topic is explained. Each detail clearly relates.	The topic is clear, but some details do not relate.	The writer is beginning to make the topic clear.	The topic is not clear. Most details do not relate.
Organization	Details follow a logical order.	Most details follow a logical order.	Organization of details is awkward.	Details are in random order.
Voice	The voice is interesting and reliable throughout the response.	The voice is interesting and reliable in most of the response.	The tone is interesting or reliable in a few sentences.	The tone is flat or mechanical, making it hard to connect to the writer.
Word Choice	Vivid, accurate words are used to express key ideas.	Vivid, accurate words are used to express most key ideas.	Vivid, accurate words are used to express one or two key ideas.	Vocabulary is limited. Some words are used incorrectly.
Sentence Fluency	A variety of sentence types is used in a pleasing rhythm.	A variety of sentence types is used, but some may be awkward.	Sentences are complete but are mostly short and simple.	Sentences are mostly short and simple or are incomplete.
Conventions	Capitalization, spelling, punctuation, and grammar are correct.	Few errors in capitalization, spelling, punctuation, or grammar are present.	Errors in capitalization, spelling, punctuation, and grammar do not prevent the reader from understanding.	Errors in capitalization, spelling, punctuation, and grammar make it hard to understand the writing.

Ch. 17 **Respond to a Narrative**

 Edit

You have made the big revisions to your paragraph. Now it's time to focus on smaller changes, such as correcting mistakes in the conventions of writing. The following mini-lesson will help you recognize and correct spelling errors in words with suffixes.

Mini-Lesson: Spelling Words with Suffixes

A few basic rules will help you spell correctly when you add a *suffix* to a word.

A **suffix** is a word part added to the end of a word to change the word's meaning or use.

base word	+	suffix	=	new word
abandon	+	ment	=	abandonment
educate	+	ion	=	education
survive	+	or	=	survivor
protect	+	ion	=	protection

➡ If the word ends in silent *e*

   drop the *e* to add a suffix beginning with a vowel.

   smile + ing = smiling

   dance + er = dancer

   keep the *e* to add a suffix beginning with a consonant.

   grace + less = graceless

   huge + ly = hugely

268 • The Writer's Studio   Level A

Respond to a Narrative Ch. 17

Give It a Try: Find Examples of This Rule

Review your response to literature to find any words that follow this rule. Write them in the box below. If you do not find examples in your paragraph, skim this chapter to find two examples. (At the end of this mini-lesson, you'll share your examples of each rule.)

→ If the word ends in a vowel plus *y*

    keep the *y* when adding a suffix:

        enjoy + able = enjoyable

        play + ful = playful

→ If the word ends in a consonant plus *y*

    change the *y* to *i* before a suffix not beginning with *i*:

        merry + ment = merriment

        beauty + ful = beautiful

Give It a Try: Find Examples of These Two Rules

Review your response to literature to find any words that follow these rules about words ending in -*y*. Write the words in the box below. If you do not find examples in your paragraph, find two examples somewhere else.

Unit 5 • **Response to Literature** • **269**

Ch. 17 Respond to a Narrative

→ To add the suffix *-ly* or *-ness*

do not change the spelling of the word if it ends in any letter but *y*:

sweet + ly = sweetly

smooth + ness = smoothness

(For words ending in *y*, follow rule 2 or 3, above.)

Give It a Try: Find Examples of This Rule

Review your response to literature to find any words that follow this rule. Write them in the box below. If you do not find examples in your paragraph, find two examples somewhere else.

→ To decide whether to double the final consonant

if the word ends in one vowel plus a consonant, double the consonant if the word is one-syllable or the accent is on the final syllable:

big + est = biggest

forgot + en = forgotten

do not double the consonant if it is preceded by more than one vowel:

dream + er = dreamer

brain + y = brainy

270 • The Writer's Studio   Level A

Respond to a Narrative   Ch. 17

Give It a Try: Find Examples of This Rule

Review your response to literature to find any words that follow this rule. Write them in the box below. If you do not find examples in your paragraph, find two examples somewhere else.

Edit Your Response to Literature. Edit the revised copy of your character sketch. The following questions will help you decide what to change, remove, or leave in place.

Conventions
- ❑ Did you capitalize proper nouns?
- ❑ Did you use a comma when beginning a sentence with an introductory element?
- ❑ Did you use a comma when joining sentences with a coordinating conjunction?
- ❑ Did you use a comma when beginning a sentence with a subordinate clause?
- ❑ Did you correct spelling mistakes, either with a friend's help or by using a dictionary?

PUBLISH

Presentation. Prepare your response for publication by writing or typing the final, edited copy.

Publish Your Response. Here are some ideas for publishing your work.
- ❑ Post a copy of the character sketch on your personal Web page or in a blog.
- ❑ Give a copy of the character sketch to a friend who would enjoy reading the short story or novel.

Unit 5 • Response to Literature • 271

Ch. 17 Respond to a Narrative

❑ Find (or create) a drawing or other image that helps to bring the character to life, such as a drawing of the character or an image of the book's cover. Get your teacher's permission to hang these on a bulletin board in the classroom.

Evaluate Your Response to Literature

Your teacher will either assess your response, ask you to self-assess your response, or ask you to switch with a partner and assess each other's work.

Evaluate the Model Response to Literature

Work with a partner to evaluate the following response to literature. Use the rubric on page 267 and write your score here: ____. In a class discussion, explain the score that you gave.

The Problem with Pleasing Others

Jonathan is a teenager who relates to others by trying to please them. In "The Writer in the Family" by E. L. Doctorow, Jonathan's father has just died. The family hides this fact from the grandmother because she is so old and fragile. They tell her that Jonathan's father moved to Arizona. To support the lie, Jonathan's aunt asks him to write letters to the grandmother, pretending to be his father. Eager to please, Jonathan writes some letters. As he does this, he starts to understand his father better. He realizes that his father always tried to please others, and everyone took him for granted. Jonathan realizes he is behaving just like his father. He writes a letter to the grandmother (pretending to be his father) saying that he is dying. This will be the last letter. Jonathan's aunt is angry with him, but Jonathan knows that he was finally true to himself.

Chapter 18

Respond to a Poem

What is your favorite song right now? What does it mean to you? Do any of your favorite songs help you to understand things about life, such as why people lie or what is the point of love?

If you've ever spent time thinking about these types of questions, then you have been thinking about themes in songs. A **theme** is the work's lesson or message about life. In the same way, you can identify and respond to themes in poetry. In this chapter, you'll write a response to a theme in a poem by an American poet. First, look at the six traits below. Notice how a response to a poem is similar to a response to a narrative, which you learned about in Chapter 17. For both kinds of writing, you need to use specific examples to prove your point. However, in the last chapter, you responded to a narrative by looking at a character, and here, you'll respond to a poem by exploring theme.

Six Traits of a Response to a Poem

Ideas	The topic is narrowed to a specific theme or other part of the poem. Each detail clearly relates to this topic.
Organization	The response has a beginning, a middle, and an end. Details follow a logical order.
Voice	The writer uses a knowledgeable and objective tone.
Word Choice	The writer refers to specific images in the poem or quotes key words or phrases in order to make ideas clear.
Sentence Fluency	A variety of sentence types and structures creates a pleasing rhythm to the writing.
Conventions	Capitalization, spelling, punctuation, and grammar are correct.

Unit 5 • Response to Literature • 273

Ch. 18 Respond to a Poem

In the following paragraph, the writer explains his interpretation of the theme of a poem about baseball.

> In the poem "The Double Play," Robert Wallace compares a double play in baseball to a poem. To show a baseball play as a poem, the poet uses several strategies. First, he uses poetic language like "sea-lit distance" to set the scene of the ballpark. Second, he uses similes to help express the action. The pitcher's arm swinging in a circle before the pitch is "winding like a clock." When the batter hits the ball, the ball moves in a fast straight line "like a vanishing string." Third, the last line of the poem compares the double play to a poem. The poet says that the empty field after the game is "the space where the poem has happened." In this poem, Wallace shows that unexpected parts of life can be poetry in motion.

Give It a Try: Examine the Model Paragraph

Answer the following questions about six traits in the model paragraph. Write your answers on separate paper.

1. **Ideas.** What is the paragraph's topic sentence?
2. **Organization and word choice.** List three transition words that draw attention to the writer's three main points.
3. **Voice.** Does the writer use the first-, second-, or third-person point of view? How do you know this?
4. **Sentence fluency.** Copy the last sentence from the paragraph. Underline the dependent clause in this complex sentence.
5. **Conventions.** List three quotations from the poem that the writer uses, including the quotation marks and periods.

Respond to a Poem   Ch. 18

Your Turn to Write: Respond to a Poem

Now you'll write your own response to a poem. Read the assignment carefully and follow the strategies and instructions for each stage of the writing process.

Assignment

April is National Poetry Month, and a bookstore in your town is hosting a weekend of poetry readings in the store. You have been invited to read a one-paragraph response to a poem's theme. Choose one of the following poems. Then write a paragraph of 100–150 words in which you examine the poem's theme.

choice 1

In Heaven

Stephen Crane

In heaven,
Some little blades of grass
Stood before God.
"What did you do?"
Then all save one of the little blades
Began eagerly to relate
The merits of their lives.
This one stayed a small way behind,
Ashamed.
Presently, God said:
"And what did you do?"
The little blade answered: "Oh, my lord,
"Memory is bitter to me
"For if I did good deeds
I know not of them."
Then God in all His splendor
Arose from His throne.
"Oh, best little blade of grass," He said.

Unit 5 • Response to Literature • 275

Ch. 18 Respond to a Poem

choice 2

The Morns Are Meeker Than They Were
Emily Dickinson

The morns are meeker than they were—
The nuts are getting brown—
The berry's cheek is plumper—
The Rose is out of town.
The Maple wears a gayer scarf—
The field a scarlet gown—
Lest I should be old fashioned
I'll put a trinket on.

Prewrite

Analyze the Prompt. Reread the assignment and answer the following questions. Use separate paper.
1. What is the purpose of this response to literature?
2. Who is the audience for this response to literature?
3. How long does the response need to be?

Choose a Topic. Carefully read both poems. Then choose one poem to write about.

Gather Ideas and Details. As your teacher directs, form a group with other students who chose the same poem. Gather ideas and details for your response to the poem by discussing the poem with one another. The following sentence starters will help you.

This poem is mainly about . . .

The part I like best is . . .

The poet probably wants us to learn that . . .

I think _____ is a symbol for . . .

I didn't understand the part about . . .

I really liked the way the poet said this . . .

A literary device (simile, metaphor, personification) used is . . .

Respond to a Poem   Ch. 18

Organize Ideas and Details. Use the suggestions in this table to create an outline for your response.

Parts of Your Paragraph	Notes
Beginning My thesis is . . .	Make a statement about the poem that your paragraph will prove.
Middle My first supporting detail is . . . My second supporting detail is . . . My third supporting detail is . . .	Refer to specific ideas in the poem, or quote key words or phrases from the poem, to prove your points.
End My closing idea is . . .	Based on the evidence in your paragraph, state (or restate) what the theme of the poems.

 Draft

Since your purpose for writing this response is to examine the poem's theme, be sure to state the theme of the poem. A theme is the life lesson that the poet wants to teach readers.

You can state the poem's theme at the beginning or end of your paragraph. In the model paragraph that begins this chapter, the writer states the theme at the end of the paragraph, as the concluding sentence.

> In this poem, Wallace shows that unexpected parts of life can be poetry in motion.

Unit 5 • Response to Literature • 277

Ch. 18   **Respond to a Poem**

Another strategy is to state the theme at the beginning of the paragraph, in the topic sentence. Here is a topic sentence that states a theme in a poem by Ralph Waldo Emerson.

> In "The Rhodora," Ralph Waldo Emerson uses descriptions of a flower to show that beauty does not have to serve any purpose other than being a delight to the eyes.

When you begin by stating the theme, you can conclude by re-stating the theme. Here is an example of how you might conclude a paragraph about "The Rhodora."

> He means that beauty is never lost in nature. Instead, beauty is nature's way of bringing delight and awe to anyone who looks at it.

State a Theme of a Poem. On separate paper, state a theme of the poem you chose to write about. Remember, a poem may contain more than one theme, and these themes may be expressed in different ways. It's okay if you don't state a theme in exactly the same way as a classmate does. The important thing is that you will explain your choice in the paragraph that you write.

Write Your Response to a Poem. Using your prewriting and the theme that you stated, write a first draft of your paragraph. Be sure to
- ❑ include a beginning, a middle, and an end
- ❑ use the third-person point of view
- ❑ refer to specific images in the poem, or quote specific words and phrases, to help make your ideas clear

 ## Revise

Have you ever picked lint off the back of someone's sweater or pointed out, "Your shoe's untied"? If so, then you know that even though people do their best to be presentable, they can overlook details. The same is true in writing. You can do your best to write a strong draft, but you may overlook weaknesses that someone else could point out to you. This is where peer feedback comes in handy.

278 • The Writer's Studio   Level A

Respond to a Poem — Ch. 18

Mini-Lesson: Getting (and Giving) Helpful Feedback

One of the most helpful things you can do as a writer is seek feedback on your work in progress. A second pair of eyes may see strengths and weakness that you've overlooked.

The key to getting (and giving) helpful feedback is to be specific about what the reviewer should do. A request such as, "Would you read this and tell me what you think?" is too vague. Your reviewer is likely to say something like, "I liked it. Great work!" This kind of response is good for the ego but not helpful for improving a composition.

> **Tip:** Even if your feedback partner is your best friend, be polite. Saying something is bad is not helpful. Instead say, "I'm having trouble finding your topic sentence," "Another detail here would help," and the like. And be sure to find *at least one* positive thing to say.

In contrast, a request such as, "Which sentence in this paragraph seems to be my topic sentence?" is specific. It will get you specific feedback such as, "I think the second sentence is your topic sentence" or "I couldn't find your topic sentence."

Give It a Try: Get Feedback on Your Work

Get out the draft of your response to a poem. Write down *three* specific questions to ask a peer reviewer. Here are some examples:

Can you tell which sentence is my topic sentence?

Can you tell which sentence expresses the theme of the poem?

Would you rate the sentence fluency as Pleasing, Okay, or Repetitive?

Now exchange drafts and questions with a classmate. If you responded to the Dickinson poem, exchange drafts with someone

Ch. 18 **Respond to a Poem**

who responded to the Crane poem, and vice versa. On the draft you receive, write answers to the writer's questions. If necessary, underline sentences or circle words in the draft to help make your feedback clear. Finally, return the draft and your feedback to the writer.

Revise Your Response to a Poem. Revise the rough draft of your paragraph. Use the feedback you received and the following checklist and rubric to guide your revision.

Ideas
- ❑ Underline the sentence in which you identify the theme of the poem.

Organization
- ❑ What method did you use to organize the reasons and examples in your response (for example, comparison-contrast or order of importance)? Write down the method. Now examine the ideas in your response. If an idea breaks this pattern of organization, move or remove it.

Voice
- ❑ Do you use an objective, knowledgeable tone?
- ❑ Did you use the third-person point of view throughout your response? If you express an idea using the first-person point of view, revise it to use the third-person point of view.

Word choice
- ❑ Circle a word or phrase that you quote directly from the poem, or an image from that poem to which you refer.

Sentence fluency
- ❑ Find a well-placed short sentence that adds variety to nearby longer sentences and write *variety* above it. If all your sentences are long, revise your work to include at least one short sentence for variety.

280 • The Writer's Studio   Level A

Respond to a Poem   Ch. 18

Response to Poetry Rubric

	4 Strong	**3** Effective	**2** Developing	**1** Beginning
Ideas	One theme is explained. Each detail clearly relates.	The theme is clear, but some details do not relate.	The writer is beginning to make the theme clear.	The theme is not clear. Most details do not relate.
Organization	The paragraph has a clear beginning, middle, and end.	The beginning or ending is unclear.	The beginning or ending is missing.	The writer's thoughts are given in random order.
Voice	The voice is objective and knowledgeable throughout the response.	The voice is objective and knowledgeable in most of the response.	The tone is objective and knowledgeable in one or two sentences.	The tone is preachy, careless, or otherwise not objective.
Word Choice	Vivid words and relevant quotes express key ideas.	Many vivid words, along with some basic ones, express key ideas.	One or two vivid words help to express a key idea.	Vocabulary is limited or does not clearly relate to the poem.
Sentence Fluency	A variety of sentence types is used in a pleasing rhythm.	A variety of sentence types is used, but some may be awkward.	Sentences are complete but are mostly short and simple.	Sentences are mostly short and simple or are incomplete.
Conventions	Capitalization, spelling, punctuation, and grammar are correct.	Few errors in capitalization, spelling, punctuation, or grammar are present.	Errors in capitalization, spelling, punctuation, and grammar do not prevent the reader from understanding.	Errors in capitalization, spelling, punctuation, and grammar make it hard to understand the writing.

Unit 5 • Response to Literature

Ch. 18 **Respond to a Poem**

 **Edit**

Edit Your Response to a Poem. Use the following checklist to edit the revised copy of your paragraph.

Conventions
- ❏ Did you capitalize each important word in the poem's title?
- ❏ Did you capitalize the poet's name?
- ❏ Did you use quotation marks to enclose the poet's exact words?
- ❏ Did you use a comma when you joined sentences with a coordinating conjunction?
- ❏ Did you use a comma when you began a sentence with a subordinate clause?
- ❏ Did you correct spelling mistakes, either with a friend's help or by using a dictionary?

PUBLISH

Presentation. Prepare your response for publication by writing or typing the final, edited copy.

Publish Your Response to a Poem. Here are some ideas for publishing your work.
- ❏ In class, at home, or in a local bookstore, host a Poetry Response Party. Each participant should read a poem aloud and then read a one-paragraph response to the poem.
- ❏ Create a video presentation by reading the poem and your response aloud while a friend films you. Post the video on a school Web site or a safe public Web site.
- ❏ Submit your response to a Web site that publishes the work of young people.
- ❏ Get permission to hang your response on a bulletin board in the classroom.
- ❏ Illustrate your response with a photograph or drawing, and share this with your teacher or classmates.

Respond to a Poem   Ch. 18

Evaluate Your Response to a Poem

Your teacher will either assess your response, ask you to self-assess your response, or ask you to switch with a partner and assess each other's work.

Evaluate a Model Response to a Poem

Work with a partner to evaluate the following model paragraph. Use the rubric on page 281 and write your score here: _____. In a class discussion, explain the score that you gave.

Why Beauty?

In "the Rhodora," Ralph Waldo Emerson uses descriptions of a flower to show that beauty does not have to serve a purpose other than being a delight to the eyes. In the poem, the speaker goes for a walk in the woods. In May. He finds a shrub of purple flowers, the rhodora, "in a damp nook." He reacts with wonder and thoughtfulnes. First, beautiful purple flower petals. Then he thinks about how much prettyer the flowers are than a bright redbird. Finaly, he speaks directly. To the flower. He says that wise people may wonder why the flower's beauty "is wasted on the earth and sky." He tells the flower that it's answer should be, "Beauty is its own excuse for being. He means that beauty is never lost in nature. Instead, beauty is natures way of bringing delight and awe to anyone who looks at it.

Unit 5 • Response to Literature

Chapter 19

Respond to a Document-Based Question

A **document-based question**, or **DBQ**, is based on two or more *primary sources* that relate to one another. A primary source is a firsthand account of an event. These are examples of primary sources:

diaries	photographs
journals	legal documents
letters	speeches
newspaper articles	maps
receipts and other records	

The primary sources in a DBQ may link to the same historical event, such as World War II. They may share a common theme, such as religious freedom. Your purpose in responding to the documents is to explain how they relate or what they say as a group. To do this, you use a combination of information in the documents and your own knowledge. This chapter shows you how to write a strong response to a DBQ.

Like other forms of writing, a response to a DBQ should show careful consideration of the six traits of writing. The table on the next page explains.

Unit 5 • Response to Literature • **285**

Ch. 19 Respond to a Document-Based Question

Six Traits of a Response to a DBQ

Ideas	The thesis links directly to the topic in the prompt. The writer uses supporting details from the documents and from previous knowledge.
Organization	The response has a beginning, a middle, and an end.
Voice	The writer uses an objective, knowledgeable tone.
Word Choice	The writer refers to specific ideas in the documents or quotes key words or phrases to make his or her points clear.
Sentence Fluency	A variety of sentence types and structures creates a pleasing rhythm to the writing.
Conventions	Direct quotes begin and end with quotation marks. Proper nouns are capitalized. Spelling, punctuation, and grammar are correct.

In the paragraph below, the writer responds to documents about women's participation in the American Civil War.

> During the American Civil War (1861–1865), women were not allowed to be soldiers, but they were allowed to nurse the wounded soldiers. The nurses bathed and dressed wounds on battlefields, in field hospitals, in army hospitals, and in homes. At first they were shocked by the blood and pain, but they soon got on with their work.

The Writer's Studio • Level A

Respond to a Document-Based Question Ch. 19

> One nurse, Kate Cumming, wrote in her journal, "None of the glories of the war were presented here" (Document 1). She also wrote that she would "never forget the poor sufferers' gratitude; for every little thing, done for them." The nurses not only cared for wounds, but they made sure the soldiers had quilts, clothing, and food. According to one receipt, the Women's Central Relief Association handed out more than 150,000 shirts to soldiers between May 1861 and November 1863 (Document 2). Without the service of women as nurses in the Civil War, far more lives would have been lost.

Give It a Try: Examine the Model Paragraph

Answer the following questions about six traits in the model paragraph you just read. Write your answers on separate paper. Then explain your answers in a class discussion.

1. **Ideas.** What historical event is the focus of this paragraph?
2. **Organization.** Identify the paragraph's beginning, middle, and end by drawing a circle around each part. Label each circle.
3. **Voice and word choice.** What do you think the writer's attitude toward Civil War nurses is? How can you tell?
4. **Sentence fluency.** Copy the last sentence of the paragraph. Circle the introductory element, underline the subject once, and underline the verb twice. Is this a simple, compound, or complex sentence?
5. **Conventions.** Why does the writer place some words inside parentheses?

Unit 5 • Response to Literature • **287**

Ch. 19 **Respond to a Document-Based Question**

Your Turn to Write: Respond to a DBQ

Now you'll write your own response to a document-based question. Read the assignment carefully and follow the strategies and instructions for each stage of the writing process.

Assignment

Historical Background

The Battle of Gettysburg took place during July 1–3, 1863. Union and Confederate troops fought near Gettysburg, Pennsylvania, and Union troops gradually won the upper hand. On July 3, Confederate forces attacked the Union's strongest position. The Confederates not only failed in their attack but also suffered a great loss in life.

Writing Prompt

Write a paragraph in which you explain to classmates how people responded to the Civil War. Use information in at least two of the documents and your own knowledge of the Civil War. Your paragraph should be 100–150 words long.

Document 1

Part of a Diary Entry

Randolph McKim, Confederate soldier

Then came General Ewell's order to assume the offensive and assail the crest of Culp's Hill, on our right.... The works to be stormed ran almost at right angles to those we occupied. Moreover, there was a double line of entrenchments, one above the other, and each filled with troops. In moving to the attack we were exposed to enfilading [moving back and forth] fire from the woods on our left flank, besides the double line of fire which we had to face in front, and a battery of artillery posted on a hill to our left rear opened upon us at short range. . . .

On swept the gallant little brigade, the Third North Carolina on the right of the line, next the Second Maryland, then the three Virginia regiments (10th, 23d, and 37th), with the First North Carolina on the extreme left. Its ranks had been sadly thinned, and its energies greatly depleted by those six fearful hours of battle that morning; but its nerve and spirit were undiminished. Soon, however, the left and center were checked and then repulsed, probably by the severe flank fire from the woods; and the small remnant of the Third North Carolina, with the stronger Second Maryland (I do not recall the banners of any other regiment), were far in advance of the rest of the line. On they pressed to within about twenty or thirty paces of the works—a small but gallant band of heroes daring to attempt what could not be done by flesh and blood.

The end soon came. . . .

Document 2

Gettysburg Address

Abraham Lincoln

November 19, 1863

Four score and seven years ago our fathers brought forth on this continent a new nation, conceived in liberty and dedicated to the proposition that all men are created equal.

Now we are engaged in a great civil war, testing whether that nation, or any nation so conceived and so dedicated, can long endure. We are met on a great battlefield of that war.

Ch. 19 Respond to a Document-Based Question

> We have come to dedicate a portion of that field, as a final resting place for those who here gave their lives that that nation might live. It is altogether fitting and proper that we should do this.
>
> But, in a larger sense, we cannot dedicate—we cannot consecrate—we cannot hallow—this ground. The brave men, living and dead, who struggled here, have consecrated it far above our poor power to add or detract. The world will little note, nor long remember what we say here, but it can never forget what they did here. It is for us the living, rather, to be dedicated here to the unfinished work which they who fought here have thus far so nobly advanced. It is rather for us to be here dedicated to the great task remaining before us—that from these honored dead we take increased devotion to that cause for which they gave the last full measure of devotion—that we here highly resolve that these dead shall not have died in vain, that this nation, under God, shall have a new birth of freedom, and that government of the people, by the people, for the people shall not perish from the earth.

Respond to a Document-Based Question   Ch. 19

Document 3
Abraham Lincoln's Address at the Dedication of the Gettysburg National Cemetery, November 19, 1863

Prewrite

Analyze the Prompt. Use the assignment on page 288 to answer the questions in the paragraphs that follow. Write your answers on separate paper.

A document-based question usually has three main sections. First, a few sentences give background information on the theme or subject of the DBQ. In the assignment above, this information is included under the heading Historical Background.

Unit 5 • Response to Literature • **291**

Ch. 19 Respond to a Document-Based Question

1. According to the Historical Background, what is the subject of this DBQ?

    After the historical background, the next section gives you a topic for your response. On page 288 this section is called Writing Prompt. It might also be called Task.

2. According to the Writing Prompt
    a. What is the purpose of this paragraph?
    b. Who is the audience for this paragraph?
    c. How long does the paragraph need to be?
    d. How many primary sources must you use?

    Finally, you'll see the documents. These are primary sources that you must use when writing your response.

3. Make a list of the titles of the primary sources in this DBQ.

Read the Documents. Reading and understanding the documents is your next step in preparing to write your response. Unless you are writing for a test, you can discuss the documents with your teacher and classmates. In addition, you can use these tips:

- **Read each document more than once.** First, read to get the big picture. What's happening? What is (are) the writer's main point(s)? Next, read to understand more completely. Figure out those areas that confused you the first time. Finally, read again to tie it all together in your mind.
- **Mark unfamiliar words and find out their meanings.**
- **Identify the writer's strategy for organizing information.** Did the writer use chronological order? A cause-and-effect pattern? A compare-and-contrast pattern? A list of reasons in order of importance? If you know how ideas are organized, you can better figure out the challenging parts.
- **Summarize. In a sentence or two, restate the writer's main idea.** Your summary could begin, "He's basically saying that . . ." or "She wants people to know/think that . . ."

Read the Documents in the DBQ. Use the reading tips above to read and understand the documents in the DBQ. Then share your

Respond to a Document-Based Question Ch. 19

ideas in a class discussion. These sentence starters may help you get the discussion going.

The diary entry tells how . . .

The purpose of the speech is to . . .

One of the unfamiliar words I looked up is . . .

I noticed that McKim (or Lincoln) used the organization method of . . .

McKim's attitude toward the events is . . .

Lincoln's attitude toward his topic is . . .

Gather Ideas and Details. In a response to a DBQ, you must use information from the documents plus your own knowledge. Gather this information by using the table below.

My purpose for Writing: _____

What the Documents Say	What I Know	What I Can Conclude Based on Both Sets of Information
your details here	your details here	your details here

Unit 5 • Response to Literature • **293**

Ch. 19 Respond to a Document-Based Question

Organize Ideas and Details. Use the suggestions in this table to create an outline for your response.

Parts of Your Paragraph	In This Part You Should . . .
Beginning My thesis is . . .	Make a statement about people's response to the Civil War. This statement is what your paragraph will prove.
Middle My first supporting detail is . . . My second supporting detail is . . . My third supporting detail is . . .	Prove your thesis. Use supporting examples from at least two of the documents, plus your own knowledge and conclusions.
End My closing idea is . . .	Summarize your information in a closing statement about your thesis.

Draft

By now, you have put a great deal of effort into understanding the DBQ and the documents in the DBQ. Moreover, you have worked to gather and organize ideas. Take a moment to appreciate how far you've come in preparing your response! You will benefit from all your preparation now that it's time to write your response.

As you write, make sure that you use quotations accurately. The following mini-lesson explains how to use quotations from documents in a DBQ.

Respond to a Document-Based Question Ch. 19

Mini-Lesson: Using Quotations

A response to a DBQ is not a summary of all the documents. Instead, the response is made up of *your ideas* about information in the documents. To show how your ideas link to the documents, you can quote key words or phrases from the sources.

In the paragraph about Civil War nurses, here is how the writer used a quotation.

> One nurse, Kate Cumming, wrote in her journal, "None of the glories of the war were presented here" (Document 1).

Notice three things about the use of the quotation.
- The writer identifies who is speaking or writing (a nurse, Kate Cumming).
- The writer places quotation marks around the quoted words.
- The writer tells which document the quote comes from (Document 1).

Give It a Try: Write Sentences That Use Quotations

Skim the documents in the DBQ. Choose three words or phrases that are especially vivid or well phrased *and* that link to your ideas for your response. On separate paper, write three sentences in which you quote words or phrases from a document. In each sentence, be sure to identify the writer or speaker, use quotation marks, and identify the document number.

Write Your Response to a DBQ. Use your prewriting, organization chart, and sentences from the mini-lesson to write the first draft of your response to the DBQ. Be sure to
- ❑ include a beginning, a middle, and an end
- ❑ write using the third-person point of view
- ❑ use examples to make your ideas clear

Unit 5 • Response to Literature • **295**

Ch. 19 Respond to a Document-Based Question

 **Revise**

Get Feedback on Your Response to a DBQ. Read your draft. Write down *three* specific requests for a peer reviewer. Here are some examples:

> Please circle my topic sentence.
>
> Can you tell whether each supporting detail comes from a document or from my own knowledge?
>
> What is the strongest sentence or idea in my paragraph?
>
> Write a question mark next to unrelated details.

Now exchange drafts and questions with a classmate. On the draft you receive, write answers to the writer's questions. If necessary, underline sentences or circle words in the draft to help make your feedback clear. Finally, return the draft and your feedback to the writer.

Revise Your Response to a DBQ. Revise the rough draft of your paragraph. Use the feedback you received and the following checklist and rubric to guide you.

Ideas
- ❑ Underline your thesis. Make sure it addresses the prompt.

Organization
- ❑ Number each of your main reasons or examples. If a detail does not relate to one of these reasons/examples, cross it out.

Voice
- ❑ Find two examples of third-person pronouns that you use. Write *third person* above each one.
- ❑ Change any first-person pronouns (such as *I* or *me*) to use the third-person point of view instead.

Word choice
- ❑ Circle two phrases that you quoted from a document.

Sentence fluency
- ❑ Find a compound sentence *and* a complex sentence in your essay, and label each one.

Respond to a Document-Based Question — Ch. 19

Response to a DBQ Rubric

	4 Strong	3 Effective	2 Developing	1 Beginning
Ideas	The thesis links to the prompt. Details come from the documents and the writer's knowledge.	The thesis links to the prompt but is weak. Most details come from the documents and the writer's knowledge.	No clear thesis. Details are all from either the documents or the writer's knowledge.	No thesis. The paragraph is not focused on one topic or does not relate to the prompt.
Organization	The paragraph has a clear beginning, middle, and end.	The beginning or ending is unclear.	The beginning or ending is missing.	The writer's thoughts are given in random order.
Voice	The voice is objective and knowledgeable throughout the response.	The voice is objective and knowledgeable in most of the response.	The tone is objective and knowledgeable in one or two sentences.	The tone is goofy, sarcastic, or otherwise not objective.
Word Choice	Vivid words and relevant quotes express key ideas.	Many vivid words, along with some basic ones, express key ideas.	One or two vivid words help to express a key idea.	Vocabulary is limited. Some words are used incorrectly.
Sentence Fluency	A variety of sentence types is used in a pleasing rhythm.	A variety of sentence types is used, but some may be awkward.	Sentences are complete but are mostly short and simple.	Sentences are mostly short and simple or are incomplete.
Conventions	Capitalization, spelling, punctuation, and grammar are correct.	Few errors in capitalization, spelling, punctuation, or grammar are present.	Errors in capitalization, spelling, punctuation, and grammar do not prevent the reader from understanding.	Errors in capitalization, spelling, punctuation, and grammar make it hard to understand the writing.

Unit 5 • Response to Literature

Ch. 19 **Respond to a Document-Based Question**

Edit Your Response to a DBQ. Edit the revised copy of your paragraph. The following questions will help.

Conventions
- ❑ Did you capitalize proper nouns?
- ❑ Did you use quotation marks to enclose words taken from a document?
- ❑ Did you use parentheses to enclose the document citation?
- ❑ Did you use a comma after a coordinating conjunction?
- ❑ Did you use a comma after an introductory element?
- ❑ Did you correct spelling mistakes?

PUBLISH

Presentation. Write or type the final, edited copy.

Publish Your Response to a DBQ. Try one of these ideas:
- ❑ With classmates, create a booklet of your responses to the DBQ. Send the booklet to a historical society that studies the Civil War. You can start by looking at the Web site of the Society of Civil War Historians (http://scwh.la.psu.edu).
- ❑ Read your paragraph to a younger student who would enjoy learning about the Civil War.
- ❑ E-mail your paragraph to friends or family members. Tell them why they might be interested in your ideas.

Evaluate Your Response to a DBQ

Your teacher will either assess your response, ask you to self-assess your response, or ask you to switch with a partner and assess each other's work.

Evaluate the Model Response to a DBQ

Work with a partner to evaluate the model paragraph about Civil War nurses, on page 286. Use the rubric on page 297 and write your score here: _____. In a class discussion, explain the score that you gave.

298 • The Writer's Studio   Level A

Chapter 20
Test Writing: The Critical-Lens Essay

What's your favorite inspirational quote? Your favorite proverb or saying? These little sentences have a way of summing up big ideas, and they speak to different people in different ways. For example, what do the following quotations mean to you?

> "It takes two to speak the truth,—one to speak, and another to hear."
> —Henry David Thoreau

> "Don't judge a man until you have walked in his shoes."
> —proverb

On a test, you may be asked to write a response to a quotation like the ones listed above. This kind of response is often called a response to a critical-lens quotation. A **critical lens** is a tool for examining life or literature. It gives you a frame of reference for talking about a truth. This chapter explains how to write a response to a critical-lens quotation.

Six Traits of a Critical-Lens Essay

Ideas	The writer interprets the quotation, agrees or disagrees with it, and explains it using examples from literature.
Organization	The response has a beginning, a middle, and an end. Details follow a logical order.
Voice	The writer uses an objective, knowledgeable tone.
Word Choice	Vivid, accurate words are used.
Sentence Fluency	A variety of sentence types and structures creates a pleasing rhythm to the writing.
Conventions	Capitalization, spelling, punctuation, and grammar are correct.

 **Test Writing: The Critical-Lens Essay**

Preparing to Write Your Test Essay

A prompt for a critical-lens response has two or three parts: your writing assignment, the critical-lens quotation, and (sometimes) a list of reminders or guidelines. Here is an example of a critical-lens prompt.

> **Instructions**
> You have 25 minutes to complete the written composition. Read the prompt below. Then use separate paper to plan and draft your composition. Only your draft will be scored.
>
> **Writing Prompt**
> Write an essay in which you discuss *two* works of literature from the perspective of the critical lens quotation. In your essay
> - give your interpretation of the quotation
> - agree or disagree with the quotation
> - support your opinion using details from *two* works of literature
>
> **Critical Lens**
> "This above all: to thine own self be true."
> —Shakespeare, *Hamlet*, Act I, scene iii
>
> **Remember to**
> - state the titles and authors of the works of literature you discuss
> - organize your ideas in a logical way
> - follow the conventions of capitalization, spelling, punctuation, and grammar

300 • The Writer's Studio   Level A

Test Writing: The Critical-Lens Essay   Ch. 20

1. Study the Prompt

Before you begin to write your essay, take a few moments to study the prompt. On separate paper, answer these important questions:

What is the purpose of the essay? The writing prompt lists three things that you must include in your response.

What should I write about? The writing prompt gives you a critical-lens quotation to respond to.

How much time do I have to write? According to the prompt, how much time is allowed for writing this response?

What other instructions are stated? According to the prompt, what are three things the writer should remember to do?

2. Plan Your Time

After studying the prompt, make a quick plan for how to use your time. If you have 25 minutes in which to write the test, you could use your time as follows:

5–7 minutes:	Study the prompt and complete the prewriting.
13–15 minutes:	Write the essay.
5 minutes:	Revise and edit the essay.

> **T!p**
>
> Although 5–7 minutes might seem like a long time for prewriting, it will make the drafting stage go smoother.

3. Prewrite

During your prewriting time, gather and organize ideas. A chart with a separate space for each part of the writing task is useful. It helps you gather ideas for the three parts of your response.

Ch. 20 Test Writing: The Critical-Lens Essay

Task Chart

Task 1: Interpret the quote.
Be faithful to what you think is right for you, even if other people don't agree with you.

Task 2: Agree or disagree.
I agree

Task 3: Give 2 examples from literature.
"Say It with Flowers" by Toshio Mori. The new sales clerk decides to stop lying to customers because he does not want to be dishonest. He loses his job but is proud of himself.

~~Bridge to Terabithia by _____. Book about boy whose best friend dies. He has to decide whether to keep their imaginary world alive, or let it die too.~~

"The Road Not Taken" by Robert Frost. The speaker takes the road that most interests him, not the road everyone else is taking.

The chart above is useful not just for gathering ideas but also for organizing your response. In your essay, include the ideas in the order in which you wrote them in the chart (Task 1, Task 2, Task 3). Then, to conclude the essay, write a sentence that restates your interpretation of the quote, using different words this time.

TOOLKIT

For organizing a response to a critical-lens quotation, useful strategies include
- a task chart
- an outline
- a beginning-middle-end table

Don't worry about whether the person who grades your essay agrees or disagrees with you. That will not affect your score. Give *your* true opinion, and be sure to back it up with persuasive examples and details.

302 • The Writer's Studio   Level A

Test Writing: The Critical-Lens Essay Ch. 20

Writing Your Test Essay

Move on to the writing stage. Follow these tips.
- Use your prewriting work to guide you. It's okay to change a detail or two as you write. However, don't stray too much from your plan, or you may create a disorganized mess.
- Follow the tips in the "Remember to" section of the prompt.
- Write neatly and leave space on the page for writing revisions. You can do this by leaving at least a one-inch margin all around, or by double-spacing your response.

Following is the rough draft of a response to the critical-lens quotation. You will probably spot numerous mistakes. However, at this point, the writer focused mainly on ideas and organization. Notice that the writer included the three key tasks.

TIP

Be sure to give your response a title. To create an effective title, you could state the theme of the quotation ("Be True to Yourself") or use a key phrase from your response ("Listen to Your Heart").

Ideas: the author and source of the quotation

Task 2: the writer's statement of agreement or disagreement with the quote

Organization: Ideas follow the order of the tasks, as listed in the writing prompt.

In *Hamlet,* Shakespeare writes, "To thine own self be true. He means that people need to do what they think is right even if other people disagree with them. This is valueble advice that should be followed. One way that a person can follow this advice is to be honest at work. In the story "Say It with Flowers" by Toshio Mori, one character has to decide whether to cheat or be honest. His name is Teruo. His boss tells him to sell old flowers but tell the customers there fresh. At first, Teruo does this, but he feels bad because it is wrong. Then he starts selling only the fresh flowers. He gets fired from the job, but he is happy because he was true to himself. In the poem The Road Not Taken by Robert Frost. The speaker comes to a spot where the road forks. He has to decide which path to take. Most people have chose the well-traveled path. The speaker feels he should take "the road less traveled." And he does. And he says it "made all the difference." As Teruo and the speaker in the poem show, being true to yourself means listening to your own heart, not to other peoples threats or opinions.

Task 1: the writer's interpretation of the quote

Task 3: first example from literature

Task 3: second example from literature

Organization: The concluding sentence restates the writer's interpretation of the quote.

Unit 5 • Response to Literature • 303

Ch. 20 Test Writing: The Critical-Lens Essay

Polishing Your Test Essay

Save approximately five minutes to polish your response. Revise sentences, add or remove details, and correct mistakes in the conventions of writing. Taking the time to do this is useful for several reasons.

- It helps you show careful consideration of *all* six traits of writing.
- It makes ideas clear for your reader.
- It helps your reader connect with your response.

Evaluating a Response to a Critical-Lens Quotation

> **Tip**
>
> Make sure that you copy the critical-lens quotation exactly, word for word, in your response.

When a teacher evaluates your response to a critical-lens quotation, he or she will check to be sure that you

- **wrote to the prompt.** This means that you included the three parts of the writing task. It also means that you did not include unrelated details, such as personal experiences.
- **included relevant details in an organized manner.** This means that you used examples from literature that clearly relate to your interpretation of the quotation. It also means that you arranged ideas in a clear, logical way.
- **paid careful attention to the conventions of capitalization, spelling, punctuation, and grammar.**

Test Writing: The Critical-Lens Essay — Ch. 20

The following rubric shows guidelines for evaluating a response to a critical-lens quotation.

Response to a Critical-Lens Quotation Rubric

	4 Strong	3 Effective	2 Developing	1 Beginning
Ideas	The writer wrote to the prompt. Each detail clearly relates.	The writer wrote to the prompt, but a few details do not relate.	The writer included some details relating to the prompt.	The writer did not write to the prompt.
Organization	Information is arranged logically.	Most information is arranged logically.	Organization of information is awkward.	Information is included in random order.
Voice	The writing style helps the reader connect to the response.	The writing style of some parts draws the reader in.	The writing style of one or two sentences draws the reader in.	Writing is mechanical, making it hard for readers to connect.
Word Choice	Most key words are vivid. Most words are used accurately.	A few vivid words are used. Most words are used accurately.	One or two vivid words are used. Vocabulary is limited.	Vocabulary is limited and difficult to understand.
Sentence Fluency	A variety of sentence types is used in a pleasing rhythm.	A variety of sentence types is used, but some may be awkward.	Sentences are complete but are mostly short and simple.	Sentences are mostly of one type or are incomplete.
Conventions	Few errors in capitalization, spelling, punctuation, or grammar are present.	Several errors in capitalization, spelling, punctuation, or grammar are present.	Errors in capitalization, spelling, punctuation, and grammar do not prevent understanding.	Errors in capitalization, spelling, punctuation, and grammar prevent understanding.

Unit 5 • Response to Literature

Ch. 20 **Test Writing: The Critical-Lens Essay**

Evaluate a Model Critical-Lens Test Essay

Work with a partner to evaluate the following response to a critical-lens quotation. Reread the prompt on page 300 and use the rubric on page 305. Write your score here: _____. In a class discussion, explain the score that you gave.

In *Hamlet*, Shakespeare writes, "~~To~~ ^This above all:^ thine own self be true." He means that people need to do what they think is right even if other people disagree with them. This is valu^a^ble advice that should be followed. One way that a person can follow this advice is to be honest at work. ^For example,^ In the story "Say It with Flowers" by Toshio Mori, one character has to decide whether to cheat or be honest. His name is Teruo. His boss tells him to sell old flowers but tell the customers ~~there~~ ^they are^ fresh. At first, Teruo does this, but he feels bad because it is wrong. Then he starts selling only the fresh flowers. He gets fired from the job, but he is happy because he was true to himself.
¶ ^Another example is^ In the poem "The Road Not Taken" by Robert Frost. The speaker comes to a spot where the road forks. He has to decide which path to take. Most people have chose the well-traveled path. The speaker feels he should take "the road less traveled." And he does. And he says it "made all the difference."
¶ As Teruo and the speaker in the poem show, being true to yourself means listening to your own heart, not to other people's threats or opinions.

---

306 • The Writer's Studio   Level A

Test Writing: The Critical-Lens Essay   Ch. 20

Write a Critical-Lens Test Essay

Try writing a response to a critical-lens quotation in a test-like setting. Respond to the writing prompt below.

Instructions
You have 25 minutes to complete the written composition. Read the prompt below. Then use separate paper to plan and draft your composition. Only your draft will be scored.

Writing Prompt
Write an essay in which you discuss two works of literature from the perspective of the critical-lens quotation. In your essay,
- give your interpretation of the quotation
- agree or disagree with the quotation
- support your opinion using details from *two* works of literature

Critical Lens
"A gem is not polished without rubbing, nor a person made perfect without hardship."
                      —Chinese proverb

Remember to
- state the titles and authors of the works of literature you discuss
- organize your ideas in a logical way
- follow the conventions of capitalization, spelling, punctuation, and grammar

---

Unit 5 • Response to Literature • 307

Response to Literature Wrap-Up

The activities and information in these pages will help you continue to strengthen your skills of writing responses to literature. In You Be the Judge, use the Response to Literature Rubric to evaluate a student's work. The Ideas for Writing are additional writing prompts you can use for practice. And finally, in the Unit 5 Reflections, you can list important ideas you have learned in this unit and set goals for future learning.

You Be the Judge

Use what you've learned about the traits of writing to evaluate a student's response to literature. First, review the traits of response writing on page 256. Next, read the student's work below. Finally, in the rubric that follows, assign the work a score for each writing trait. In the space provided, explain each score that you assign.

Uglies
by Emily N., Omaha, NE

Scott Westerfeld is the author of the Uglies Series (Uglies, Pretties, Specials, and Extras). This book was a New York Times Bestseller.

In their world you start as an Ugly. When you are an Ugly you are just normal, average, but then when you turn sixteen you have a life changing surgery that turns you into a pretty. You get a new face, new hair, an entirely new look and the best part of all you get to live in Pretty Town. In Pretty Town there are parties every night and you have no responsibilities except to have fun. Tally Youngblood meets a new friend, Shay. Shay runs away from town so that she will not have to have the surgery. When Tally goes into have her surgery done they say she will not be turned into a pretty until she finds her friend and brings her back to town to have the surgery. So, Tally takes off to find her friend, but that is not all she finds. She finds out about how being turned into a pretty might not be a glamorous as it seems.

I think that this book was very creative and imaginative. I love all of the future technologies like hover boards, hover cams, and 'hole in the wall' that gives you anything you need like clothes, or food. I also like the cool futuristic language they use. It really helps you understand what it would be like to live in their world. This book is full of adventures and twists that keep you wondering what will happen next.

This is a great book for people whom like adventure or fantasy books.

Response to Literature Rubric

	4 Strong	3 Effective	2 Developing	1 Beginning
Ideas Score____	explanation:			
organization Score____	explanation:			
voice Score____	explanation:			
word choice Score____	explanation:			
sentence fluency Score____	explanation:			
conventions Score____	explanation:			

Unit 5 • **Response to Literature** • **309**

Ideas for Writing

The assignments on this page will give you additional practice with literary-response writing. Your teacher may choose one or let you pick one that's most interesting to you.

1. Write a letter to an author explaining your response to a particular work that he or she wrote. In your letter, be sure to

- include a beginning in which you identify the title of the work and the focus of your response
- a middle in which you give examples from the work to support your response; you might also ask a question about the work that you were unable to answer
- an ending in which you give a final thought about the work

Your letter should be approximately 300 words long.

2. An English teacher at your school is starting up a literary magazine. She wants students to write all the articles, stories, and poems. For this magazine, write a 150-word response to a poem in which you examine the theme, a character's personality, *or* a character's change during the poem.

3. Page through your history book and select two or three primary sources that relate to a single event or theme. Write a 150-word response to the documents in which you explain how they relate (a theme, a topic, etc.) and what they say about this theme or topic as a group. Give a copy of your response to your history teacher and to classmates who may be interested.

4. An old proverb says, "Great oaks from little acorns grow." Write a 350-word essay in which you explain the meaning of this proverb and discuss how you can apply the statement to characters from two different works of literature that you have read.

Unit 5 Reflections

How are you different as a writer now that you have completed this unit on writing responses to literature? What new knowledge do you have? How is your writing stronger? What kinds of things could you work on to make your responses to literature even more effective? Use the following space to reflect on your work in this unit and to set goals for the future.

Focus on Me: My Achievements in Writing Responses to Literature

What I've learned about responding to literature in this unit:

Ways my writing is stronger now:

Things I can do to practice my skills of responding to literature:

Conventions Handbook

Sentences　　　　　　　　　　page 313
The Eight Parts of Speech　　　page 313
How Words Work in Sentences　page 314
Punctuation　　　　　　　　　page 314

Sentences

comma splice   Two or more sentences joined with only a comma.

complex sentence   A sentence containing one main clause and at least one subordinate clause.

compound sentence   A sentence containing two or more main clauses and no subordinate clauses.

compound-complex sentence   A sentence containing at least two main clauses and at least one subordinate clause.

fragment   A word group punctuated as a sentence yet lacking a subject, a verb, or both.

run-on   Two or more sentences run together without punctuation or a conjunction between them.

simple sentence   A sentence containing one subject and one verb (one main clause).

The Eight Parts of Speech

adjective   Part of speech used to modify a noun or a pronoun.

adverb   Part of speech used to modify a verb, an adjective, or another adverb.

conjunction   Part of speech used to link words, phrases, clauses, or sentences.

interjection   Part of speech used to express sudden, strong feeling. It usually stands alone before a sentence.

noun   Part of speech that names a person, place, thing, or idea.

preposition   Part of speech that shows the relationship between its object(s) and another word in the sentence.

pronoun   Part of speech that takes the place of a noun in a sentence.

verb   Part of speech that expresses action or links the subject to another word in the sentence.

Words in Sentences

How Words Work in Sentences

agreement   The subject and its verb are both expressed in the same number (singular or plural); a pronoun and its antecedent are both expressed in the same number and gender (male, female, or neuter).

antecedent   The word or word group to which a pronoun refers.

clause   A related sequence of words that has a subject and a predicate. A *main clause* can stand alone as a sentence, but a *subordinate clause* cannot stand alone as a complete sentence.

direct object   A noun that receives the action of a verb.

indirect object   A noun that is indirectly affected by the action of the verb.

metaphor   A figure of speech that makes a comparison indirectly by saying that one thing *is* the other thing. Example: His fingers were thick sausages.

modifier   A word, phrase, or clause that describes a word or word group. Modifiers are either adjectives or adverbs.

object of a preposition   The noun that a preposition links to another word in the sentence.

phrase   A related sequence of words that does not have a subject and/or a predicate and that is used as a single part of speech.

predicate   The part of a sentence that says something about the subject.

simile   A figure of speech that makes a comparison by using the word *like, as,* or *than*. Example: His fingers were thick as sausages.

subject   The word or word group about which the predicate says something.

tense   Used in reference to a verb, indicates the time of the action or of the state of being (past, present, future).

transition   A word or phrase that connects two ideas, sentences, or paragraphs in a written work. Examples: *first, second, in addition, therefore*

verb   Part of speech that expresses action or links the subject to another word in the sentence. The verb is part of the predicate in a sentence.

Punctuation

apostrophe   Used to form contractions and possessives.

colon   Used to call attention to what follows, such as when the first clause in a sentence announces a second clause or a list, often with

314 • The Writer's Studio   Level A

the words *the following*. Used to separate the hour and minutes in written time. Used after the salutation in a business letter. Used to separate the city and the publisher in a bibliographic entry.

comma Used to separate items in a series. Used before a coordinating conjunction that joins sentences. Used after certain introductory words and word groups. Used to set off most interrupting words and expressions.

exclamation point Used to end expressions of strong feeling.

hyphen Used in some spelled-out numbers. Used to link two or more words that work as a single adjective before a noun. Used to link the parts of some compound words. Used to show a break between syllables in a word broken at the end of a line of writing.

italics Slanted type used to punctuate titles of long works and as emphasis. Handwriting uses underlining instead of italics.

period Used to end statements, polite requests, and commands.

semicolon Used to join sentences that are not connected by a coordinating conjunction. Used to join items in a series when one or more items include a comma.

question mark Used to end questions.

quotation marks Used to enclose a speaker's exact words and the titles of short works.

Mini-Lessons Taught in This Book

Sentence Fluency (Chapter 1)	1
Using Introductory Elements (Chapter 2)	26
Using Transition Words and Phrases (Chapter 3)	38
Using a Consistent Point of View (Chapter 5)	73
Writing a Thesis Statement (Chapter 6)	85
Using Complete Sentences (Chapter 7)	99
Using Pronouns Correctly (Chapter 9)	138
Writing Topic Sentences (Chapter 10)	151
Writing Titles (Chapter 11)	168
Using a Consistent Tense (Chapter 13)	201
Forming Paragraphs in a Story (Chapter 14)	217
Capitalization in Poetry (Chapter 15)	234
Spelling Words with Suffixes (Chapter 17)	268
Getting (and Giving) Helpful Feedback (Chapter 18)	279
Using Quotations (Chapter 19)	295

Acknowledgments

Grateful acknowledgment is made to the following sources for having granted permission to reprint copyrighted materials. Every effort has been made to obtain permission to use previously published materials. Any errors or omissions are unintentional.

6 Traits model. Developed by Education Northwest, 101 Southwest Main, Portland, OR 97204. http://educationnorthwest.org/traits.

Excerpt from "Top Ten Things You Can Do to Reduce Global Warming" by Larry West © 2010 Larry West (http://environment.about.com/). Used with permission of About Inc., which can be found online at www.about.com. All rights reserved. Page 128.

Excerpt from *Gullible Gus* by Maxine Rose Schur. Used by permission of the author. Page 193.

Excerpt from *Children's Literature in the Elementary School*, 8th ed. by C. Huck, et al. Copyright © 2004 by McGraw-Hill Education. Used by permission. Page 257.

Photo of Lincoln's address at the dedication of the Gettysburg National Cemetery, November 19, 1863. Courtesy of the Library of Congress. Page 291.

"Made in Thailand" (p. 55), "Sailing" (p. 120), "No Gym" (p. 185), "At Attention" (p. 249), and "*Uglies* Book Review" (p. 308). Reprinted with permission of Teenink.com and *Teen Ink* magazine.

Index

A
Adding, transition words and phrases for, 39
Adjectives, 313
  capitalization of proper, 234
Adverbs, 313
Agreement, 314
  pronoun-antecedent, 138–139
Antecedent, 138
Apostrophe, 314
Asimov, Isaac, 192

B
Beginning in personal narrative, 204
Beginning-middle-end tables, 242, 243, 277, 294, 302
Biographies, 191
Blind writing, 22–23
Blogs, 63–64
Body paragraphs, in drafting description of a place, 24–25
Body sentences, in drafting description of a person-, 10–11
Brainstorming, 69–70, 134
Brainstorming table, 70

C
Campfire stories, 252
Capitalization
  of first, last, and major words in title, 168
  of first word in direct quotation, 234
  of first word in line of poetry, 235
  of first word in sentence, 234
  of *I*, 234
  in poems, 234–235
  of proper nouns and adjectives, 234
Cause, transition words and phrases to show, 39
Character map, 262–263
Character sketches, 259
Checklist
  in editing, 104
  in revising, 13–14, 166, 220
Clause, 314
Closing sentences, in drafting description of a person, 11
Colon, 314–315
Commas, 315
  in forming compound sentences, 12
  with quotation marks, 207
Comma splice, 313
Comparison, transition words and phrases to show, 39
Comparison-contrast essays, 93–107
  drafting, 98–99
  editing, 104
  evaluating, 105–107
  looking at model of, 94
  prewriting, 95–98
  publishing, 105
  revising, 99–102
  rubric for, 103
  traits of, 93
Complex sentences, 313
Compound-complex sentences, 313
Compound sentences, 12, 313
Conclusion, in drafting description of a place, 25
Conjunctions, 313
  coordinating, 12
Contractions, 72
Contrast, transition words and phrases to show, 39
Conventions
  in compare-contrast essay, 93, 94, 104
  in describing a person, 2, 5
  in describing a place, 19, 21
  in describing a scientific subject, 33, 34
  in descriptive test essay, 45
  in editorial, 131, 133
  in explanatory essays, 81, 82
  in expository test essay, 109
  in expository writing, 63, 68
  in literary writing, 193
  in narrative test essay, 239
  in personal narrative, 195, 197, 207
  in persuasive essays, 145, 146, 156
  in persuasive test essay, 173
  in persuasive writing, 127
  in response to a document-based question, 298
  in response to a narrative, 259, 261, 271
  in response to a poem, 273, 274, 282
  in response to literature, 256
  in reviews, 159, 161
  in short stories, 211, 213, 214, 222
Conventions handbook, 313–315

319

Coordinating conjunctions, in forming compound sentences, 12
Crane, Stephen, 275
Creative writing, 191
Critical lens, defined, 299
Critical-lens essay
   drafting, 303
   evaluating a response to, 304–307
   planning time for, 301
   polishing, 304
   preparing to write, 300–302
   prewriting, 301–302
   rubric for, 305
   traits of, 299
Critical-lens quotation, defined, 299
Critical thinking skills, 173

D

Descriptive writing, 1–60
   defined, 1
   getting ready to write, 4
   ideas for, 58–59
   learning tips, 4
   listening for, 4
   of a person, 5–17
      drafting, 9–11
      editing, 14–15
      evaluating, 17
      looking at model of, 6
      prewriting, 7–9
      publishing, 15
      revising, 11–14
      rubric for, 16
      traits of, 5
   of a place, 19–32
      drafting, 24–25
      editing, 30
      evaluating, 31–32
      looking at model of, 20
      prewriting, 22–23
      publishing, 30–31
      revising, 25–29
      rubric for, 29
      traits of, 19
   practicing, 4
   real-world examples of, 3
   reflections on, 60
   of a scientific subject, 33–44
      drafting, 37–38
      editing, 42
      evaluating, 43–44
      looking at model of, 34
      prewriting, 35–37
      publishing, 42
      revising, 38–41
      rubric for, 41
      traits of, 33
   sensory details in, 1–2
   as a test, 45–59
      drafting, 49–50
      evaluating, 51–52, 53
      planning time for, 47
      prewriting, 48
      revising, 50–51
      rubric for, 52
      studying prompt, 46
      traits of, 45
   traits of, 2, xii
   watching for, 4
   words that signal, 46
   wrapping up, 55–59
Details. *See also* Sensory details
   gathering, in prewriting, 8, 22–23, 48, 70, 83–84, 96–97, 112, 134–135, 147, 163, 176, 215–217, 243, 276, 293
   organizing, in prewriting, 8–9, 23, 48, 71, 84–85, 97–98, 135, 147–150, 163–164, 177, 215–217, 277, 294
Dialogue, defined, 192
Dickinson, Emily, 276
Dictionaries, 14
   online, 14
Direct object, 314
Direct quotation
   capitalization of first word in, 234
   quotation marks for, 295
Document-based questions
   primary sources in, 285
   sections of, 291–292
Donne, John, x

Drafting
   in comparison-contrast essay, 98–99
   in describing a scientific subject, 37–38
   in describing a person, 9–11
   in describing a place, 24–25
   in descriptive test essay, 49–50
   in editorials, 136–137
   in explanatory essays, 85–87
   in how-to articles, 71–72
   in personal narratives, 200–204
   in persuasive essays, 151–153
   in poems, 230–231
   in response to a document-based question, 294–295
   in response to a narrative, 264–265
   in response to a poem, 277–278
   in reviews, 165
   in short stories, 217–219
   topic sentences in, 9–10

E

Editing
   in describing a place, 30
   in describing a person, 14
   in a descriptive test essay, 50–51
   in editorials, 142
   in explanatory essays, 89
   in how-to articles, 77
   in personal narratives, 207
   in persuasive essays, 156
   in poems, 234–236
   in response to a document-based question, 298
   in response to a narrative, 268–271
   in response to a poem, 282
   in reviews, 168–169

in scientific description, 42
in short stories, 222
Editing marks, 50, 51, 115
Editorials, 131–144, 145
   drafting, 136–137
   editing, 142
   evaluating, 143–144
   looking at model of, 132–133
   prewriting, 133–136
   publishing, 142
   revising, 138–141
   rubric for, 141
   traits of, 131
Effect, transition words and phrases to show, 39
Emerson, Ralph Waldo, 278
End, in personal narrative, 204
Everything on a Waffle (Horvath), 3
Exclamation mark, 315
   with quotation marks, 207
Explanatory essays, 81–91
   drafting, 85–87
   evaluating, 89–91
   looking at model of, 82
   prewriting in, 83–85
   revising, 87–88
   rubric for, 88
   traits of, 81
Expository writing, 61–124
   comparison-contrast essays, 93–107
      drafting, 98–99
      editing, 104
      evaluating, 105–107
      looking at model of, 94
      prewriting, 95–98
      publishing, 105
      revising, 99–102
      rubric for, 103
      traits of, 93
   defined, 61
   drafting, 98–99
   editing, 104
   evaluating, 105–107
   explanatory essays, 62, 81–91
      drafting, 85–87
      evaluating, 89–91
      looking at model of, 82
      prewriting in, 83–85
      revising, 87–88
      rubric for, 88
      traits of, 81
   getting ready to write, 65
   how-to articles, 62, 67–79
      drafting, 71–72
      editing, 77
      evaluating, 78–79
      looking at model of, 68
      prewriting, 69–71
      publishing, 77
      revising, 73–75
      rubric for, 76
      traits of, 67–68
   ideas for, 123
   kinds of, 62
   learning tips, 65
   prewriting, 95–98
   publishing, 105
   real-world examples of, 63–64
   reflections, 124
   revising, 99–102
   rubric for, 103
   as a test, 109–122
      evaluating, 116–118
      planning time for, 111
      polishing, 114–115
      preparing to write, 110–111
      prewriting, 112–113
      rubric for, 117
      studying prompt for, 110–111
      traits of, 109
      writing, 113–114
   thesis statements in, 61
   traits of, 63, 93
   watching for, 4
   wrap-up, 120–124

F

Facts, double-checking, 165
Feedback
   getting and giving helpful, 14, 279–280
   getting in response to a document-based question, 296
   peer, in revising, 153, 278–279
Fiction, narrator in, 192
Figurative language, 226
   defined, 192
First-person point of view, 20, 73, 200–201, 204
First-person pronouns, 20, 73, 200
5 Ws plus H, 199
Fragment, 313
Freewriting, 22, 47, 176
Future tense, 201

G

Graphic organizers
   beginning-middle-end tables, 177, 242, 243, 277, 294, 302
   brainstorming tables, 70
   character map, 262
   5 Ws plus H, 199
   idea webs, 163
   listings, 7, 23, 47, 48, 70, 112, 176, 198
   opinion table, 126, 177
   outlining, 48, 135, 163–164, 177, 302
   persuasive maps, 148–150, 153
   pro-con charts, 176
   sensory detail table, 8, 47
   sequence chain, 71
   story map, 215–217, 242, 243
   task chart, 302
   T-charts, 96–97, 134–135, 176, 198–199
   3Ws table, 36, 37
   three-column chart, 162, 293
   timeline, 200, 242, 243
   Venn diagrams, 97–98
Gullible Gus (Schur), 193

H

Horvath, Polly, 3
How-to articles, 62, 67–79
   drafting, 71–72
   editing, 77
   evaluating, 78–79
   looking at model of, 68

prewriting, 69–71
publishing, 77
revising, 73–75
rubric for, 76
traits of, 67–68
Hyphen, 315

I

I (pronoun), capitalization of, 234
Ideas
  in compare-contrast essay, 93, 94, 102
  in describing a person, 2, 5, 13
  in describing a place, 19, 20, 28
  in describing a scientific subject, 33, 34, 40
  in descriptive test essay, 45
  for editorial, 131, 132, 140
  in explanatory essays, 81, 82, 87
  in expository test essay, 109
  in expository writing, 63
  gathering, in prewriting, 8, 22–23, 48, 70, 83–84, 96–97, 112, 134–135, 147, 163, 176, 215–217, 243, 276, 293
  in how-to writing, 75
  in literary writing, 193
  in narrative test essay, 239
  organizing, in prewriting, 8–9, 23, 48, 71, 84–85, 97–98, 135, 147–150, 163–164, 177, 215–217, 277, 294
  in personal narrative, 195, 196, 205
  in persuasive essays, 145, 146, 154
  in persuasive test essay, 173
  in persuasive writing, 127
  in poems, 225, 226
  in response to a document-based question, 296
  in response to a narrative, 259, 260
  in response to a poem, 273, 274
  in response to literature, 256
  in reviews, 159, 160, 166
  in short stories, 211, 213, 219
Imperative sentence, 47
Importance, transition words and phrases to show, 39
Independent clause, 12
Indirect object, 314
Information, organizing, in prewriting, 112–113
"In Heaven" (Crane), 275
Interjections, 313
Introduction, in drafting description of a place, 24–25
Introductory elements, using, 26–27
Italics, 315
  for long titles, 168

L

Listings, 7, 23, 48, 70, 112, 176, 198
Literary terms, 192
Literary writing, 191–253
  defined, 191
  getting ready to write, 194
  ideas for, 252
  learning tips, 194
  personal narratives, 191, 192, 195–209
    defined, 195
    drafting, 200–204
    editing, 207
    evaluating, 208–209
    looking at model of, 196–197
    prewriting, 197–200
    publishing, 208
    revising, 204–206
    rubric for, 206
    traits of, 195
    verb tense in, 202
  poems, 191, 192, 225–237
    capitalization in, 234–235
    drafting, 230–231
    editing, 234–236
    evaluating, 236–237
    looking at model of, 226
    narrative, 252
    prewriting, 227–230
    publishing, 236
    revising, 231–233
    rubric for, 233
    traits of, 225
  real-world examples of, 193–194
  reflections on, 253
  short stories, 191, 192, 211–224
    drafting, 217–219
    editing, 222
    forming paragraphs in, 217–219
    looking at model of, 213
    marking paragraph breaks in, 218–219
    prewriting, 214–216
    publishing, 222
    revising, 219–221
    rubric for, 221
    traits of, 211
  terms in, 192
  traits of, 193
  wrap-up, 249–256
Location, transition words and phrases to show, 39

M

Main clause, 314
Metaphors, 192, 314
Middle, in personal narrative, 204
"The Morns Are Meeker Than They Were" (Dickinson), 276

N

Narrative poems, 252
Narrative point of view, 201
Narratives
  defined, 192

personal, 191, 192, 195–209
  defined, 195
  drafting, 200–204
  editing, 207
  evaluating, 208–209
  looking at model of, 196–197
  prewriting, 197–200
  publishing, 208
  revising, 204–206
  rubric for, 206
  traits of, 195
  verb tense in, 202
as a test essay, 239–252
  evaluating, 245–246
  planning time for, 241
  polishing, 244–245
  preparing to write, 240–241
  prewriting, 241–243
  rubric for, 246
  studying the prompt, 240–241
  traits of, 239
  writing, 243–244
  words that signal response to, 240
Narrators, defined, 192
"Night Fright," 226
Nonfiction, narrator in, 192
Nouns, 313
  capitalization of proper, 234
Novels, 191

O

Object of a preposition, 314
Online dictionaries, 14
Opinion table, 126, 177
Order of importance, 9
  transition words and phrases to show, 39
Organization
  in compare-contrast essay, 93, 94, 102
  in describing a person, 2, 5, 13
  in describing a place, 19, 20, 28
  in describing a scientific subject, 33, 34

in descriptive test essay, 45
in editorial, 131, 132, 140
in explanatory essays, 81, 82, 87
in expository test essay, 109
in expository writing, 63
in literary writing, 193
in narrative test essay, 239
order of importance in, 9
in personal narrative, 195, 196, 205
in persuasive essays, 145, 146, 154
in persuasive test essay, 173
in persuasive writing, 127
in poems, 225, 226
in response to a document-based question, 296
in response to a narrative, 259, 261
in response to a poem, 273, 274
in response to literature, 256
in reviews, 159, 160, 166
in short stories, 211, 213, 219
spatial order in, 9
time order in, 9, 23
Outlining, 48, 135, 163–164, 177, 302

P

Paragraphs
  body, in drafting description of a place, 24–25
  forming, in short stories, 217–219
  marking breaks in a story, 218–219
Parts of speech, 313
Past tense, 201, 203, 204
Peer feedback in revising, 153, 278–279
Periods, 315
  with quotation marks, 207

Person, describing a, 5–17
  drafting, 9–11
  editing, 14–15
  evaluating, 17
  looking at model of, 6
  prewriting, 7–9
  publishing, 15
  revising, 11–14
  rubric for, 16
  traits of, 5
Personal narratives, 191, 192, 195–209
  defined, 195
  drafting, 200–204
  editing, 207
  evaluating, 208–209
  looking at model of, 196–197
  prewriting, 197–200
  publishing, 208
  revising, 204–206
  rubric for, 206
  traits of, 195
  verb tense in, 202
Persuasive essays, 145–158
  drafting in, 151–153
  editing in, 156
  looking at model of, 146
  prewriting in, 147–150
  publishing, 156
  revising, 153–155
  rubric for, 155
  traits of, 145
  words that signal, 174
Persuasive map, 148–150, 153
Persuasive writing, 125–189
  defined, 125–126
  editorials, 131–144
    drafting, 136–137
    editing, 142
    evaluating, 143–144
    prewriting, 133–136
    publishing, 142
    revising, 138–141
    rubric for, 141
    traits of, 131
  getting ready to write, 128–129
  ideas for, 187–188
  learning tips for, 129

persuasive essays,
145–158
  drafting in, 151–153
  editing in, 156
  looking at model of,
146
  prewriting in, 147–150
  publishing, 156
  revising, 153–155
  rubric for, 155
  traits of, 145
persuasive test essay,
173–187
  evaluating, 180
  planning time for, 175
  polishing, 179–180
  preparing to write,
173–178
  prewriting, 176–178
  studying the prompt,
174–175
  traits of, 173
  writing, 178–179
real-world example,
127–128
reflections on, 189
reviews, 159–171
  drafting, 165
  editing, 168–169
  evaluating, 169–170
  looking at model of,
160–161
  prewriting, 161–164
  publishing, 169
  revising, 165–167
  rubric for, 167
  traits of, 159
rubric for, 167
thesis statement in, 126
thinking about prior
experience, 126
traits of, 127
wrap up, 185–189
Phrase, 314
Place, describing a, 19–32
  drafting, 24–25
  editing, 30
  evaluating, 31–32
  looking at model of, 20–21
  prewriting, 22–23
  publishing, 30–31
  revising, 25–29

rubric for, 29
traits of, 19
Poems, 191, 192, 225–237
  capitalization in, 234–235
  drafting, 230–231
  editing, 234–236
  evaluating, 236–237
  looking at model of, 226
  narrative, 252
  prewriting, 227–230
  publishing, 236
  revising, 231–233
  rubric for, 233
  traits of, 225
Point of view
  defined, 73
  first-person, 20, 73,
200–201, 204
  narrative, 201
  second-person, 20, 72, 73
  third-person, 73
  using consistent, 73–74
Predicate, 314
Prepositions, 313
Present tense, 201, 203,
204
Prewriting
  in comparison-contrast
essays, 95–98
  in descriptive writing,
7–9, 22–23, 35–36
  in editorials, 133–136
  in explanatory essays,
83–85
  in how-to articles, 69–71
  in narrative test essay,
241–243
  in personal narratives,
197–200
  in persuasive essays,
147–150
  in poems, 227–230
  in response to a document-based question,
291–294
  in response to a narrative, 262–264
  in response to a poem,
276–277
  in reviews, 161–164
  in short stories, 214–216

Prewriting strategies
  analyzing prompts, 7, 22,
35, 69, 83, 133–134,
147, 161, 197–198, 214,
276, 291–293
  choosing topics, 7–8, 22,
35–36, 69–70, 96, 134,
147, 161–162, 198–199,
214, 242, 276
  gathering ideas and
details, 8, 22–23, 48,
70, 83–84, 96–97, 112,
134–135, 147, 163, 176,
215–217, 243, 276, 293
  organizing ideas and
details, 8–9, 23, 48,
71, 84–85, 97–98, 135,
147–150, 163–164, 177,
215–217, 277, 294
Primary sources, 285
  in a document-based
question, 285
  examples of, 285
Pro-con charts, 176
Prompt
  analyzing, in prewriting,
7, 22, 35, 69, 83, 133–134, 147, 161, 197–198,
214, 276, 291–293
  studying
    for descriptive test essay, 46–47
    for expository test essay, 110–111
    for narrative test essay,
240–241
    for persuasive test essay, 174–175
Pronouns, 138–140, 313
  antecedent for, 138
  agreement with,
138–139
  defined, 138
  first-person, 20, 73, 200
  second-person, 20, 73
  third-person, 73
Proper adjectives, capitalization of, 234
Proper nouns, capitalization of, 234
Publishing
  in describing a person, 15

in describing a place, 30–31
in editorials, 142
in explanatory essays, 89
in how-to articles, 77
in personal narratives, 208–209
in persuasive essays, 156
in poems, 236
in response to a document-based question, 298
in response to a narrative, 271–272
in response to a poem, 282
in reviews, 169
in scientific description, 42
in short stories, 222
Punctuation, 314–315

Q

Question marks, 315
  with quotation marks, 207
Quotation marks, 315
  for direct quotations, 295
  to enclose spoken words, 207
  for short titles, 168
Quotations
  capitalization of first word in, 234
  quotation marks for, 295
  using, 295

R

Responding to literature
  defined, 255
  document-based questions, 285–298
    drafting, 294–295
    editing, 298
    evaluating, 298
    looking at model of, 287
    prewriting, 291–294
    publishing, 298
    revising, 296–298
    rubric for, 297
    traits of, 286
    writing, 288–291
  getting ready to write, 258
  ideas for, 255–311
  learning tips, 258
  narratives, 259–272
    drafting, 264–265
    editing, 268–271
    looking at model of, 260–261
    prewriting, 262–264
    publishing, 271–272
    revising, 266–267
    rubric for, 267
    traits of, 259
  poems, 273–284 (*See also* Poems)
    drafting, 277–278
    editing, 282
    looking at model of, 274
    prewriting, 276–277
    publishing, 282
    revising, 278–281
    rubric for, 281
    traits of, 273
  purpose of, 255
  real-world examples of, 256–257
  traits of, 256
  wrap-up, 308–311
Reviews, 159–171
  drafting, 165
  editing, 168–169
  evaluating, 169–170
  looking at model of, 160–161
  prewriting, 161–164
  publishing, 169
  revising, 165–167
  rubric for, 167
  traits of, 159
Revising
  in comparison-contrast essays, 99–102
  in describing a person, 11–14
  in describing a place, 25, 26–27
  in describing a scientific subject, 38–41
  in editorials, 138–141
  in explanatory essays, 87–88
  in expository writing, 73–75
  in how-to articles, 73–75
  in personal narratives, 204–206
  in persuasive essays, 153–155
  in poems, 231–233
  in response to a document-based question, 296–298
  in response to a narrative, 266–267
  in response to a poem, 278–281
  in reviews, 165–169
  in short stories, 219–221
"The Rhodora" (Emerson), 278
Rubrics
  Comparison-Contrast essay, 103
  Descriptive Article, 41
  Descriptive Essay, 29
  Descriptive Paragraph, 16
  Descriptive Test Essay, 52
  Editorial, 141
  Explanatory Essay, 88
  Expository Test Essay, 117
  How-To Article, 76
  Narrative Test Essay, 246
  Personal Narrative, 206
  Persuasive Essay, 155
  Persuasive Test Essay, 181
  Poem, 233
  Response to a Critical-Lens Quotation, 305
  Response to a DBQ, 297
  Response to Literature, 267
  Response to Poetry, 281
  for a Review, 167
  Story, 221
Run-on sentences, 313

S

Schur, Maxine Rose, 193
Science fiction stories, 252
Scientific language
  defined, 37
  using, 37–38
Scientific subject, describing a, 33–44
  drafting, 37–38
  editing, 42
  evaluating, 43–44
  looking at model of, 34
  prewriting, 35–37
  publishing, 42
  revising, 38–41
  rubric for, 41
  traits of, 33
Scientific writing, 33–44
Second-person point of view, 20, 72, 73
Second-person pronouns, 20, 73
Semicolons, 315
Sensory details, in descriptive writing, 1–2
Sensory detail table, 8, 47
Sentence(s)
  capitalization of first word in, 234
  complex, 313
  compound, 12, 313
  compound-complex, 313
  imperative, 47
  run-on, 313
  simple, 12, 313
  using complete, 99–102
  variety in, 25, 26–27
Sentence fluency
  in compare-contrast essays, 93, 94, 102
  defined, 11
  in describing a person, 2, 5, 14
  in describing a place, 19, 21, 28
  in describing a scientific subject, 33, 34, 41
  in descriptive test essay, 45
  in editorials, 131, 132, 140
  in explanatory essays, 81, 82, 88

  in expository test essay, 109
  in expository writing, 63
  in how-to writing, 75
  in literary writing, 193
  in narrative test essay, 239
  in personal narratives, 195, 197, 205
  in persuasive essays, 145, 146, 154
  in persuasive test essay, 173
  in persuasive writing, 127
  in response to a document-based question, 296
  in response to a narrative, 259, 261
  in response to a poem, 273, 274
  in response to literature, 256
  in reviews, 159, 160–161, 166
  in short stories, 211, 213
Sequence chain, 71
Short stories, 191, 192, 211–224
  drafting, 217–219
  editing, 222
  forming paragraphs in, 217–219
  looking at model of, 213
  marking paragraph breaks in, 218–219
  prewriting, 214–216
  publishing, 222
  revising, 219–221
  rubric for, 221
  traits of, 211
Simenon, Georges, 2
Similes, 192, 314
Simple sentence, 12
Simple sentences, 313
Spatial order, 9
Speaker, defined, 192
Spell Check, problems with, 14

Spelling words with suffixes, 268–271
Stanza, defined, 192
Stendhal, 61
Stories. *See* Short stories
Story map, 215–217, 242, 243
Subject, 314
  defined, 100
  placement of, in sentences, 26
Subordinate clause, 314
Suffixes
  defined, 268
  spelling words with, 268–271

T

Table, 293
Task chart, 302
T-charts, 96–97, 134–135, 176, 198–199
Tense, 314. *See also* Verbs
  future, 201
  past, 201, 202, 204
  present, 201, 202, 204
  using consistent, 201–204
Test essays
  critical-lens, 299–307
    drafting, 303
    evaluating, 304–305, 306–307
    planning time for, 301
    polishing, 304
    preparing to write, 300–302
    prewriting, 301–302
    rubric for, 305
    traits of, 299
  descriptive, 45–59
    drafting, 49–50
    evaluating, 51–52, 53
    planning time for, 47
    polishing, 50–51
    preparing to write, 46–46
    prewriting, 48
    revising, 50–51
    rubric for, 52
    traits of, 45
  expository, 109–122
    evaluating, 116–118

326 • The Writer's Studio

planning time for, 111
polishing, 114–115
preparing to write, 110–111
prewriting, 112–113
rubric for, 117
traits of, 109
writing, 113–114
narrative, 239–252
evaluating, 245–248
planning time for, 241
polishing, 244–245
preparing to write, 240–241
prewriting, 241–243
rubric for, 246
traits of, 239
writing, 243–244
persuasive, 173–187
evaluating, 180, 182–183
planning time for, 175
polishing, 179–180
preparing to write, 173–178
prewriting, 176–178
rubric for, 181
traits of, 173
writing, 178–179, 183–184
Theme, defined, 192
Thesis statements, 126
defined, 85
in expository writing, 61
writing, 85–87, 151
Third-person point of view, 73
Third-person pronouns, 73
Thoreau, Henry David, 299
3Ws table, 36, 37
Three-column chart, 162
Time
planning, for descriptive test essay, 47
planning, for expository test essay, 111
planning, for narrative test essay, 241
planning, for persuasive test essay, 175
transition words and phrases to show, 39

Timeline, 200, 204, 217, 242, 243
Time order, 9, 23
Titles
capitalization for first, last, and major words in, 168
giving to stories, 208
quotation marks for short, 168
underlining or italics for long, 168
writing effective, 87
Tool kits, 47, 176, 177, 242, 302. *See also* Graphic organizers
Topic, choosing, in prewriting, 7–8, 22, 35–36, 69–70, 96, 134, 147, 161–162, 198–199, 214, 242, 276
Topic sentences
in drafting description of a person, 9–10
writing, 151–153
Transitions, 72, 314
to add, 39
defined, 38
to show cause or effect, 39
to show comparison or contrast, 39
to show importance, 39
to show location, 39
to show time, 39

U
Underlining, for long titles, 168
Unity, defined, 192

V
Venn diagrams, 97–98
Verbs, 313, 314. *See also* Tense
defined, 100
placement of, in sentences, 26
Voice
in compare-contrast essays, 93, 94, 102
in describing a person, 2, 5, 13

in describing a place, 19, 20–21, 28
in describing a scientific subject, 33, 34, 41
in descriptive test essay, 45
for editorials, 131, 132, 140
in explanatory essays, 81, 82, 87
in expository test essay, 109
in expository writing, 63
in how-to writing, 75
in literary writing, 193
in narrative test essay, 239
in personal narratives, 195, 196, 205
in persuasive essays, 145, 146, 154
in persuasive test essay, 173
in persuasive writing, 127
in poems, 225, 226
in response to a document-based question, 296
in response to a narrative, 259, 261
in response to a poem, 273, 274
in response to literature, 256
in reviews, 159, 160, 166
in short stories, 211, 213, 219
Vonnegut, Kurt, 126

W
West, Larry, 127–128
Wikipedia, 63
Word choice
in compare-contrast essay, 93, 94, 102
in describing a person, 2, 5, 14
in describing a place, 19, 21, 28
in describing a scientific subject, 33, 34

Index • **327**

in descriptive test essay, 45
in editorials, 131, 132, 140
in explanatory essays, 81, 82, 87–88
in expository test essay, 109
in expository writing, 63, 68
in how-to writing, 75
in literary writing, 193
in narrative test essay, 239
in personal narratives, 195, 196, 205
in persuasive essays, 145, 146, 154
in persuasive test essay, 173
in persuasive writing, 127
in response to a document-based question, 296
in response to a narrative, 259, 261
in response to a poem, 273, 274
in response to literature, 256
in reviews, 159, 160, 166
in short stories, 211, 213, 219

Words, use of expressive yet balanced, 136–137
Writer's network, x–xi
Writing
   blind, 22–23
   reasons for studying, xi
   thinking about, ix–x
Writing studio, ix